Hellenic Studies 80

In Her Own Words

Recent Titles in the Hellenic Studies Series

IN HER OWN WORDS

THE LIFE AND POETRY OF AELIA EUDOCIA

by
Brian P. Sowers

CENTER FOR HELLENIC STUDIES
Trustees for Harvard University
Washington, DC
Distributed by Harvard University Press
Cambridge, Massachusetts, and London, England
2020

In Her Own Words: The Life and Poetry of Aelia Eudocia
   By Brian P. Sowers
Copyright © 2020 Center for Hellenic Studies, Trustees for Harvard University
All Rights Reserved.
Published by Center for Hellenic Studies, Trustees for Harvard University, Washington, D.C.
Distributed by Harvard University Press, Cambridge, Massachusetts and London, England
Printed by Total Printing Systems, Newton, IL
Cover Design: Joni Godlove
Production: Kerri Cox Sullivan

Library of Congress Cataloging-in-Publication Data

Names: Sowers, Brian P., author.
Title: In her own words : the life and poetry of Aelia Eudocia / by Brian P. Sowers.
Other titles: Eudocia
Description: Washington, D.C. : Center for Hellenic Studies, Trustees for Harvard University, 2020. | Series: Hellenic studies ; 80 | Revision of author's thesis (doctoral)--University of Cincinnati, 2008 titled: Eudocia : the making of a Homeric Christian. | Includes bibliographical references and index.
Identifiers: LCCN 2019021515 | ISBN 9780674987371
Subjects: LCSH: Eudocia, Empress, consort of Theodosius II, Emperor of the East, -460--Criticism and interpretation. | Christian poetry, Greek--History and criticism.
Classification: LCC PA3972.E86 S69 2019 | DDC 881/.01--dc23
LC record available at https://lccn.loc.gov/2019021515

Contents

Contents

Acknowledgements

This book would not have been possible without the support of many people. I would like to thank Scott Johnson and everyone at the Center for Hellenic Studies, particularly Jill Curry Robbins and Jason Harris, for their encouragement and assistance with the manuscript. I would like to thank the anonymous readers who took time out of their schedules to read through the manuscript and provide invaluable suggestions that helped clarify the scope of the project. David Schur, Kimberly Passaro, and Sylvia Czander graciously read various portions of the manuscript throughout the process. Scott and Ann Ellis and Seth and Sally Lundgren generously hosted me during a prolonged research trip to Cincinnati where the librarians and staff at the John Miller Burnam Classical Library at the University of Cincinnati assisted me in countless ways.

To my colleagues at Brooklyn College of the City University of New York and elsewhere, thank you for giving me the opportunity to work through and develop my ideas. In particular, I would like to thank David Schur, Katherine Lu Hsu, Lauren Mancia, Gianfranco Agosti, Scott McGill, Marco Formisano, Aaron Pelttari, Daniel Osland, Kristine Trego, Tom Garvey, Peter van Minnen, Craig Williams, Jim Pletcher, Danielle Kellogg, Liv Yarrow, Phil Thibodeau, John van Sickle, Gail Smith, and Dee Clayman. Funding for travel and other associated costs was generously provided by my professional union (PSC CUNY) and through a Tow Faculty Travel Fellowship at Brooklyn College. Finally, I would like to thank my friends and family, too many to name, for all their support and encouragement. Rick, Sandra, Sean, Katie, Ray, Debbie, Melissa, Jeff, Sarai, Dan, Alicia, and, especially, Marvin and Rachel have always been there to provide a constant and unwavering light, even on the darkest days.

Introduction

THE DATE WAS June 7th, 421 CE, and Theodosius II had just married. His choice of bride would have scandalized the Constantinopolitan court and church, had she not been hand-picked by his sister and chief advisor, Pulcheria. Theodosius' bride neither came from the local aristocracy, nor did she secure a marriage alliance between the eastern and western halves of the empire. In fact, she was hardly well-born at all—she was from Athens, a city long past its prime, where her father had served as *rhetor*. Thanks to her father's background, Theodosius' bride had a superior education—for a woman. After her father's death, his sons, enticed by the opportunity to fleece their sister of her inheritance, had forced her to seek imperial support in Constantinople. During that trip, she had impressed Pulcheria, who quickly arranged a marriage between her brother and this exceptional young woman.

So begins one version about the life and times of Aelia Eudocia, née Athenais.[1] Accounts, both ancient and modern, that begin this way usually focus on Eudocia/Athenais' family, the implicit political interests behind her engagement to Theodosius, the influential bureaucratic positions that she orchestrated, her role in the intrigue and gossip of the imperial court, her fall from favor, her exile from Constantinople, her life in Jerusalem, her building programs, or her involvement in the Nestorian controversy.[2] Such approaches, by necessity, rely on multiple ancient sources to reconstruct Eudocia's involvement in the fifth-century East, from Athens and Constantinople to Antioch and Jerusalem. That nearly all these sources were written by men, usually aristocratic men, and reflect their aristocratic male interests, is a product of the ancient world, which disproportionately silences or elides over female voices and female perspectives. Based on this surviving evidence, Eudocia played a key role in fifth-century society and was a central figure, albeit briefly, in the Constantinopolitan court. After leaving the imperial capital, she remained a generous imperial patron and funded building projects throughout the Greek East, especially in Jerusalem and its environs.

---

[1] Compare Mazzarino 1946; Beck 1966; Haffner 1996; Leppin 1998; Haffner 1999.

[2] Cameron 1965; Cameron 1982; Holum 1982; Hunt 1982; Biers 1989–1990; Burman 1994; Cameron 2000.

In addition to these exceptional accomplishments, Eudocia was also one of the most prolific female poets of antiquity. Although most of her poems no longer survive, nearly 3,500 lines do, about three times as many as Sappho, antiquity's most celebrated female poet. This remarkable survival rate sets Eudocia apart from most other ancient female poets, whose works typically survive piecemeal as citations in later, male readers and critics.[3] Because so much of her poetry survives, we are afforded a unique opportunity to hear her in her own words, not mediated by redactors and epitomizers.

This book examines Eudocia's life and times by focusing on her poetry and her choice of self-presentation. Surprisingly, such a study about Eudocia's stories—the one she lived and those she wrote—currently does not exist. Most studies about Eudocia focus either on her historical life, at the expense of her literary works, or on individual poems or poetic types, at the expense of a wider understanding of her literary agenda. My approach is intentionally the opposite of these other studies, in that I attempt, first and foremost, to recover the literary Eudocia. For that reason, I do not provide a complete biographic account of her life, although readers interested in this can find the relevant sources in the notes and bibliography. When discussing historical events, I attempt to limit myself only to details that directly contextualize and elucidate Eudocia's poetry. For that reason, my discussion of her travels in and around Jerusalem are rather brief. Despite this selectivity, this book fills a glaring gap in the scholarship on ancient women and female poets. It is my hope that it will be of interest to scholars in multiple fields, particularly my fellow classicists, experts in late antique poetry, and colleagues in women and gender studies.

Moreover, my approach situates Eudocia's poetry within the context of her late antique milieu. Those centuries collectively referred to as late antiquity, roughly 200–600 CE, were a period of significant and long-lasting political, social, and cultural change. Just a few decades ago, scholars working on this period had to justify their academic interests and the legitimacy of the literature written during these centuries. Over the past few decades, however, research on late antiquity has flourished, and scholars increasingly view late antiquity as a pivotal moment in history that anticipates the medieval world in the Roman West and the Byzantine world in the Roman East. Moreover, because late antiquity is, in part, defined by its continuity with the "classical" past, it encapsulates the development of classical literary and cultural practices, even as this literature and culture underwent continued development and innovation. It is this unique blend of continuity with the classical past and innovation

---

[3] For Eudocia's place in recent works on women poets of antiquity, see Homeyer 1979; Wilson-Kaster 1981; Snyder 1989; Balmer 1996; Plant 2004; Greene 2005; Stevenson 2005.

foreshadowing a medieval/Byzantine future that makes late antiquity, particularly late antique literature, a valuable field of study in its own right.

Eudocia's words provide modern readers a glimpse into the innovative world of late antique poetry, one in which authors, including female authors, wrote creative and dynamic stories, even when those stories had already been written before. As a product of this late antique literary culture, Eudocia evidences a literary style representative of her time. First, her poetry fits within late antiquity's paraphrastic habit, whereby popular literary works or stories were rewritten, revised, and updated to speak to new audiences and to conform to new aesthetic and ideological interests. The most obvious examples of this paraphrastic tendency are the multiple retellings of Christian scriptures, including verse paraphrases that transform the Bible, particularly the Gospels, into classical epics. In his catalogue of Eudocia's corpus, the Byzantine bibliophile Photius informs us that Eudocia wrote numerous verse paraphrases: a Homeric cento (a retelling of Genesis and the Gospels using lines from Homer's *Iliad* and *Odyssey*), verse paraphrases of the Hebrew Bible books of Daniel and Zechariah, an extended poetic paraphrase of the first eight books of Hebrew Bible, and an epic retelling of the *Martyrdom of Cyprian*. In addition to these paraphrastic poems, Photius also mentions two verse panegyrics, one in honor of Antioch and one commemorating Theodosius' victory against the Persians. Other than Eudocia's Homeric cento and Cyprian epic, these poems are lost and survive only as lines in Photius' catalogue. As a result, it remains unclear how Eudocia's Hebrew Bible paraphrases interpreted and revised these canonical texts to make them accessible to her late antique audience.

Second, like other late antique authors, Eudocia's poetry reconciles and conflates the classical past with early Christian literature, especially biblical texts that had, by the fifth-century, been canonized and codified. Moreover, Eudocia uses equally classicizing language when describing her imperial projects, which gives them an explicitly Homeric quality. Her interpretations of Christian scriptures and her paraphrases about the lives of Christian holy men and women equally blend sacred texts and values with Homeric and classicizing forms and content. By reading Eudocia's poetry against her Homeric models, this project elucidates her literary and political programs.

The first chapter, "Homeric Euergetism," focuses on Eudocia's two chronologically and geographically fixed works: her 438 CE speech given in Antioch and her panegyric poem from the bath complex at Hammat Gader. Unlike her other poems that survive in the manuscript tradition, these works require wider context about Eudocia's life. Toward that end, this chapter opens with a brief introduction to Eudocia's childhood and education, her marriage to Theodosius, and her two pilgrimages to Jerusalem, the first as part of a vow associated with their daughter's marriage to Valentinian III in 437 CE and the second associated with a fallout between Eudocia and Theodosius in the early 440s. Although she never returned to Constantinople after this second trip, Eudocia maintained her imperial retinue and funded many euergetistic programs, including the bath complex at Hammat Gader.

While a good deal of information about Eudocia's eastern travels survives in later accounts written by male authors, her speech in Antioch and her seventeen-line panegyric from Hammat Gader allow Eudocia's own euergetistic agenda and self-presentation to emerge without male mediation and interpretation. Taken as a whole, this material underscores how she adapted classical models, particularly the Homeric epics, to express her imperial benefactions, especially when her audience had diverse identities and interests. By structuring Eudocia's travels around specific moments when her own words survive, this chapter advances a more nuanced model of her euergetistic and alimentary programs and complicates how Eudocia expressed her religious identity to diverse, non-Christian/Orthodox audiences.

Chapter Two, "The Homeric Cento: Paraphrasing the Bible," examines Eudocia's most popular poem—her Homeric cento, a biblical paraphrase that appropriates Homeric lines to retell the beginning of Genesis and selections from the Gospels. Building on the recent proliferation of critical editions and commentaries on Homeric and Vergilian centos, the first half of this chapter places Eudocia within the wider cento tradition, a tradition that culminated during late antiquity. I begin by introducing the Vergilian centos written by Proba and Ausonius and their paratextual prefaces, after which I situate Eudocia's literary aims and poetic aesthetics, articulated by Eudocia herself in her own paratextual preface, within and against this wider tradition. In my reading, Eudocia describes her cento as a sacred text, rhetorically equal to the Bible, and consequently follows a path first blazed by Proba. Despite Eudocia treating her cento as a holy book, her critical aesthetics, on the other hand, more closely adhere to those expressed by Ausonius in his preface to the *Cento Nuptialis*. Eudocia's complex balance between sacred texts and critical evaluation, redaction, and emendation reflects an equally complex understanding of the relationship between an author and her product.

In the second half of this chapter, I provide a close reading of Eudocia's retelling of the Samaritan woman at the well episode from the Gospel of John. My main interest in this section is to demonstrate how Eudocia adapts this canonical story into one more ethically relevant to a fifth-century audience. She accomplishes this process by expanding on the Samaritan woman's role in the passage and, in the process, gives her a more public voice, while also highlighting her sexuality. By reading this biblical story against the lines Eudocia uses to tell it, the Samaritan woman and her concomitant sexuality become increasingly complicated, as she is intertextually transformed into a remixed Penelope-Nausicaa hybrid—two exceptional Homeric women equally defined, albeit in different ways and toward different ends, by their sexuality and chastity. This reading nuances Eudocia's engagement with her biblical characters, especially female characters, and their Homeric models, all of which underscore Eudocia's exegetical agency implicit in her paraphrastic versification of the Bible.

Chapter Three, "The Conversion: Constructing the Feminine Ideal," examines the first book of Eudocia's epic, the *Martyrdom of Cyprian*. The *Conversion* tells the story of a fictional Antiochene magician who converts to Christianity after his erotic magic fails to seduce a young Christian woman, Justa. Although following a fourth-century prose version of the Cyprian legend, Eudocia's *Conversion* also intertextually engages earlier Christian narratives, particularly the second-century Christian novel, the *Acts of Paul and Thecla*, and the third-century *Martyrdom of Perpetua and Felicitas*. After situating the Cyprian legend within the context of early Christian prose fictions and providing a close reading of Eudocia's verse paraphrase of the *Conversion*, this chapter uses Victor Turner's theory of social drama to elucidate the differences between Eudocia's epic and these earlier stories. By modeling Justa and the physical/sexual assaults against her on Thecla and Perpetua, Eudocia contrasts Justa with exceptional women from previous generations, which sets the recurring themes of sexual ambiguity and reversal found within those texts against her *Conversion*. Through this intertextual juxtaposition, Eudocia subtly comments on the early Christian feminine ideal and the depiction of that feminine ideal in early Christian literature.

Compared to Thecla and Perpetua, who reject the patriarchal trappings of marriage and family by increasingly adopting masculine physical characteristics, Eudocia's Justa is a simple protagonist: she never breaks from the authority of her father's house, and she never adopts masculine characteristics. In terms of social drama theory, Eudocia tells a story in which "nothing happens," despite reasonable expectations for such drama based on the story's intertextual allusions and the many demonic attacks that Justa overcomes. Not only does Eudocia characterize Justa in ways that disrupt Turner's theory, she also creates a female character with exceptional agency and spiritual power. In the final section of this chapter, I argue that Eudocia's Justa emerges as a new type of feminine ideal, intertextually distinct from and superior to those of previous generations. Along with my reading of the Samaritan woman at the well episode in the second chapter, this section advances the view that Eudocia actively influenced literary depictions of late antique Christian women.

Introduction

In the fourth chapter, "*The Confession*: Competing with Magic," I focus on the second book of Eudocia's *Martyrdom of Cyprian*, which takes the form of an apologetic speech given by the newly converted Cyprian to the Antiochene Christians to demonstrate the legitimacy of his conversion. During this speech, Cyprian traces how and where he learned magic—a journey that begins in Athens and spans the eastern half of the Mediterranean. After brief stops at the major religious centers of Greece and Asia Minor, Cyprian travels to Egypt and Babylon, where he advances to the position of Satan's lieutenant, before settling in Antioch, where he is hired to seduce Justa. While the details Eudocia provides about these cult centers and their associated rituals may not reflect historical reality, they do clarify the competitive rhetoric that late antique Christians used to discredit their ideological rivals.

The first section of this chapter traces the obscure ritual and cultic details of Cyprian's Mediterranean journey and situates them within the context of this late antique religious competition. In the second section, I compare the vastly different accounts of Justa between the *Confession* and the *Conversion* and argue that Eudocia gives her epic a thematic unity around her revisionist reading of Justa by adding to her *Confession* further allusions to the *Acts of Paul and Thecla*. In the final section of this chapter, I examine the literary origins of Cyprian's character and compare him to Pythagoras and Apollonius of Tyana, among others. Like Justa, Cyprian emerges as a type of literary bricolage who intertextually surpasses previous generations of itinerant wonderworkers. By employing this type of allusive competition, Eudocia anticipates Cyprian and Justa's martyrdom (in the third book of her epic, now lost) and gives her story more ideological force. Included after these chapters is my translation of Eudocia's Cyprian epic, its first complete English translation.

What follows is a long overdue study on Aelia Eudocia's life and poetry. Despite my attempts to allow Eudocia's own words to guide the organization and structure of each chapter, I am acutely aware that my own active hand as (male) reader and interpreter is present throughout. I ask for my reader's patience, with an understanding about the challenges associated with recovering the voices of ancient women, many of whom were silenced by oppressive and unjust forces. It is my hope this book on Eudocia's poetry does her justice and presents her as an exceptional late antique woman, courageous enough to challenge countless social, religious, and literary boundaries.

1

Homeric Euergetism

Introduction

IN 1981, YIZHAR HIRSCHFELD and Giora Solar published an initial report on their first three seasons of excavations at Hammat Gader, a site located along the Yarmuk River on the eastern border of modern-day Israel.[1] While their initial investigation of the epigraphic evidence was cursory, they claimed to have discovered a previously unknown poem by the empress Aelia Eudocia.[2] The following year, a more thorough analysis of the Greek inscriptions from the bath complex appeared and included a seventeen-line hexameter poem by Eudocia. This poem, dating between 437 CE, when Eudocia first traveled to Judea, and her death in 460 CE, is a rare piece of contemporary evidence for her activities outside Constantinople. In addition to this inscription, Evagrius Scholasticus writes that Eudocia gave a speech in Antioch that ended with a Homeric-sounding line.[3] These two pieces of evidence speak toward Eudocia's literary aptitude and her involvement in broader social, political, and religious projects.[4] By approaching Eudocia's travels and activities primarily through the lens of her surviving words, this chapter adds to previous studies of her travels to and euergetistic campaigns in Syria and Palestine, some of which have elicited comparison to Helena, mother of Constantine. My approach, therefore, addresses how late antique euergetism was performed and models a way to interpret Eudocia's public, literary productions.[5]

This literary program beyond Constantinople clarifies how Eudocia's pilgrimage to and subsequent exile in Jerusalem—despite some similarities to Helena's activities—originate from a nuanced appreciation for late antique

---

[1] The archaeological reports for Hammat Gader can be found in Hirschfeld and Solar 1981; Hirschfeld 1997; Broise 2003.

[2] SGO 21/22/01 (SEG 32.1502).

[3] Evagrius *Ecclesiastical History* 1.20.

[4] Green and Tsafrir 1982:83, 86 recognize Eudocia's engagement with Homeric models.

[5] The reports of the excavation likely were written too late for Hunt to consider. Recent studies on mosaics in the Holy Land (e.g. Baumann 1999) also do not discuss the Hammat Gader inscription.

imperial travel with all of its associated complexities, not from a desire to appear as a "new Helena."[6] Eudocia's deliberateness becomes more evident when her Hammat Gader poem and speech in Antioch are situated within their larger literary and euergetistic context(s). Removing the poem and speech from these contexts leads to confusion and a distorted picture of her travels. For instance, Bury suggests that, during her stay in Antioch, Eudocia "posed as one trained in Greek rhetoric and devoted to Hellenic traditions and proud of her Athenian descent [rather] than as a pilgrim on her way to the great Christian shrine."[7] This suggestion creates a false dichotomy between literary culture (*paideia*) and religious devotion and implies an inherent chasm between classical erudition and Christian piety. Based on her extant poems, Eudocia demonstrates an effortless ability to shift between different ideological registers. Simultaneously empress, *euergetes*, pilgrim, and poet, Eudocia presents herself both as every woman and as an exceptional one. Her speech in Antioch and the poem at Hammat Gader pivot on these various registers, as Eudocia communicates in a way that is quintessentially late antique, while also demonstrably unconventional.

As Christian pilgrim, Eudocia visits all the "must see" destinations; as imperial benefactress on a tour of the eastern empire, she stops at strategic urban centers, where she oversees or financially supports *ad hoc* building campaigns. In this regard, she imitates Helena but distinguishes herself from other imperial women, pilgrims, and *euergetai* by selecting a decidedly Homeric mode of communication. Her epigraphic and encomiastic winks and nods to classical epic open an intertextual dialogue between her late antique contexts and her Homeric content; at times these Homeric allusions clarify, other times they bemuse. Despite the inherent challenges of interpreting Eudocia's literary play, her euergetistic programs suggest that she never lost sight of fifth-century necessities. Through a distinct combination of Christian values and classical *paideia*, Eudocia emerges as a unique type of late antique *euergetes*, a Homeric one. This chapter focuses on the theme of Eudocia as Homeric *euergetes* and situates this theme both in its immediate context (Antioch and Hammat Gader) and in the wider context of Eudocia's life, beginning with her adolescence and marriage to Theodosius.

---

6   Eudocia's itinerary does mirror Helena's. See Hunt 1982; Holum 1990; Limberis 1996:60; Brubaker 1997; Elsner 2005. The title of "new Helena" was given to Pulcheria, Eudocia's sister-in-law, after the council of Chalcedon in 451 CE (Holum 1982:216; Brubaker 1997:62).

7   Bury 1923:226.

Eudocia's Early Life, Marriage, and Family

As daughter of the Athenian sophist Leontius, Aelia Eudocia, née Athenais, received the best classical education available and earned a reputation as an accomplished poet at a young age. Her unique education and literary aptitude, along with her connection to Leontius, advanced the assumption that she had been raised a "pagan." This assumption, however, is reflected in, although not entirely supported by, contemporary accounts and is difficult to reconcile with our knowledge about Theodosius' sister, Pulcheria, who influenced the young Theodosius and likely had some say in whom he married. For that reason, Eudocia and her family possibly had ties to Christianity.

The evidence for Eudocia's early life is sparse and contradictory. For example, the *Chronicon Paschale* (in its entry for 420 CE) lists her father as Heraclitus, a detail directly contradicted by her contemporary and Constantinopolitan insider, Socrates Scholasticus.[8] Despite this error, the *Chronicon Paschale* is not entirely unreliable, as it explains why Athenais initially visited Constantinople, where she met Pulcheria and Theodosius. According to this story, after Leontius' death, Athenais' brothers, Gessius and Valerius, by attempting to deprive her of her inheritance, forced her to travel to Constantinople to seek assistance from the imperial family. Impressed by Athenais, Pulcheria quickly arranged her engagement to Theodosius. Shortly before their wedding, Athenais adopted the imperial name Aelia Eudocia and, as the story goes, converted to Christianity.

Some scholars question this version of the story and downplay Pulcheria's influence as presented in the *Chronicon Paschale*.[9] According to this view, details of Eudocia's "rags to riches" story seem exaggerated, especially her need for imperial support from greedy brothers. That these same brothers held significant imperial positions shortly after her marriage is difficult to reconcile with such familial tension. Those who question the *Chronicon Paschale* instead posit that Eudocia's family had already risen to prominence before her arrival in Constantinople and that her brother Valerius had even held the governorship of Thrace. Pulcheria's opponents under the leadership of Paulinus preferred Hellenism (i.e. "paganism") to Christianity and, seeking to weaken Pulcheria's influence on Theodosius, arranged his engagement to the "pagan" Eudocia behind Pulcheria's back. While reconciling the difficulties surrounding Eudocia's family, this view stresses a growing conflict between Constantinopolitan Hellenizers and Christians and situates Eudocia as a central figure in their dispute. With so much conflicting evidence bound up with religious fervor and

---

[8] Socrates Scholasticus *Ecclesiastical History* 7.21.
[9] Holum 1982:112–121.

court intrigue, the reality behind Eudocia's early life may be irrevocably lost or shrouded in mystery.

Eudocia married Theodosius II on June 7, 421 CE and gave birth in the following year to their first child, Licinia Eudoxia, named after Theodosius' mother, Aelia Eudoxia. Perhaps through Pulcheria's direction, the infant Eudoxia was betrothed to Valentinian III, the child emperor in the West who needed eastern support against a usurper. Having given birth to an heir and secured an alliance with the West, Eudocia adopted the title Augusta on Jan 2, 423 CE. It has been suggested that she also bore a son, Arcadius, who, although never mentioned by imperial historians, was thought to be named in one inscription and the verse dedication of Proba's cento gifted to the Theodosian family.[10] Critics counter that this Arcadius must be the father of Theodosius, not his otherwise unattested son, a reading that is now the standard view.[11] Sometime during her first decade of marriage, Eudocia gave birth to a second daughter, Flacilla, who died in 431 CE.[12] Theodosius and Eudocia spent these early years with their two daughters in Constantinople, although she likely maintained ties with Athens and perhaps even supported building programs there.[13]

During these years in Constantinople, Eudocia augmented her reputation as an accomplished poet. After Theodosius' victory against the Persians in 421 CE, she, along with other court literati, recited encomia to commemorate the event. In his account of the recitation, Socrates claims that Eudocia's encomium stood out from the others, because it was in heroic verse.[14] As this Persian ode, like most of her poetry, does not survive, its precise content and form remain uncertain. Unlike most of Eudocia's poetry, however, the fairly secure date for her Persian ode allows us to situate it within its precise socio-historical context. Eudocia might have composed her Homeric cento, her Cyprian epic, or her versified paraphrases of Hebrew Bible (Pentateuch, Joshua, Judges, Zechariah, and Daniel) before leaving for Jerusalem in 438 CE, although it is equally possible that she wrote them later in life.

---

[10] ILS 818; *Dedication to Proba's Cento* 13–14 (Schottenius Cullhed 2015:190); Bury 1923:220; Clark and Hatch 1981:98–99; Cameron 1982:267. For more on the dedication, see Usher 1997:315; McGill 2007; Whitby 2007:216–217; Curran 2012:328–329; Kelly 2013b:34–35; Schottenius Cullhed 2015:59; Whitby 2016:229–230.

[11] Holum 1982:178; Burman 1994:84.

[12] Marcellinus Comes *Chronicon* 431.

[13] The Theodosian family spent more time in the imperial capital and less time traveling abroad than other imperial dynasties (Mitchell 2007:104–105). For possible Eudocian building programs, including a palace and basilicas, see Mommsen 1868:68, 127; Pagano 1988–1989; Burman 1994:82–83.

[14] Socrates Scholasticus *Ecclesiastical History* 7.21.

After securing prominent political positions for her male relatives, Eudocia encouraged them to promote religiously moderate and tolerant legislation. Her maternal uncle, Asclepiodotus, consul in 423 CE and praetorian prefect between 423–425 CE, issued a series of laws that discouraged violence against Jewish and pagan communities by granting these communities triple or quadruple restitution.[15] Considering the religious intolerance of the Theodosian emperors, these laws may represent Eudocia's moderating influence. The similarity of these edicts to those passed by Constantinian emperors in the preceding decades may also indicate that they had little actual effect beyond the world of late antique legal study. On the other hand, at least one militant Christian leader noticed these laws protecting pagan and Jewish communities and complained. In a threatening letter, St. Simeon the Stylite protested to Theodosius, and Asclepiodotus shortly thereafter was removed as praetorian prefect.[16] If these events are related, they underscore fifth-century ecclesiastic influence and the limitations of Eudocia's moderating voice.

On October 29, 437 CE, Licinia Eudoxia and Valentinian III married, an event that, along with those regions of Illyricum promised to Theodosius, secured an alliance between the eastern and western empires.[17] To commemorate the wedding, Theodosius and Eudocia commissioned an inscription for San Pietro in Vincoli in Rome: *Theodosius pater Eudocia cum coniuge votum, cumque suo supplex Eudoxia nomine solvit* (Theodosius, father, with his wife Eudocia and Eudoxia, as suppliant, in her own name, completed their vow).[18] That spring (438 CE), Eudocia went on pilgrimage to Jerusalem, either to fulfill her own vow or to alleviate tensions with Pulcheria.[19] Theodosius did not join her, a fact that fueled speculation about this trip and Eudocia's eventual exile from Constantinople.[20] Because Melania the Younger was in Constantinople visiting a sick relative and planned to return to Jerusalem around the same time Eudocia set out, the two women travelled together.[21]

[15] *Codex Theodosianus* 16.5.59, 16.8.26, 16.9.5, 16.10.22 (Holum 1982:123–124).
[16] *Life of St. Simeon Stylites* 130–131 (Holum 1982:125).
[17] Cassiodorus *Variae* 11.1.9; Jordanes *De gestis Romanorum* 329.
[18] ILCV 1779.
[19] Socrates *Ecclesiastical History* 7.47 states that Eudocia's journey fulfilled a vow connected with Licinia's marriage, whereas Mitchell 2007:108 suggests that her rivalry with Pulcheria forced Eudocia to leave Constantinople.
[20] Clark 1982:147–148.
[21] Evagrius *Ecclesiastical History* 1.20 and *Vita Melaniae Junioris* 55–56. See also the *Vita Petri Hiberi* and its summary in Horn 2004.

Eudocia in Antioch

Because Eudocia left Constantinople a few days before Melania, their arrangement to meet in Sidon gave Eudocia an opportunity to visit the Syrian capital of Antioch, a traditional stopping point for the imperial family.[22] While there, she recited an encomium that ended with ὑμετέρης γενεῆς τε καὶ αἵματος εὔχομαι εἶναι (I claim to be of your race and blood).[23] Influenced by her other verse encomia, especially the ode commemorating Theodosius' Persian victory, some scholars suggest that this speech was entirely in meter, either a hexametric panegyric (πάτρια) or a Homeric cento.[24] This view is supported by external evidence. For example, in his summary of Eudocia's poetry, Photius lists a panegyric to Antioch, although it is unclear if this panegyric is the same as the speech Eudocia gave in 438 CE.[25] Because only this Homeric ending survives, the remainder of Eudocia's speech, including its form and content, remains conjectural.[26]

Public or semi-public speeches given by ancient women are intrinsically valuable, not least because they were more infrequent and less likely to survive than those given by men. For that reason, speeches analogous to Eudocia's are rare. Of the few oratorical examples from Athens (Aspasia of Miletus), Rome (Sempronia, Hortensia), and elsewhere (Maesia of Sentinum, Carfania), most elicited harsh criticism, in particular those given by Hortensia, Maesia, and Carfania.[27] Speeches from female philosophers, Pythagoreans in particular, are more common, although these typically date to the classical or Hellenistic period.[28] Because the socio-cultural factors that produced these female philosophers were no longer at play in the fifth century CE, female Pythagoreans do

---

[22] Compare Eudocia's nondescript visit to Helena's, which was marked by some disagreement with Antioch's bishop, Eustathius (Hunt 1982:36; Chadwick 1948), Julian's tensions in Antioch are well known and related in his *Misopogon* (Downey 1951; Gleason 1986; Wiemer 1995; Lieu 1989:44–46).

[23] Evagrius *Ecclesiastical History* 1.20.

[24] Cameron 1970:8–12 and Hunt 1982:229 suggest that Eudocia's speech was a πάτρια. Ludwich 1882:207 proposes a cento.

[25] Photius *Bibliotheca* 183–184 (Henry 1959:2.195–199).

[26] Cameron 1982:278; Horn 2004:199.

[27] For Aspasia and her audience comprised of Socrates and his followers, see Plutarch *Life of Pericles* 24; Jarratt and Ong 1995. For Sempronia, see Appian *Civil Wars* 1.20; Valerius Maximus 3.8.6; 9.7.1; 9.15.1. For Hortensia, the first Roman woman to give a public speech, see Appian *Civil Wars* 4.32–33; Bauman 1992:78. According to Quintilian (*Institutio Oratoria* 1.1.6), Hortensia's speech was still read for its oratorical value. Quintilian also mentions a speech by Laelia, but it is unclear whether she gave her speech publicly. See Cicero *Brutus* 58.211–212; Bauman 1992:47–48. Valerius Maximus 8.3.3 lists Hortensia, Maesia, and Carfania as the three notable women who publicly pleaded cases.

[28] Haskins 2005:315–319.

not adequately account for educated and influential late antique women, such as Eudocia. Preeminent among all educated women, arguably throughout antiquity, was Hypatia, the closest analog, chronologically and socially, to Eudocia.[29] From the various, convoluted accounts about her life and death, Hypatia gave semi-public lectures on scientific or philosophical topics and was an active participant in fifth-century Alexandrian politics.[30] That she died so prematurely and violently underscores the real risks ancient women took when participating in public life. Similar to Hypatia's activity in Alexandria, Eudocia's public and political orations likely turned a few heads.

Most modern treatments of Eudocia's speech focus on what *intentions* or *desires* led her to make this Homeric allusion. According to one view, Eudocia had an affection for the cultured Antiochene aristocracy, a welcome reprieve from Constantinople's Trinitarian experts.[31] This view makes at least two significant assumptions about Eudocia, Antioch, and Constantinople. First, it assumes that Antioch was less engaged in theological controversy than Constantinople, which was frequently immersed in Trinitarian conflicts, in large part because of imperial involvement in these debates. Nevertheless, Antioch was also deeply involved in heresiological matters, particularly those involving Nestorius, and Antiochene Christians made as many theological contributions in the fifth century as Christians from Constantinople.

Second, this view assumes that Eudocia found herself alone in Constantinople without the type of cultured friends available in Antioch, despite the fact that Hellenism was no more common in Antioch than in Constantinople—by the fifth century, neither city had a sizeable pagan community compared to Alexandria, Aphrodisias, or Athens.[32] Moreover, equating Eudocia's *paideia* and her so-called pagan background risks the unverifiable conclusion that she never felt comfortable among Constantinople's Christian aristocracy. Her poetry and later involvement in the Monophysite controversy, especially as it intensified in Jerusalem, evince a seamless blend of theological and classical interests. Of course, we may move too far in the opposite direction and view Eudocia's speech as exclusively literary and entirely removed from her pilgrimage, a model that also risks creating two opposing Eudocias: the learned poet and the Christian pilgrim.[33]

Since Eudocia's intentions and feelings are ultimately unknowable, my approach focuses on the surviving speech, Antioch's response, and their developing relationship. According to the *Chronicon Paschale*, the Antiochenes

---

[29] For more on Hypatia and the expansive bibliography on her, see Cameron 2016; Watts 2017.
[30] Watts 2017:82–92.
[31] Bury 1923:226–227.
[32] Bowersock 2006:175. For late antique Antioch more generally, see Downey 1961; Matthews 2006.
[33] Hunt 1982:229.

applauded Eudocia's speech and commissioned two statues in her honor, a gold statue for the curia and a bronze statue for the museum.[34] A few essential observations can be made from this reaction. First, Eudocia's speech communicated more about her relationship with Antioch than about her ability to almost quote the *Iliad*. If Antioch erected multiple statutes to anyone able to (mis) quote Homer, their magistrates would have had time or money for little else. Second, her Homeric flourish communicated some message, however subtle, to the Antiochenes; for this message to be most effective, it necessarily contained multiple, complementary registers, simultaneously Homeric and late antique. Third, Antioch's commissioning of multiple statues reveals its response to her message as communicated through this Homeric allusion. In other words, the city's response is an equally multivalent Homeric wink, but one that follows late antique conventions and reveals late antique concerns. Honored by these statues, Eudocia funded multiple building campaigns, which further augmented her relationship with Antioch and indicates that there was more to her Homeric allusion than meets the eye.[35]

Poetic allusion was part of Eudocia's repertoire, and she routinely adapted Homeric lines to suit her literary or social agenda. In this instance, her engagement with Homer has multiple registers—literary and contextual—and adds an aesthetic touch to her speech. Even if one is unable to identify the exact location of the line in Homer, this language is unmistakably epic and adds *gravitas* to her performance. By concluding in this way, she also opens an intertextual conversation that frames her entire speech vis-à-vis Homer. For those able to identify the reference, her conclusion not only adds literary authority but also activates an intertextual engagement between her Homeric source and her agenda in Antioch. Audience members cultured enough to understand the allusion thus could have interpreted it as an indication of Eudocia's wider imperial program.

That Eudocia visited Antioch, or any city, is remarkable. Compared to the heirs of Constantine, the Theodosian emperors infrequently left Constantinople, a practice that likely alienated them from cities, including Antioch, that had previously benefited from periodic imperial visits.[36] Having access to the emperor's ear and purse appealed to the urban elite, despite the challenges, for citizens and emperor, associated with hosting the imperial court. A decade after Julian's fiasco with Antioch's grain supply, Valens funded a building campaign

---

[34] *Chronicon Paschale* (Dindorf 1831:585; Whitby and Whitby 1989:74–75; Bury 1923:131–132. Evagrius *Ecclesiastical History* 1.20, following John Malalas, only mentions the bronze statue. See Whitby and Whitby 1989:75; Downey 1961:451–452.

[35] John Malalas *Chronographia* 14 (Dindorf 1831:352–358; Thurn 2000:272–278); Evagrius *Ecclesiastical History* 1.20; Downey 1941:207–13.

[36] Mitchell 2007:323.

and established a grain distribution system that lasted two centuries.[37] Through these projects, Valens conflated two essential roles: as imperial benefactor, he modeled euergetism at the local level; as temporary resident of Antioch, he met the physical and religious needs of the city.[38] Late Roman emperors frequently addressed such social needs, especially when their host city exhausted its grain reserves.[39]

By comparing Eudocia's involvement in Antioch to previous imperial programs, the euergetistic implications behind her encomium come into sharper focus. As self-proclaimed kin to the Antiochenes—some have argued that her father was an Antiochene citizen residing in Athens—and as imperial benefactress, she provided tangible, civic assistance to Antioch.[40] Shortly after her arrival, she funded the construction of a basilica, the restoration of a bath complex, an extension of the city's wall, and a system to feed the city's poor.[41] Since such projects typically fell to local *euergetai*, Eudocia's assistance may suggest a scarcity of local elites who were contributing to the city's needs.

Just fifty years earlier, in a homily about charitable giving, John Chrysostom implied that Antioch's abject poor made up a very small part (about two percent) of the city's population.[42] Despite this hyperbolic depiction of urban poverty, it seems that "cheerful givers" in late antique aristocratic circles had become—to borrow a phrase from Peter Brown—*rarae aves*.[43] As a result, urban poor flocked with great expectation whenever a "rare bird" migrated to their city. For instance, when Melania and Pinianus arrived in northern Africa, the Christian communities of Hippo eagerly welcomed and courted them.[44] If Antioch's citizens were similarly on the lookout for external patrons, such as Eudocia, they would have publicly recognized euergetistic generosity. In general, such honors augmented a patron's prestige and social capital, which advanced her future interests and secured a mutually beneficial relationship marked by public benefactions and public gratitude. In my view, Eudocia's speech fits within and perhaps even initiates this social give-and-take.

---

[37] Downey 1951:382–383; Liebeschuetz 1972:129–130.

[38] For a discussion on the changes in late antique euergetism, especially the increasing concern for the poor, see Patlagean 1977; Holman 2001; Brown 2002:26–32; Holman 2008; Brown 2012; Brown 2015:85–88; Brown 2016.

[39] Wiemer 1995:190–194.

[40] Holum 1982:117–118; McClanan 2002:20.

[41] *Chronicon Paschale* (Dindorf 1831:585; Whitby and Whitby 1989:74–75); Evagrius *Ecclesiastical History* 1.20; Downey 1941:207–213; Downey 1961:451–452; Whitby and Whitby 1989:75.

[42] John Chrysostom *Homilies on Matthew* 66.3. See also Augustine *Expositions on the Psalms* 149.10. Patlagean 1977:207–214; Patlagean 1997:15–25; Brown 2002:14; Mayer 2006a; Mayer 2006b; Mayer 2008; Brown 2015:90–91.

[43] Brown 2002:48; Finn 2006; Brown 2015:87.

[44] *Vita Melaniae Junioris* 21; Augustine *Epistle* 126.7; Clark 1985:22–25; Brown 2002:55–56.

If Eudocia's brief stay in Antioch began an ongoing socio-cultural exchange with the city, then the beginning of this interaction, specifically her words "ὑμετέρης γενεῆς τε καὶ αἵματος εὔχομαι εἶναι," invariably clarifies but also, perhaps, complicates her euergetistic program. For that reason, it is constructive to identify her possible Homeric source, to analyze the allusion in its Homeric context, and to reconstruct the implications of making this allusion in a public speech.

The exact line, ὑμετέρης γενεῆς τε καὶ αἵματος εὔχομαι εἶναι, is not attested in the Homeric corpus. In fact, ὑμετέρης is never positioned first in a Homeric hexameter; the closest example is γαίης ὑμετέρης (*Odyssey* 7.269). No form of ὑμέτερος opens an Iliadic line, although it is infrequently found as part of a prepositional phrase at the beginning of lines (e.g. *Iliad* 5.686, ἐν πόλει ὑμετέρῃ, and *Iliad* 20.116, ἐν φρεσὶν ὑμετέρῃσιν). It can begin a line in the *Odyssey* but never in the feminine singular genitive. It stands to reason, therefore, that Eudocia either wrote her own Homeric sounding line or modified a line from the *Iliad* or the *Odyssey*. Manipulating Homeric lines came easily to Eudocia, as her cento demonstrates.[45] The closest analog to ὑμετέρης γενεῆς τε καὶ αἵματος εὔχομαι εἶναι is *Iliad* 6.211 and 20.241: ταύτης τοι γενεῆς τε καὶ αἵματος εὔχομαι εἶναι. These lines, both from heroic speeches immediately preceding battle, would require minimal lexical change, a substitution of ὑμετέρης for ταύτης τοι.[46] By examining each in turn, *Iliad* 6.211—part of the famous exchange between Glaucus and Diomedes—emerges as the preferred source for Eudocia's encomium.

Meeting in the field of battle, Diomedes sarcastically and insultingly asserts that he neither knows Glaucus nor has seen him fighting in the vanguard (*Iliad* 6.124–127), a claim that prompts Glaucus to summarize his illustrious ancestry (*Iliad* 6.151). For his part of this traditionally Homeric tête-à-tête, Glaucus traces his line from Aeolus through Sisyphus, Glaucus, and Bellerophon to his own father, Hippolochus, and concludes with, "ταύτης τοι γενεῆς τε καὶ αἵματος εὔχομαι εἶναι" (*Iliad* 6.211). Upon learning Glaucus' race and blood, Diomedes joyfully drives his spear into the ground and declares that, because his grandfather, Oeneus, once hosted Bellerophon, they were guest-friends (ἦ ῥά νύ μοι ξεῖνος πατρώϊός ἐσσι παλαιός). *Xenia*, a crucial social contract in Homeric society that discouraged conflict between guest-friends, was commonly sealed with mutual gift exchange. Accordingly, Glaucus and Diomedes agree not to fight each other and ritually reinstitute their relationship with an exchange of gifts: Glaucus trades his golden armor for Diomedes' bronze armor.[47]

---

[45] For more on Eudocia's Homeric cento, see the following chapter.

[46] Based on their shared line, Kirk 1990:171 draws connections between these Homeric episodes.

[47] Kirk 1990:190–191 suggests this bizarre end resists literal and realistic interpretation.

Iliad 20.241 appears in the middle of a battle scene between Aeneas and Achilles (20.75–352), an episode that contains a simile depicting Achilles as a gentle lion, an image inconsistent with the bloodthirsty warrior found in this portion of the *Iliad*.[48] Similar to Glaucus and Diomedes in *Iliad* 6, Aeneas boasts of his birth and accomplishments, in the middle of which he says, "ταύτης τοι γενεῆς τε καὶ αἵματος εὔχομαι εἶναι." Unlike Glaucus, Aeneas immediately challenges Achilles to fight, but Poseidon intervenes and steals Aeneas to safety, the second contest between them to end this way.[49]

When compared to Eudocia's speech, three features support the conclusion that *Iliad* 6.211 was her likely source. First, by ending her speech with this Homeric allusion, Eudocia mirrors the speech of Glaucus more than that of Aeneas, who continues for another sixteen lines. That Eudocia echoes not only the words but also the structure of Glaucus' speech evinces the complexity of her intertextual play. Second, the general tone of her oration parallels Glaucus' speech. Despite the martial context of both passages, the confrontation between Glaucus and Diomedes ends in a recognition scene and a reinstitution of *xenia*, marked by mutual gift exchange and an agreement to avoid each other in battle. Aeneas and Achilles, in contrast, already know each other's ancestry (*Iliad* 20.203). After Aeneas reminds Achilles of his birth, he requests that they stop speaking (*Iliad* 20.244) and test each other with weapons (*Iliad* 20.257–258). Considering this was likely Eudocia's first visit as Augusta to Antioch, her public address, comparable to Glaucus', served as a formal introduction. Third, Antioch's response suggests that someone attributed her allusion to *Iliad* 6.211 and decided to play along with the intertextual game. While only the literary elite would have recognized or appreciated her echo and its Homeric context, they knew Homer well enough to make equally cultured gestures. In fact, Antioch's official response was equally Homeric—their two statues, gold for the curia, bronze for the museum—subtly echo Glaucus and Diomedes' armor exchange.

Eudocia's commitment to fund building projects and an alimentary program is consistent with late antique euergetism, as is the city's response. Their honorific statues, likely unfinished when Eudocia left Antioch for Jerusalem, were to remain in the city, not to return with Eudocia to Constantinople. The entire interaction—statues in return for a basilica, bath, walls, and grain— is one whereby a wealthy benefactor provides functional monuments and commodities in exchange for honorific monuments. This exchange is consistent with late antique euergetism, not with Homeric *xenia*. While both parties

---

[48] Leaf 1902:2, 348–349 and Combellack 1976:49–53 contrast this "normal" Achilles with the blood-thirsty one after Patroclus' death. Edwards 1991:301–329 argues that this imagery is consistent with rest of the *Iliad*.

[49] *Iliad* 20.90–93, 188–194.

offer tangible and valued objects, neither abandons late antique mores for a less valuable, Homeric substitute. What distinguishes this event, therefore, is how Eudocia opens her euergetistic program with a Homeric allusion, to which Antioch responds in equally Homeric fashion. Similar to Glaucus and Diomedes' exchange of armor in *Iliad* 6, Eudocia's exchange of gifts with Antioch is equally imbalanced. Rather than simply flaunting her *paideia*, Eudocia fulfills her imperial obligations while making a culturally meaningful reference to their shared, classical past. In doing so, she simultaneously presents herself as Homeric *euergetes* and Antiochene guest-friend.

Eudocia in Jerusalem

After leaving Antioch, Eudocia joined Melania at Sidon and traveled from there to Jerusalem, where she continued her euergetistic program by funding a cross for the Church of the Holy Sepulchre and food for Jerusalem's poor.[50] Based on the accounts of Eudocia's pilgrimage to Jerusalem, she situated herself within a social and religious tradition dating back to Constantine and Helena.[51] Unfortunately, the surviving evidence is selective and often contradictory. For example, Eudocia's support of monophysite Christianity earned her the sympathy of Gerontius, the Greek author of Melania's *vita*, although he interprets events favorably for Melania and never allows Eudocia's activity in Jerusalem to overshadow Melania. Gerontius' Eudocia is, therefore, a type of imperial sidekick who remains securely in Melania's shadow. The author of Melania's Latin *vita*, in contrast, is less concerned with Nestorian partisanship and adds at least one unflattering story about Eudocia.[52] In addition to the narratives focused on Melania, John Rufus' life of Peter the Iberian contains episodes, unavailable to or omitted by Gerontius and his Latin translator/redactor, that clarify Eudocia's interactions with local church leaders in Jerusalem other than Melania. Although it is difficult to reconcile all these events, which present an incomplete and slightly muddled picture of Eudocia's time in Jerusalem, they underscore her relationship with Melania and their involvement in the cult of the saints.

According to John Rufus, on May 15th, 438/439 CE, Eudocia presided over the dedication of a basilica to St. Stephen, built just north of the Jerusalem wall

---

[50] For late antique travel and travel accounts, see Wilkinson 2002; Matthews 2006; Johnson 2012b; Johnson 2016b.

[51] *Vita Melaniae Junioris* 58-59; Hunt 1982:228–229; Brubaker 1997:62. Clark 1982:147, building on John Rufus *Plerophoria* 11, critiques the details of Eudocia's first visit to Jerusalem.

[52] Clark 1984:23.

to house his relics in her possession.[53] Cyril, bishop of Alexandria, was also in attendance, but Juvenal, bishop of Jerusalem, seemingly was not.[54] As Juvenal was not part of the eastern monophysite circle made up of Melania, Eudocia, and Cyril, whom he had opposed during the Nestorian controversy, Eudocia perhaps publicly preferred Cyril over Juvenal. It is equally possible that Juvenal was present for the dedication, although his participation was omitted by John Rufus, who sided with the Monophysites.[55] The following day, Eudocia attended the dedication of a second martyrium to St. Stephen built by Melania on the Mount of Olives, which housed additional relics of St. Stephen, as well as relics of the Forty Martyrs of Sebaste and of some unspecified Persian martyrs, whose bones Peter the Iberian had brought to Jerusalem.[56] Our sources here differ significantly. The pro-Melanian Gerontius deemphasizes Eudocia's involvement, whereas John Rufus mentions an inscription commemorating her financial support.[57]

Since our sources do agree that Eudocia and Melania each funded a martyrium to house St. Stephen's relics and that the commemoration services for these projects took place on concurrent days, there is either some confusion or some unexpressed tension. Either these accounts are mistaken, and the relics of Stephen were housed in only one Jerusalem martyrium, or St. Stephen's bones were the object of contention between Melania and Eudocia. In order to reconcile these details, Clark suggests that Eudocia used the bones of Stephen to gain local and imperial legitimacy and prestige, despite Theophanes' ninth-century account that the bishop of Jerusalem had already sent St. Stephen's hand to Theodosius II and Pulcheria in the 420s CE, years before Eudocia went on pilgrimage.[58] Clark follows the late antique accounts, which attest that Eudocia transported some of these relics to Constantinople in 439 CE and deposited them in the Basilica of St. Lawrence.[59] Because this basilica was built by Pulcheria and

[53] *Vita Petri Hiberi* 33 (Raabe 1895:37). The precise date of Eudocia's trip is debated. Clark 1982:147 and Holum 1982:184–185 suggest 438 CE, whereas Hunt 1982:230 argues that 439 CE is preferable, since Eudocia's arrival at Jerusalem in May of 438 CE is too early. Holum and Clark's dates are consistent with the pilgrimage timeline depicted in the *Itinerarium Burdigalense* 571.6-8 (Cuntz 1929).

[54] Clark 1982:153.

[55] For Eudocia's entourage, see Hunt 1982:230–232; Clark 1986b:63–64; Burman 1994; Horn 2004:200–201.

[56] Melania had housed these relics near her female monastery on the Mount of Olives as early as 431 CE (*Vita Melaniae Junioris* 48). By December 26, 439 CE, she celebrated the festival to St. Stephen in the martyrium (*Vita Melaniae Junioris* 64).

[57] *Vita Melaniae Junioris* 58–59; *Vita Petri Hiberi* 37.

[58] Clark 1982:143; Theophanes *Chronographia* 5920 (de Boor 1980:1:86–87); Holum and Vikan 1979:119, 128.

[59] Marcellinus Comes *Chronicon* 439.2 (Mommsen 1894:80); Holum and Vikan 1979; Brubaker 1997:56. For Pulcheria's role in the cult of the saints, see Holum 1982:136–137.

was located in a city district named after her, Eudocia's decision to deposit these relics there can be seen as a form of imperial competition.[60]

More generally, Eudocia brought relics back to Constantinople that helped secure her and her family's position. These include the chains Herod used to bind St. Peter, which Licinia Eudoxia deposited in the Roman basilica eventually named St. Peter ad Vincula.[61] According to Theodorus Lector, Eudocia sent Pulcheria a portrait of the Virgin presumed to be the work of Luke the Evangelist, although the reliability of this account is disputed.[62] As a way to further augment her participation in the cult of the saints, she wrote verse paraphrases of saints' lives and prophetic texts. It is not a coincidence that, while Melania publicly venerated the bones of the prophet Zechariah, Eudocia rewrote the book of Zechariah into Greek verse. This paraphrase can also be viewed as a literary rival to Pulcheria's basilica for Isaiah in Constantinople built around the time Eudocia returned.[63] It is equally tempting to interpret her epic paraphrase of Cyprian of Antioch as a literary participation in the cult of Cyprian and Justina, especially as the cult spread across the empire.[64]

At some point during this trip—the Greek and Latin versions of the *Life of Melania* disagree on the particulars—Eudocia twisted her foot so seriously that prayers for her recovery were made in the Church of the Holy Sepulchre.[65] After she recovered well enough to travel, she left Jerusalem, accompanied by Melania as far as Caesarea. Her injured foot and her possession of St. Stephen's bones were soon conflated so much that an epigraphic forgery claims that Eudocia dedicated St. Stephen's foot in the Basilica of St. Stephen in the Paphlagonian town of Safranbolu.[66] Based on this forged inscription, at least one person imagined Eudocia depositing bones of St. Stephen along her return route to Constantinople.

---

[60] Clark 1982.

[61] This is the same church where the inscription (ILCV 1779) that mentions a dedication by Eudocia and Theodosius II was found. See Bury 1923:227; Burman 1994:72.

[62] Theodorus Lector *Historia Tripartita* 353; Holum 1982:142; Burman 1994:72. Compare with Acts 12:6.

[63] Marcellinus Comes *Chronicon* 439.2, 453; Theodorus Lector *Historia Tripartita* 363; Holum 1982:137.

[64] Sowers 2017. See also chapters three and four.

[65] *Vita Melaniae Junioris* 59. For the differences between the Greek and Latin *vitae*, see Clark 1984:192.

[66] Doublet 1889; Halkin 1953; Livrea 1996. On the history of this inscription and its influence on scholarship, see Mango 2004.

Eudocia in Exile

A few years after Eudocia returned to Constantinople, she found herself estranged from Theodosius and his immediate circle of advisors.[67] By the early 440s CE, her conflicts with Pulcheria increased enough that they allowed the court eunuch, Chrysaphius, to isolate Pulcheria and to force her suburban retirement, which lasted until he lost imperial favor and was exiled in 450 CE.[68] After removing Pulcheria, Chrysaphius turned his attention to Eudocia, whose reputation he ruined by persuading Theodosius that she had an affair with Paulinus, master of offices and rival of Chrysaphius.[69] Paulinus' intimacy with the imperial family—he served as παράνυμφος in Theodosius' wedding—had already promoted an earlier charge of sexual impropriety with Pulcheria.[70] It appears Paulinus' political/religious opponents used his familiarity with imperial women against him, and his fall from favor occurred at the same time Theodosius exiled Eudocia, a fact that further incited court gossip. After removing Paulinus, Chrysaphius facilitated the replacement of the popular city prefect, fellow poet, and close friend of Eudocia, Cyrus of Panopolis, who resigned from the city prefecture in 441 CE. Shortly thereafter, Theodosius confiscated Cyrus' property and exiled him to the bishopric of Cotyaeum.

These events clarify the legendary account of Eudocia's exile related by John Malalas.[71] According to this story, the emperor bought an apple of such remarkable size that he sent it as a gift to Eudocia. She, in turn, gifted the apple to Paulinus, who, equally impressed by the magnificent fruit, gave it to Theodosius. The emperor immediately recognized that it was the same apple he had given Eudocia. Suspicious, Theodosius asked Eudocia about the apple, and, when she insisted that she had eaten it, he produced the apple and accused Paulinus and Eudocia of having an affair. The folk-tale motif of this "apple of discord" story has been much discussed and variously resolved.[72] Some assume Paulinus' involvement in Eudocia's exile but dismiss the apple narrative.[73] Others see in the narrative an exculpatory purpose—a literary reaction to court

---

[67] My purpose here is not to revise the account of Eudocia's exile, which is discussed in detail in Cameron 1982; Clark 1982; Holum 1982; Burman 1994.

[68] Bury 1923; Holum 1982.

[69] Cameron 1982:256 lists Cyrus of Panopolis and Paulinus as Chrysaphius' victims. Burman 1991:55–56, 1994:67–69 argues that the sources may equally refer to a scandal between Paulinus and Eudocia, Paulinus and Pulcheria, or Honoria and Eugenius.

[70] This charge, leveled against Pulcheria by Nestorius, survives in Theodorus Lector *Historia Tripartita* 340 (Hansen 1995:97). See also Holum 1982:193.

[71] John Malalas *Chronographia* 14 (Dindorf 1831:352–358; Thurn 2000:272–278).

[72] Littlewood 1974; Cameron 1982:258–259, 270–279; Holum 1982:114; Scharf 1990; Burman 1994:64–69.

[73] Bury 1923.

gossip—that simultaneously exonerates Eudocia and vilifies the overly jealous Theodosius.[74] At the very least, Malalas' account reveals how Eudocia's dismissal from Constantinople was interpreted, although we should note that Theodosius did not send her away in disgrace. She retained the title Augusta until her death and retained an imperial retinue, at least during the early years of her exile.[75] Eudocia never returned to Constantinople and remained in Jerusalem, even after the death of Theodosius in 450 CE.

Eudocia at Hammat Gader

During her Holy Land exile between 440 and 460 CE, Eudocia visited the springs at Hammat Gader and composed the honorific poem that opened this chapter. These springs were a popular source of therapeutic relief beginning in the second century CE, when the bath was built as a Roman army spa.[76] By the third century CE, the bath enters the literary record; these descriptions complement and, occasionally, clarify the archaeological record.[77] In his treatment of Iamblichus' visit, Eunapius describes the springs as the second most popular therapeutic site in the Mediterranean and as having two springs named Eros and Anteros, a detail partially corroborated in Eudocia's poem.[78] From Epiphanius, bishop of Salamis, we also learn that the bath had co-ed bathing facilities, a feature that elicited concern among some late antique Christians.[79]

The Piacenza Pilgrim of 570 CE adds to this picture by describing the bath's layout and its overnight accommodations for visitors suffering from various skin diseases, especially leprosy.[80] Such incubation rooms were full of natural vapors, a treatment recommended by Galen that could also induce the type of nocturnal visions associated with incubation cults.[81] The following morning, priests prescribed additional bathing rituals for visitors to perform until they experienced relief. Corroborating the Piacenza Pilgrim's description, recent

---

[74] Cameron 1982:258–259.

[75] Theodosius withdrew this retinue in 444 CE, when they had a further falling-out. According to court rumor, Eudocia killed Theodosius' agent, Satornilos, who had killed two of her clerics. See Marcellinus Comes *Chronicon* 444; Priscus Fragment 8 (Given 2014:78); Cameron 1982:260; Burman 1994:69.

[76] Eck 2014:212–214; Renberg 2016:808.

[77] Origen's *Commentary on John* 6:41 is the earliest extant reference to the bath complex (Schürer 1974–1987:100–104).

[78] Eunapius *Lives of the Philosophers* 459; Hirschfeld and Solar 1981:202.

[79] Epiphanius *Panarion* 30.7.

[80] Piacenza Pilgrim *Itinerarium Antonini Placentini* 7 (Cuntz 1965:132; Wilkinson 2002:133). Milani 1977:34–36; Johnson 2016c; Renberg 2016:808–814.

[81] Bourdy 1992:31–35. Renberg 2016:808–814 explains how the incubation ritual at Hammat Gader differed from those elsewhere.

excavations have discovered a small room equipped with a pool, whose water source ran separate from the rest of the complex.

Not every visitor to Hammat Gader suffered from skin diseases, despite the trend in late antique healing cults to specialize in specific ailments. Other natural springs, such as the military bath at Bourbonne-les-Bains, never took on any ritual significance.[82] Based on the literary and archaeological evidence, Hammat Gader welcomed a diverse range of patrons, from guests looking to enjoy a day at the bath to those desperate for a healing touch.[83] When Eudocia composed her poem in honor of the bath and its springs, the religious identities of its guests would have been equally diverse, from Christian and Jewish to traditionalist or "pagan." Her poem must then be understood within these divergent, perhaps competing, ideological and economic contexts.

The inscription itself was found *in situ* in the southern end of the building's largest room, the Hall of Fountains, and would have been visible as one entered from the west (room A).[84] It has a height of 71 cm, a thickness of approximately 2 cm, and an original length of 184–186 cm; where the right edge is broken, the length is 181 cm. It is uncertain whether the inscription was designed as part of a wider decorative program for the room, but it does contain one controversial feature: the crosses flanking Eudocia's name. In 427 CE, Theodosius outlawed crosses on areas with pedestrian traffic, including mosaic floors.[85] As a result, some have questioned whether Eudocia knew about the crosses or their placement in a major thoroughfare.[86] Considering the time necessary to commission, to fabricate, and to install an inscription of this size, Eudocia likely would not have been present for its "unveiling." The inscription reads as follows:

1   Εὐδοκίας Αὐγούστης
Πολλὰ μὲν ἐν βιότῳ κ' ἀπίρονα θαύματ' ὄπωπα,
τίς δέ κεν ἐξερέοι, πόσα δὲ στόματ', ὦ κλίβαν' ἐσθλέ,
4   σὸν μένος, οὐτιδανὸς γεγαὼς βροτός; Ἀλλά σε μᾶλλο(ν)
ὠκεανὸν πυρόεντα νέον θέμις ἐστὶ καλεῖσθαι,
Παιάνα καὶ γενέτην, γλυκερῶν δοτῆρα[87] ῥεέθρων.
ἐκ σέο τίκτεται οἶδμα τὸ μυρίον, ἄλλυδις ἄλλη,
8   ὅππῃ μὲν ζεῖον, πῇ δ' αὖ κρυερόν τε μέσον τε.
τετράδας ἐς πίσυρας κρηνῶν προχέεις σέο κάλλος·

---

[82] Ronot 1973; Troisgros 1994; Sauer 2005.
[83] Muir 2006 discusses the ideological competition inherent to healing across religious traditions.
[84] Broise 2003:219.
[85] Codex Justinianus 1.8.1.
[86] Green and Tsafrir 1982:82.
[87] Read δωτῆρα (Bevegni 1990). Compare Eudocia's *Martyrdom of Cyprian* lines 115 and 406.

Ἰνδή· Ματρώνα τε· Ῥεπέντινος· Ἠλίας ἁγνός·
Ἀντωνῖνος ἐύς· δροσερὰ Γαλάτια· καὶ αὐτή
12 Ὑγεία· καὶ χλιαρὰ μεγάλα· χλιαρὰ δὲ τὰ μικρά·
Μαργαρίτης· κλίβανος παλεός· Ἰνδή τε· καὶ ἄλλη
Ματρώνα· βριαρή τε Μονάστρια· κ᾽ ἡ Πατριάρχου.
ὡδείνουσι τεὸν μένος ὄβριμον ἠνε[κὲς ἀιέν,]
16 ἀλλὰ θεὸν κλυτόμητιν ἀείσο[μαι - - - - -]
εἰς εὐεργεσείην μερόπων τε χ[ρ - - - - - -]⁸⁸

1   By Eudocia Augusta,
I have seen many countless wonders in my lifetime,
But who, how many mouths, o good *clibanus*,
4   What worthless mortal could proclaim your might? But rather,
It is fitting to call you a new fiery ocean,
Paean and begetter, dispenser of sweet streams.
From you is born the boundless swell, one here, another there,
8   In some parts a boiling (swell), in others a cold and tepid (swell).
In four tetrads of springs, you pour forth your beauty:

Indian woman and Matrona, Repentinus and St. Elijah,
good Antoninus, dewy Galatea and
12   Hygeia herself, the great warm (baths) and the small warm (baths),
the Pearl and old *clibanus*, Indian woman, and another
Matrona, the strong Nun, and the spring of the Patriarch.
For those who are in anguish, your mighty strength is eternal,
16   but I will sing of God, famous in skill,
for the benefit and ... of mortals.⁸⁹

This seventeen-line poem blends panegyric and ekphrastic features to honor the bath, its springs, and its furnace or *clibanus*, a tank boiler similar to a modern hot-water heater.⁹⁰ In this poem, Eudocia followed an established late antique tradition of praising hot springs and baths.⁹¹ Claudian's *fons Aponi* (*Carmina*

---

⁸⁸ Meimare 1983 reconstructs the final two lines:
ἀλλὰ θεὸν κλυτόμητιν ἴσο[μαι ὄφρα σε σῴζω]
εἰς εὐεργεσείην μερόπων τε χρ[ῆσιν ἀείνων].

⁸⁹ The translation is my own. I avoid including any of the various reconstructions for the last two lines, since they are uncertain.

⁹⁰ Green and Tsafrir 1982:83–85; Yegül 1992:373; Becker 1995; Boehm 1995; Busch 1999:84–98; Christian 2015:340–354.

⁹¹ Busch 1999 provides a complete list of these praises, including many in the *Latin Anthology* (331–344).

Minora 26), for example, describes the beauty and therapeutic function of the springs of Abano.[92] A century later, Ennodius and Cassiodorus composed similar poems for the springs at Abano and drew inspiration from Claudian's *fons Aponi*.[93] Similar to Claudian, Eudocia compares the springs at Hammat Gader to various healing deities, although her poem focuses on the bath's man-made features, rather than its natural location and beauty.

Structurally, the poem contains multiple lists, a common poetic feature of late antiquity that Eudocia preferred. For instance, her Homeric cento begins with the creation story, itself a catalogue of sorts, and borrows heavily from the Shield of Achilles, the first and archetypical ekphrasis in the western literary tradition.[94] This type of generic hybridity was quite popular in Late Antiquity.[95] Christodorus of Coptus, one of the so-called "wandering poets," composed a verse inventory, "On the pupils of the great Proclus," as well as a 416-line ekphrastic poem of nearly eighty statues at the bath of Zeuxippus in Constantinople.[96] Writing within this tradition of ekphrastic panegyrics about springs or baths, Eudocia adopts the perspective of the viewer but also innovates on this tradition by directly addressing the *clibanus*.[97]

The poem opens with two Homerisms that give the entire encomium an epic tone.[98] In line 2, Eudocia introduces the theme of healing or wonders, central to the poem and the site's reputation, by transforming *Odyssey* 15.79 (πολλὴν ἐπ' ἀπείρονα γαῖαν) into πολλὰ καὶ ἀπίρονα θαύματα. Since visitors of various religious backgrounds, including traditionalists (e.g. *Odyssey* 9.190), Hellenistic Jews (Josephus *Jewish Antiquities* 9.182; Philo *On the Life of Moses* 1.180), Christians (Mark 5:20 and Luke 11:14), and even philosophers or thaumaturges, would have been comfortable with the ideologically ambiguous θαύματα, its use here may suggest an awareness of the bath's diverse clientele.

In the following two lines (3–4), Eudocia confesses her inability to adequately describe the *clibanus'* strength (μένος), even with countless mouths—a firmly established literary trope by the first century.[99] Unlike the ideologically neutral θαύματα above, this allusion is decidedly more classicizing and Homeric. First, μένος—the force/anger endowed upon gods, humans, and, less frequently, inanimate objects—is comparatively less common in later authors, especially

---

92 Martial *Satires* 6.42.4; Lucan *Civil War* 7.193.
93 Kennell 2000:96–98; Majani 2006; Consolino 2017:119–120.
94 Usher 1999:1–2; Schembra 2007b:5–6.
95 Formisano 2017:225–227; Rees 2017:315.
96 *Palatine Anthology* 2; Cameron 1965:475, 481, 489; Busch 1999:98; Whitby 2003:598–599; Bassett 2004:51–58, 160–185; Kaldellis 2007; Agosti 2009.
97 Didot 1872; Kendall 1998:24n16; Thébert 2003:485–521.
98 The term Homerism comes from Fournet 1995:302. See also Christian 2015:342–343.
99 Busch 1999:88–89.

Christians.[100] Within its original Homeric contexts, the request for ten tongues opens the Catalogue of Ships (*Iliad* 2.489), another paradigmatic ancient list, and had become commonplace in Greco-Roman literature, used by Cicero, Vergil, Ovid, and Persius, among others, and by Jewish authors, including Philo, Baruch, and Yohanan ben Zakkai.[101] Eudocia here anticipates her catalogue of springs and situates it within the classical tradition through this allusion.

The appearance and identity of the poem's sixteen fountains have been much discussed, mostly because Eudocia names only fifteen distinct objects, a few of which are certainly not fountains.[102] Her list can be divided into four types: general descriptions of people, specific historical figures, religious/mythological figures, and architectural features of the bath. First, Eudocia twice mentions an Indian woman and a Matrona, along with a strong Nun and a Patriarch.[103] These are likely based on the physical appearances or clothing of sculptures in the complex. It is tempting to compare these two Matronas with the Matrona healing cult near Antioch, a possibly Jewish incubation cult.[104] The Patriarch is likely a reference to a Jewish patriarch, not the Christian bishop, Juvenal of Jerusalem.[105]

Second, Eudocia lists specific individuals, Repentinus and Antoninus the Good, tentatively identified as Antoninus Pius, who might have been local/imperial benefactors honored with sculptures near the fountains.[106] Next are religious or mythological figures associated with healing centers: Helias the Holy (the biblical prophet Elijah), whom the Piacenza Pilgrim associates with the bath, along with Galatia and Hygeia, two classical healing deities commonly linked with eastern springs. Finally, Eudocia mentions four architectural features of the bath: the small and large warm-water pools, the old *clibanus*, and a room described as the Pearl.[107] Why Eudocia chose to include these specific features of the bath in her poem, especially the old *clibanus*, is unclear. Nevertheless, the

---

[100] Hainsworth 1993:318–319; Janko 1994:102–103.

[101] Vergil *Aeneid* 6.625–627; Vergil *Georgics* 2.42–44; Ovid *Fasti* 2.119; Persius *Satires* 5.1–5; Macrobius *Saturnalia* 5.7.16. For more on this commonplace and even more examples, see Scheiber 1984:180–181; Hinds 1998:34–47; Robinson 2011:140–142.

[102] Green and Tsafrir 1982:86–91.

[103] Green and Tsafrir 1982:90 suggest, quite improbably, that Μονάστρια refers to Eudocia. For other late antique uses of μονάστρια, see John Chrysostom *Epistle* 14.2; Isidorus of Pelusium *Epistle* 1.367; Justinian's *Novellae Constitutiones* 123.36; Joannes Moschus *Pratum spirituale* 60; Sophronius Hierosolymitanus *Narratio Miraculorum Cyri et Iohannis* 44; *Chronicon Paschale*; Council of Nicaea (787).

[104] John Chrysostom *Orations against the Jews* 1.6; Trzcionka 2007:130; Renberg 2016:778.

[105] Green and Tsafrir 1982; Habas 1996:114; Demandt 2007:521–522; Appelbaum 2013.

[106] Hirschfeld 1997:4, 11.

[107] Green and Tsafrir 1982:89.

bath's decorative program clearly was quite diverse and likely reflects the site's equally diverse clientele.

After insisting that mortal words fail to adequately describe the *clibanus'* strength, Eudocia proceeds to praise it with three metaphors: a new fiery ocean, Paean, and an emanating source of sweet streams.[108] As a vestige of the popular honorific epithet found in encomiastic acclamations, comparing the *clibanus* to a new fiery ocean (ὠκεανὸν πυρόεντα νέον) communicates along political and poetic registers.[109] For instance, there is some evidence that *prytaneis* received this acclamation and that Homer, as inspiration for all subsequent poets, was compared to the ocean by the Hellenistic period.[110] Closer to Eudocia's time, John Chrysostom used this epithet in his treatment about vainglory and the ambitious urban patron eager for civic praise.[111] Within Chrysostom's imagined scenario, urban citizens congregate in the theater to praise their patron, whose beneficence they successively compare to the Nile and the ocean, metonyms for late antique euergetism and the predictable services *euergetes* provide.[112] In the same way, by employing this oceanic metaphor, Eudocia gestures to Homer as her poetic model and applies euergetistic imagery to the *clibanus*. As a type of local patron, the *clibanus* provides essential and appreciated therapeutic services for the local community.[113] Its beauty and architectural aesthetics quickly recede to the background, as Eudocia highlights its therapeutic benefits. Through this simile, ekphrasis yields to panegyric.[114]

In addition to a euergetistic ocean, the *clibanus* is a source of physical wonders (θαύματα, 2), a late antique Paean (6) for its patrons.[115] Undoubtedly classicizing, Paean can refer to a number of ancient physicians or healing divinities, including Apollo, Asclepius, or Hygeia. Eudocia identifies one of her sixteen "fountains" as Hygeia, alongside Elijah and Galatia, whose miraculous powers

---

[108] Green and Tsafrir 1982:85 suggest an omitted τε in line 6 to be read Παιάνα καὶ γενέτην γλυκερῶν τε δοτῆρα ῥεέθρων (thus with four images present).

[109] Peterson 1929; Méautis 1931; Merkelbach 1988; Blume 1989; Wiemer 2004; Kruse 2006; Christian 2015:344–345.

[110] P. Oxy. 1305, 1413. Brink 1972:553–556.

[111] John Chrysostom *Address on Vainglory and the Right Way for Parents to Bring Up Their Children*; Schulte 1914; Laistner 1951; Roskam 2014.

[112] Each flood season, the Nile rose sixteen cubits, a predictable and reliable level that afforded security to the Egyptian agrarian economy and is even found on imperial coinage (Bonneau 1964:336–337). Similar to the Nile's floodwaters, Hammat Gader's sixteen fountains consistently supported the local economy.

[113] Compare Renberg 2016:811.

[114] In his reading of this section, Ovadiah 1998 emphasizes κάλλος and situates it within late antique Neoplatonism.

[115] Compare Claudian *Fons Aponi* 67–70; Busch 1999:96.

made them recurring characters in ancient healing cults.[116] By closing with the sick receiving comfort from the *clibanus* (15), the poem ends where it began, with an emphasis on the site's power. Similar to Chrysostom's Antiochenes, Eudocia compares the *clibanus* to a euergetistic ocean—the source and dispenser (γενέτην and δοτῆρα) of pleasant waters and good gifts. For the bath's ailing patrons, these good gifts take the form of curative miracles (ἀπίρονα θαύματα).

This emphasis on physical healing and miracles is consistent with Eudocia's broader interest in the cult of the saints and their accompanying healing cults. According to contemporary accounts of her first pilgrimage to Jerusalem, Eudocia had personally been healed after praying in the Church of the Holy Sepulchre. Late antique saints' lives, including those of Menas of Cotyaeum, Cyrus and John at Menouthis, and Artemius, Cosmas, and Damian of Constantinople, frequently emphasize healings and miracles. Partially because of these miracle accounts, each *vita* became inextricably bound within the ritualized space associated with its saint, who occasionally "specialized" in healing specific diseases.[117] For instance, the cults of Cyrus and John were centers for ophthalmic miracles, and sites associated with Saint Artemius were known to alleviate genital-based diseases/maladies. Other holy men, such as Saint Menas, were jack-of-all-trades saints and could heal a variety of ailments. Based on the description provided by the Placenza Pilgrim, along with its surviving epigraphic record, Hammat Gader was a destination for those seeking relief from various skin conditions, particularly leprosy.[118] While the Piacenza Pilgrim attributes the site's healing power to the prophet Elijah, we know, in part from Eudocia's poem, that the site incorporated holy figures from diverse religious backgrounds.[119]

Considering this religious diversity, Eudocia's language appears inclusive, even when, in the poem's final lines, she directs her reader's attention from the bath's μένος to the god's (θεόν). In line 16 (ἀλλὰ θεὸν κλυτόμητιν ἀείσο...), Eudocia draws from the *Homeric Hymn to Hephaestus* (Ἥφαιστον κλυτόμητιν ἀείσεο, 20.1) and opens an intertextual conversation with it.[120] In context, *Homeric Hymn* 20 celebrates the technical skills, especially architectural technology, that Hephaestus taught humans, which equip them to build houses and leave their cave-abodes. In terms of Eudocia's poem, this same skill promotes the building of the bath complex and the ability to heat water, which

---

[116] Käppel 1992:372–374. Not mentioned are the Graces, who were associated with healing cults and were represented on Gader's coinage (Dvorjetski 2007:355–359; Renberg 2016:812).

[117] Deubner 1907; Drescher 1946; Festugière 1971; Marcos 1975; Parmentier 1989; Crisafulli and Nesbitt 1997; Montserrat 2005; Gascou 2006; Frankfurter 2010.

[118] Piacenza Pilgrim *Itinerarium Antonini Placentini* 7 (Cuntz 1965:132; Wilkinson 2002:133); Di Segni 1997.

[119] Compare Sigerist 1961; Román López 1995; Dvorjetski 1997.

[120] Compare IG 14.1015.

consequently provides added services. This line also has euergetistic implica-
tions, as κλυτόμητις was a popular epithet for late antique political and reli-
gious benefactors.[121] In fifth-century Bostra, the local religious leader and self-
described defender of orthodoxy, Antipater, calls himself κλυτόμητις for his role
in building a church.[122] In Smyrna, the city publicly proclaimed their proconsul
Damocharis a κλυτόμητις.[123] Eudocia's Homeric allusion has added euergetistic
force, when she thanks the god for the εὐεργεσεία he provides (17). This creates
two complementary *euergetes* at Hammat Gader: the *clibanus*, which heats the
bath's pool, and the god, who heals the bath's patrons.

And yet, Eudocia does not explicitly praise Hephaestus. By replacing his
name with the ambiguously imprecise θεόν, she welcomes readers to bring their
own perspectives to the poem. She could equally be speaking about the Judeo-
Christian god or a deity from any number of pantheons, whether Hephaestus
or one more closely associated with eastern healing cults.[124] Moreover, traces of
Neoplatonic language in the poem allow for the possibility that Eudocia blurs
the line between god (as an emanating force that permeates all matter) and the
natural spring.[125] These radically divergent interpretive options can be resolved
in various ways, depending in large part on the reader's perspective.

Eudocia's engagement with the various ideologies represented at Hammat
Gader is remarkably elusive. Only in her list of sixteen fountains do we catch a
glimpse of the communities that frequented the bath, many undoubtedly to be
healed. That portions of the complex were named after illustrious visitors from
diverse backgrounds speaks toward their importance to the bath and its wide
range of patrons. Through her ambiguous language, Eudocia neither dismisses
these various interest groups nor questions the bath's therapeutic virtues. In
fact, she might have traveled there to take advantage of them.[126] Rather, Eudocia
directs her reader, first to the wonders of the bath, its various rooms, its springs,
and patrons, and second to the healing potential of the site, its ἀπίρονα θαύματα.
Here, she interpretively focalizes her reader's attention toward a single divine
source for these wonders.

From our knowledge of her religiosity, Eudocia likely attributed the bath's
therapeutic power to the Christian god but chose to express that power in

---

[121] Feissel 1998:132; Agosti 2014a:27; Agosti 2016.
[122] IGLS 13.9119a-d.
[123] *Palatine Anthology* 16.43.
[124] The site, as a whole, does not look like a traditional "pagan," Jewish, or Christian healing sanc-
tuary (Renberg 2016:813–814).
[125] Ovadiah 1998:391–392 argues in favor of these Neoplatonic ideas in the poem without ever
addressing the identity of the θεόν in line 16. See Proclus *The Elements of Theology*, proposition
126 and 162; Dodds 1963.
[126] Meimare 1983; Habas 1996:112–113.

classicizing terms.[127] Her other poems similarly juxtapose Christian theology with classical allusion. Despite promoting religious tolerance within the fairly intolerant and theologically conservative Theodosian court, Eudocia here solely acknowledges a god's active hand.[128] Considering the bath boasts diverse patrons, including an emperor, a Jewish patriarch, the prophet Elijah, an unnamed nun, as well as two mythological figures associated with healing cults and bath complexes, her emphasis on a singular god is striking. By the end of the poem, she has directed her reader's attention to this god and his miraculous power, which leaves the bath's benefactors with little credit for their euergetistic services. Despite Eudocia's peripatetic tour of the bath's features and her acknowledgement of the active hand various patrons played in its history, including that of the *clibanus* itself, her κλυτόμητις θεός has subsumed all possible rivals and has relegated them to a list of sixteen fountains. God, even if a slightly ambiguous one, acts as *euergetes* par excellence and receives all the credit. In this regard, Eudocia is similar to other members of the Theodosian family.[129]

This section has situated Eudocia's ekphrastic encomium at Hammat Gader within the context of the bath's role as therapeutic destination for a diverse group of visitors. A popular healing location, the springs were understood to provide essential services for local patrons and for visitors who traveled long distances in search for physical relief. While living in Jerusalem, Eudocia visited the bath and fulfilled her role as imperial benefactor by writing a poem in honor of the bath and commissioning its installation in a fairly prominent location. Through her various Homeric allusions about the site's water heater (*clibanus*), Eudocia praises its beauty and its therapeutic power, which she metaphorically compares to ocean and Paean, images that underscore its therapeutic and euergetistic qualities. Her poem provides an encomiastic tour of the bath, including its sixteen "fountains," which, I have argued, neither total sixteen nor are fountains. Eudocia's list, however, clearly confirms the diverse clientele and an equally diverse list of Christian, Jewish, and pagan benefactors at Hammat Gader. By the end of the poem, however, Eudocia credits God as preeminent *euergetes*, ultimately responsible for the site's miracles.

Conclusion

Rather than recounting a traditional historical introduction to Eudocia's life that heavily relies on male-authored texts and their attendant court intrigue

---

[127] Green and Tsafrir 1982:91.
[128] Limberis 1996:41–45.
[129] Holum 1982; Flower 2013; Watts 2013.

and gossip, this chapter instead has focused on Eudocia's surviving words, particularly her speech in Antioch and her poem at Hammat Gader. This approach elucidates Eudocia's early life and her active participation in imperial benefactions by putting them in terms she herself expressed. As a result, some of Eudocia's interests or values, such as her propensity for writing socially engaging poetry and her interest in civic building programs, emerge more clearly to the fore. Other dimensions of her personal life, although historically important, recede into the background. This selectivity is not to suggest that these unmentioned parts of her life were unimportant to Eudocia; rather, my approach in this chapter (and those that follow) allows Eudocia to dictate her own story and to advance her ideas about herself.

Although only a single line from Eudocia's Antioch speech survives, it reveals a great deal about how she adapts Homeric lines into new contexts. By altering *Iliad* 6.211, Eudocia gestures to Glaucus' encounter with Diomedes, along with its recognition scene and re-institution of *xenia*. Eudocia engages Glaucus' speech on multiple registers, as both the content and form of her speech mirror his. I argue that the response from the Antiochene aristocracy is equally Homeric. By commissioning two statues, one golden and one bronze, Antioch echoes Glaucus and Diomedes' armor exchange. This is not merely intellectual banter between groups of educated elites. Their interaction begins a mutually beneficial "friendship" shared between Antioch and Eudocia, who funds building projects and alimentary programs. These projects, consistent with late antique euergetism, should come as no surprise. What distinguishes Eudocia's euergetistic agenda is her choice to express her civic engagement in Antioch in decidedly Homeric terms, which the Antiochenes appreciate and respond to in equally Homeric terms.

Eudocia continues in this Homeric mode in her one definitively exilic poem, the ekphrastic panegyric at Hammat Gader. Incorporated into the site's floor design, the poem as a physical object patronizes the therapeutic bath and adds to its beauty. Instead of commemorating her own role as imperial benefactor, Eudocia instead chooses to describe the bath's furnace, or *clibanus*, as a source of healing for its diverse patrons. Her Homeric allusions underscore the magnitude of the *clibanus*' favor and the site's beauty. The mere enumeration of the site's features requires a Homeric catalogue with added divine assistance. Moreover, by metaphorically comparing the *clibanus* to Paean and the ocean, Eudocia creatively blends euergetistic and therapeutic imagery. Despite recognizing the diverse clientele who depend on the bath for comfort and relief, Eudocia concludes by crediting a god with the miracles that occur there. This line simultaneously alludes to the *Homeric Hymn to Hephaestus* and to late antique euergetistic acclamations that further blend religious and secular, classical and contemporary imagery into a unified whole.

By engaging Eudocia's words with an eye toward their immediate and intertextual contexts, this chapter sets the stage for those that follow. Eudocia frequently advanced her personal and imperial agenda through poetry and Homeric allusion. In the case of her Hammat Gader poem, she was interested in supporting social and religious centers, similar to her various building programs in Constantinople, Jerusalem, and Antioch. As a strategic eastern city, Antioch was equally important to the imperial family, an importance that Eudocia acknowledged with financial support and a Homeric offer of friendship. Her choice to express that friendship in a decidedly Homeric mode speaks toward the depth of her classical erudition and her ability to use that erudition to meet contemporary needs. The continuing view of Homeric epics as preeminent authorities in the fifth century CE is evident in the following chapter, which examines Eudocia's reuse of Homer to paraphrase the Bible.

2

The Homeric Cento

Paraphrasing the Bible

EUDOCIA IS BETTER known for her Homeric cento than for her Antiochene euergetism or her ekphrastic poem from Hammat Gader. This chapter examines Eudocia's Homeric cento alongside her prefatory poem that explains how and why she paraphrased the Bible with lines from the *Iliad* and *Odyssey*. After briefly introducing centos as a poetic form, I contextualize Eudocia's poetic agenda against those of Faltonia Betitia Proba and Decimus Magnus Ausonius. Proba's preface to her Vergilian cento and Ausonius' prefatory letter to his *Cento Nuptialis* provide contrasting perspectives about cento aesthetics and the literary communities interested in reading and writing them. Frequently treated as the ancient model for the ideal(ized) cento, Ausonius' paratextual epistle is particularly constructive to read against Eudocia's preface and the Christian cento tradition. Because the Homeric biblical centos have a convoluted textual history, including four different recensions and multiple manuscript traditions, this chapter focuses primarily on Eudocia's paratextual reflections on redacting a cento. It concludes with a reading of a single episode from Eudocia's cento that illustrates how she critically interpreted the Bible by paraphrasing it.

A cento is a patchwork poem composed of reconstituted whole or half lines from a preexisting poet, typically Homer or Vergil. While there are early "proto-centos" from the classical period, most centos date to late antiquity, a period characterized by textual literariness, a "relationship with the written word."[1] As a result of its inherent dynamism, late antique literature, including centos, crosses traditional generic boundaries, both in form and function. Metrically epic, Vergilian and Homeric centos frequently blur these lines—epic epithalamia, gospel epics, epic tragedies, tragic gospels, and mythological epyllia all survive. Of the sixteen extant Latin centos, four are Christian in content, while the remaining twelve cover a wide range of non-religious topics, from

---

[1] Formisano 2007. Formisano and Sogno 2010 suggest that centos are representative, not poetic outliers, of late antique literature. See also Elsner 2017:177–182.

Greco-Roman mythology to baking bread.[2] Fewer Greek centos survive. In addition to the longer Christian centos associated with Eudocia, most Greek centos are found in the Palatine Anthology or within earlier literature.[3] Cento poets were as geographically diverse as their subject matter; Gaul, Italy, Constantinople, and North Africa all produced at least one. This geographical diversity suggests that the appeal of centos was not limited to isolated parts of the Mediterranean.

Several decades ago, scholars treated centos as relatively obscure—unknown, unread, and unappreciated, little more than parlor tricks.[4] For that reason, centos and cento poets were cited as representative examples of cultural decadence or decline, popular contemporary models for late antiquity in general. Within the past few decades, however, classical scholars have engaged postmodern theories that have helped develop critical methodologies less focused on poetic aesthetics. These emerging methodologies, particularly useful when studying late antique literature, have resulted in a proliferation of scholarship on Greek and Latin centos.[5] Only within the past twenty years, two dozen critical editions and monographs on cento poetry have been published by Italian, French, German, Spanish, and Anglophone authors.[6] To date, most scholarly attention has focused on producing critical editions, translations, and analyses about cento compositional techniques, along with several studies on individual centos or cento "traditions," such as secular or Christian centos.[7]

---

[2] The four Christian centos are Faltonia Betitia Proba's *Cento Probae* (Petschenig 1888; Schenkl 1888:568–609; Clark and Hatch 1981; Badini and Rizzi 2011; Sineri 2011; Schottenius Cullhed 2015), Pomponius' *Versus ad Gratiam Domini* (Schenkl 1888:609–615; Arcidiacono 2011), *De Verbi Incarnatione* (Schenkl 1888:615–620), and *De Ecclesia*, perhaps by Mavortius (Schenkl 1888:621–627; Damico 2010). The secular centos include Hosidius Geta's *Medea* (Lamacchia 1958; Rondholz 2012), Luxurius' *Epithalamium* Fridi (Baehrens 1882:237–240; Happ 1986), Mavortius' *Iudicium Paridis* (Baehrens 1882:198), *De Panificio* (Baehrens 1882:191), *De Alea* (Baehrens 1882:192–197), *Narcissus* (Baehrens 1882:197; Elsner 2017:182–183), *Hippodamia* (Baehrens 1882:199–205; Paolucci 2006), *Hercules et Antaeus* (Baehrens 1882:205), *Progne et Philomela* (Baehrens 1882:206), *Europa* (Baehrens 1882:207), *Alcesta* (Baehrens 1882:208), and Ausonius' *Cento Nuptialis* (Green 1999). McGill 2005 is the standard treatment on Latin secular centos.

[3] These include Aristophanes, Lucian, Arius, Diogenes Laertius, and Irenaeus (Salanitro 1997:2326–2328). See also Palatine Anthology 9.381, 382, 361; ABV 7; SEG 51.1735 (Jonnes 2001). Domínguez 2010 provides an exhaustive treatment of the Greek centos.

[4] Compare the dismissive comments in Crusius 1899; Evelyn-White 1919:xvi–xvii; Schelkle 1954; Macklin Smith 1976:266–267; Salanitro 1997.

[5] Bažil 2009:17–19; Formisano and Sogno 2010; Hinds 2014.

[6] More complete bibliographies can be found in McGill 2005; Paolucci 2006; Schembra 2006; Schembra 2007a; Schembra 2007b; Bažil 2009; Harich-Schwarzbauer 2009; Damico 2010; Domínguez 2010; Formisano and Sogno 2010; Arcidiacono 2011; Badini and Rizzi 2011; Sandnes 2011, Sineri 2011; Malamud 2012; Rondholz 2012; Hinds 2014; Schottenius Cullhed 2015.

[7] Compare Usher 1998; McGill 2005; Rondholz 2012; Schottenius Cullhed 2015. For the relationship between centos and ancient Christian poetry more generally, see Wilken 1967; Roberts 1985; Roberts 1989b; Roberts 1993; Green 2006.

Of this scholarship, Scott McGill's *Virgil Recomposed: The Mythological and Secular Centos in Antiquity* marks a watershed moment. In McGill's view, the particular appeal of centos lies in their intrinsic allusiveness, which he situates within the Latin ludic tradition.[8] Taking a slightly different approach, Karla Pollmann identifies two overarching yet divergent types of centos: serious (exegetical) ones, such as the Christian biblical paraphrases written by Proba and Eudocia, and parodic ones, such as Ausonius' *Cento Nuptialis*.[9] Seeing this use of "parodic" as indistinct, Marco Formisano and Christiana Sogno define parody as the process of recontextualizing an "object so as to make it serve tasks contrary to its original tasks."[10] Therefore, by the very nature of its composition, every cento, regardless of content, is parodic. Formisano and Sogno's use of parody to describe a cento's composition unifies seemingly disparate poems (serious and ludic, Christian and pagan), an approach that frees modern readers to appreciate each cento within the context of its author's literary aims.

One unanswered, perhaps unanswerable, question about cento poetics is how readers should resolve a cento's "intertextual overload," inevitable with any poem literally composed out of another author's words.[11] Working within this unlimited allusive potential, modern interpreters invariably select lines or hemistiches they deem most interesting or useful. Selection is akin to interpretation, and modern cento scholars, who readily admit that their analysis cannot be exhaustive, are restricted by their own selectivity. As a result, many interpretations highlight fruitful and obvious allusions, at the expense of those less obvious or relevant, and spoliate the centos as much as centos themselves spoliate the classical past.[12] Exploring every potential allusion, while possible, risks obscuring more than clarifying. Reading centos, therefore, becomes a delicate balancing act to find the sweet spot between their intertextual limitlessness and limitations.

Proba and the Christian Cento Tradition

Eudocia certainly was not the first to use the cento form to paraphrase the Bible. In addition to having in hand the Homeric cento written by Patricius, which she essentially rewrites, Eudocia also had a Latin model in the Vergilian cento of

---

[8] McGill 2005.
[9] Pollmann 2004:79–80.
[10] Formisano and Sogno 2010. See also Bright 1984:80–81.
[11] Hinds 2014:182. See also Formisano and Sogno 2010; Schottenius Cullhed 2010:44; Dykes 2011:33–34.
[12] Elsner 2004; Liverani 2011; Agosti 2014b:160–162.

Faltonia Betitia Proba.[13] Little is known about Proba or her poetry beyond her Vergilian cento, a 694-line paraphrase of select scenes from Genesis (creation and fall) and the Gospels (Jesus' birth, ministry, execution, and resurrection).[14] Her overall literary agenda can be deduced from paratextual remarks within the cento itself, especially in her preface (*Cento* 1–23), where she apologizes for the graphic and violent content of her previous epics.[15] This *recusatio* serves double duty as a *captatio benevolentiae* and situates Proba's cento within her late antique milieu.[16] For instance, by gesturing to Lucan (*Civil War* 1.225) within her apology, Proba rhetorically distances her cento from Roman political or heroic epic and, through her allusively charged preface, rejects imperial violence and embraces religious peace (*Cento* 9–12).[17]

To give her poem a definitively Christian quality, Proba invokes God and asks him to receive her divine poem.[18] As addressee of and inspiration for her cento, God replaces the classical Muse, a substitution that transforms the cento into a sacred hymn sung in praise of the pious feats of Christ (*pia munera Christi*).[19] Proba here follows an emerging Christian epic tradition begun by Juvencus, the first Latin poet to paraphrase the Bible in epic meter.[20] Early Christian poetry's dependence on the classical epic tradition belies Proba and Juvencus' rhetorical posture against it. The influence of Vergil and other epic poets on Juvencus is well attested, and literally every line of Proba's poem derives from and points

---

[13] I follow Stevenson 2005:64–71, 532–535, and Cameron 2011:327–337, who attribute authorship of the Vergilian Christian cento to Faltonia Betitia Proba and not to her granddaughter. Shanzer 1986, Shanzer 1994, and Barnes 2006, by arguing that Proba the cento poet is the granddaughter of Faltonia Betitia Proba, thus move the date of the cento's composition back some forty years. The confusion between the two dates back at least to the fifteenth century. See Badini and Rizzi 2011:13–19; Sineri 2011:20–26; Schottenius Cullhed 2014:206.

[14] External evidence is limited to a few comments made by Isidore of Seville (*De viris illustribus* 22; *Etymologiarum* (*De originibus*) 1.39.26), not including notices appended to her cento (Clark and Hatch 1981:97–98; Schottenius Cullhed 2015:61).

[15] This cento is frequently assumed to have been an epic in honor of Constantius II's victory over Magnentius in 353 CE. See Schottenius Cullhed 2015:114–117 for the complete history and bibliography. There is a parallel here between Proba and Eudocia, in that they are both said to have composed historical/military epics earlier in their literary career.

[16] Schottenius Cullhed 2015:117–118.

[17] Green 1997:550; Sandnes 2011:149–150; Hinds 2014:186–187. Bažil 2009:121–122 suggests this Lucanic echo is also in conversation with early Christian epic.

[18] Pollmann 2004:80; Formisano and Sogno 2010:380. Not all classical poetry found inspiration from Clio or Calliope, as it could invoke Apollo, a philosophical god, Cupid, Venus, a lover, or the emperor (Pollmann 2017:216–217).

[19] Compare Juvencus *Praefatio* 19–27; Paulinus of Nola *Carmina* 15.30–33; Arator *De actibus apostolorum* 2.577–581. See also Green 2006:300–301; Schottenius Cullhed 2010:45; Badini and Rizzi 2011:151–152; Sandnes 2011:151–152; Schottenius Cullhed 2015:119–123.

[20] Green 2006:16–17; Bažil 2009:121–123; Hecquet-Noti 2009:202–205; Dykes 2011:154–161; McGill 2016a. For the ways Proba distances herself from Juvencus, see Pollmann 2004:89–90.

back to the very tradition she explicitly rejects.[21] That being said, both Proba and Juvencus mark for their readers that their poems will be different.

These attempts to rhetorically distance herself from the secular epic tradition notwithstanding, Proba admits that her cento fuses Vergil with new, biblical content.[22] As poet-prophet (*vatis*), Proba is divinely inspired to perform the cento and reveal mysteries (*arcana*), yet Vergil also actively participates in the performance (*vergilium cecinisse loquar pia munera Christi*).[23] The cento, along with its message, here becomes a duet sung by both Proba and Vergil, centuries removed and with unequal airtime.[24] Within the remainder of the preface (*Cento* 24–55), the repetition of first-person singular markers foregrounds Proba as soloist and seemingly relegates Vergil to backup singer, although the increased use of Vergilian lines gives him the loudest voice. By the end of the preface, we are firmly in the world of cento poetry, with every line of Proba's prophetic song coming directly from Vergil's mouth. This performative duet underscores the intersection between cento and source text. For Proba, cento poetics is not intertextually neutral—her source text and its original author are inextricably bound to her new product, no matter how divinely inspired or focused on peace and love she claims it to be.[25]

The wider Christian community more generally had mixed reactions to Proba's poem and centos. In his epistle to Paulinus of Nola, Jerome lists cento poets as an example of irresponsible biblical exegetes.[26] Jerome's concern over proper biblical exegesis and his use of centos within that discussion are part of a long-standing Christian tradition found also in Irenaeus' *Against Heresies* (1.9.4).[27] Unlike Irenaeus, who cites a previously unattested Homeric cento on Heracles, Jerome's example, both its original Vergilian lines and its new biblical contexts, identically correspond to Proba's cento and strongly suggest that he

---

[21] For more on Juvencus, see Roberts 2004; McGill 2007; Dykes 2011:159; McGill 2016a:14–17; McGill 2016b; Müller 2016:16.

[22] Pollmann 2004:80, 87–90 situates Proba as an example of an exegetical cento poet.

[23] Compare Ovid *Ars Amatoria* 3.549; *Fasti* 6.5; *Epistulae ex Ponto* 3.4.93. The *vates* in manuscript P (Paris, Bibliothèque Nationale, lat. 7701) more explicitly references Proba, although Schottenius Cullhed 2015:192–193 interprets the *vatis* as Vergil. See also Dykes 2011:155–156; Pollmann 2017:217.

[24] By late antiquity, Vergil and his poetry had already been appropriated within a definitively Christian context. MacCormack 1998; Pollmann 2004:89; Rees 2004b; Bažil 2009:97–105; Hinds 2014:177, 187; Pollmann 2017.

[25] Dykes 2011:156–157. Compare Genette 1982:14–15. Hinds 2014:184 asserts that late antique literary consciousness is marked primarily by literary appropriation.

[26] Jerome *Epistle* 53. The scholarly debate about the relationship between Jerome's letter and Proba continues. See Wiesen 1971; Clark and Hatch 1981:104–105; Sandnes 2011:134–136; Sineri 2011:13; Rondholz 2012:23–24; Schottenius Cullhed 2014:200–201.

[27] Wilken 1967; Domínguez 2010:98–111; Sandnes 2011:132–134.

has her in mind, without explicitly naming her.[28] Influenced by the polemical writings of Irenaeus and Jerome, among others, the late antique and medieval church generally viewed centos with suspicion, which in turn influenced their modern reception. On the other hand, Proba and the Christian Vergilian cento tradition provided Eudocia with a pre-existing conceptual framework around issues of divine inspiration and the cento poet's relationship with the classical past. It is within a slightly modified version of this conceptual framework that Eudocia situates her (and Patricius') cento.

Ausonius and the Cento Legacy

In addition to being influenced by the Christian cento tradition, Eudocia's reflections on cento aesthetics and compositional techniques evince an awareness of other ancient metaliterary theories on writing centos, especially Decimus Magnus Ausonius' preface to the *Cento Nuptialis* (hereafter the *PCN*), which, in my view, complements Eudocia's explicit metapoetic agenda. Ausonius' literary corpus is as diverse as his various careers—he served as grammarian in Bordeaux, imperial tutor to the young Gratian, and held imperial posts, even rising to the consulship in 379 CE.[29] Among his poems is the *Cento Nuptialis*, a 131-line Vergilian epithalamic cento introduced by a lengthy prefatory epistle, through which, as is his habit, Ausonius commissions a trusted friend with the task of critically evaluating his newest poem. He also wrote a prose digression that precedes the cento's sexually explicit conclusion, as well as a prose postscript to preemptively defend himself from the charge of sexual impropriety. Because the *PCN* contains the most complete ancient discussion of cento poetics, it has been used from the time of Erasmus as a type of cento primer.[30] In my view, because Ausonius' prefaces, including the *PCN*, advance his immediate literary agenda and are not primarily guides for aspiring poets, modern readers are cautioned about over-extrapolating details within them. On the other hand,

---

[28] Dykes 2011:156. Schottenius Cullhed 2014 challenges this traditional assumption by arguing that Jerome's invective against a "garrulous granny" earlier in the epistle is a rhetorical trope, not a veiled allusion to Proba, as it is popularly seen. While Schottenius Cullhed argues this point persuasively, she does not address the overlap between Jerome and Proba's cento lines.

[29] Green 1991 is standard. See also Evelyn-White 1919; Prete 1978; Green 1999. For Ausonius' career, see Matthews 1975:56–87; Sivan 1993; Amherdt 2004:9–12; Watts 2015; Aull 2017:132–134.

[30] Erasmus *Adages* 2.4.58 (Mynors 1991:221–222). The clearest use of Ausonius as a guide to writing centos, post McGill 2005, is Sandnes 2011:108–113, who reads the PCN in a straightforward way. The tendency to invoke the PCN persists, even by authors who express doubt whether it is a universalizing model. For instance, Schottenius Cullhed 2015:94 expresses her doubt about the PCN as model but on pages 137–138 uses Ausonius' comparison of centos to the *stomachion* game. See also Formisano and Sogno 2010:380, 386–389; Malamud 2012:162, 175; Hinds 2014:171, 176, 185, 188–190; Pelttari 2014:64, 96–112 for a few recent representative examples.

since Eudocia echoes cento aesthetics expressed in the *PCN*, the comparison of Eudocia and Ausonius, despite their obvious differences, is constructive.

Ausonius' prefaces often take the form of epistolary communications to *amici*, with whom he shares his newest works.[31] From the surviving prefaces and epistles, a pattern emerges that suggests a carefully constructed literary etiquette shared between Ausonius and his friends. Because these prefaces elaborate on the shared responsibilities of authors and recipients, they provide valuable information about late antique literary *amicitia*, specifically the ways in which Ausonius' coterie wrote, edited, and circulated their writings, often by situating their literary activities within the Roman tradition of *docta studia*.[32] Despite some variation, the following pattern emerges. In a letter to a trusted friend, Ausonius (1) insists that the attached poem is worthless. Nonetheless, he invites this friend (2) to read the poem and (3) to edit or to evaluate it. In a moment of lighthearted reversal, Ausonius (4) challenges his friend to join in the poetic process, either by writing a similar poem or by un-writing his poem. Of all Ausonius' prefatory correspondences, the *PCN* adheres most closely to this pattern.

Ausonius addresses the *PCN* to Axius Paulus, a trusted literary friend and recipient of two poems and seven epistles.[33] Beyond his typical self-deprecations and insistence that the cento is worthless and written hastily, Ausonius claims that he only composed it because the emperor, Valentinian, compelled him.[34] While there is enough evidence to suspect that Valentinian was bookish enough to compose a cento had he wanted to, this reference about him in the *PCN* is likely a carefully constructed fiction.[35] Ausonius frequently invents poetic contexts that wrong-foot his addressees or himself and reinforce the ludic persona that he wears and forces members of his coterie to wear in turn.[36] In this metaliterary fiction, Ausonius expresses anxiety about being publicly challenged to a poetic competition by Valentinian. As client to the imperial family and court poet, he depends on Valentinian's support. He must, therefore, accept

---

[31] For the role of prefaces in late antique literature, see Pavlovskis 1967; Pelttari 2014.

[32] McGill 2009; Pelttari 2011; Sowers 2016.

[33] In addition to the *Cento Nuptialis*, Paulus is the addressee in the preface to the *Bissula*. Green 1991:514–515, 518, 606–608.

[34] McGill 2014 examines Ausonius' trope of writing hastily, often during a single night. On Ausonius' self-presentation, see Kleinschmidt 2013:71–95.

[35] For Valentinian's education and exceptional memory, see Ammianus Marcellinus 30.9.4; Pseudo-Aurelius Victor *Epitome de Caesaribus* 45.5–6; Matthews 1975:49; Sivan 1993:105–106; McGill 2005:94. On memory and cento poetics in general, see Quintilian *Institutio Oratoria* 1.1.36 and 11.2.40–41; Fortunatianus *Ars Rhetorica* 3.13; Bright 1984:81–82; Comparetti 1997:53; McGill 2005:10–11.

[36] Lowe 2013:337–338; McGill 2014; Sowers 2016.

the challenge and perform well, but not so well that he upstages Valentinian or offends him.[37]

Ausonius is also aware of the critical gaze of the imperial court—the anonymous others (*aliorum*) present for his performance. He mentions elsewhere that drinking parties, social gatherings, and getaways to country villas provide ideal occasions for composing and reciting ludic poetry.[38] Such recitations may include playful banter and agonistic ribbing among friends, but only friends within his carefully curated literary circle. The hostile terms that Ausonius uses for the unknown judges in the PCN position them outside his coterie, trusted to provide supportive critiques of preliminary drafts of his poems. As outsiders, the unpredictable and uncontrollable reactions of these hostile onlookers elicit further anxiety.[39] In this regard, Ausonius constructs his idealized literary community on models advanced by Pliny the Younger and other imperial literary elites.[40]

Despite repeatedly insisting that he is an ill-equipped teacher and novice cento poet, Ausonius spends over half of the PCN outlining in detail the compositional rules and aesthetics of writing centos. Above all, he insists, an ideal cento draws from various Vergilian contexts and joins two half-lines into a single line or joins a hemistich with one-and-a-half consecutive lines into two lines.[41] Half-lines refer to line segments, divided at all epic caesurae. Using two consecutive lines marks an inferior cento, while using three is utterly ridiculous (*merae nugae*).[42] Although Ausonius never explicitly permits cento poets to use single whole lines, the practice was evidently quite common: 37 percent of the *Cento Nuptialis* and 28 percent of Vergilian centos consist of non-sequential, whole Virgilian lines.[43]

Throughout the PCN, Ausonius describes centos as a game, a *ludus*. The force of this ludic language is two-fold. On the one hand, as *ludus*, the cento fits within Ausonius' wider poetic persona as ludic poet, a gesture to the golden age of Latin poetry, particularly that of Catullus, Horace, and Ovid.[44] On the other hand, Ausonius applies this ludic imagery to the method of composing centos, especially when he compares centos to a geometric puzzle designed by

[37] This type of anxiety produced by *amicitia* and patronage is discussed by White 1978:76; Coleman 1988:177; White 1993:14; Konstan 1997:144–145.

[38] For example, *Praefatio ad Bissulam, Moselle* 448–453, *Prefatio ad Technopaegnion, Praefatio ad Griphum* 17–33, and *Epistle* 1. See White 1993:5; Nicholson 2014:241, 249–250; Sowers 2016:518–521.

[39] Sowers 2016:527–534.

[40] Sowers 2016, building on Frye 2003:186–189 and Johnson 2010. Compare White 1978:85; Saller 1989:58–61; White 1993:13–14; Konstan 1997:147–148; de Blois 2001; Anderson 2002:183–234.

[41] This phrase is not without difficulty (Bright 1984:84; Green 1991:520–521).

[42] Ausonius uses sequential lines three times (*Cento Nuptialis* 25–26, 75–76, and 97–98), although he generally follows his own rules (Bright 1984; Green 1991:518).

[43] Bright 1984:84–86.

[44] McGill 2005; Pucci 2016; Sowers 2016. Compare Rücker 2009; Rücker 2012:67.

Archimedes, the *stomachion*.[45] According to Ausonius, a regulation *stomachion* set consists of fourteen bones of fourteen different geometric shapes re-arranged into various shapes, ranging from elephants to tankards. Similar to the *stomachion* player, Ausonius has rearranged Vergil's lines to create an epithalamium that, if composed well, does not reveal its constituent pieces.[46] In other words, accomplished cento poets so adroitly depict an epithalamic Vergil or Homeric Jesus that their audiences forget that they are reading lines from Homer or Vergil, just as one sees an elephant in the stomachion and forgets that it is built from individual bones.

Ausonius insists that the challenge inherent to composing poems from isolated line segments is to conceal their seams, joints, and original Vergilian contexts. While this objective may be attractive in theory, it is impossible in practice, especially within a literary culture that prioritized memorizing the "best authors," particularly Homer and Vergil.[47] In fact, its intertextual engagement with well-known texts is part of a cento's appeal, similar to other late antique paraphrases and epitomes.[48] To appreciate its hyper-allusiveness, a cento's ideal audience must have been equally learned, "full-knowing readers" adept at recognizing the "intertextual noddings, winks, and gestures" literally built into every line on the page.[49]

Eudocia's Homeric Cento

This brief treatment of Proba and Ausonius' paratextual comments about their centos anchors Eudocia's cento within its wider context and allows us to contrast her poetic agenda with theirs. What sets Eudocia's cento apart from theirs is the convoluted nature of the Homeric centos. In her verse preface, Eudocia claims that she received and edited a preexisting cento, and we know that this revised

---

[45] Archimedes designed the *stomachion* to be played differently than Ausonius suggests (Netz and Noel 2007:240–241; Netz 2009:17–20, 35–36; Malamud 2012:162). Crawford 2002 compares the *stomachion* to the Chinese tangram.

[46] Malamud 1989:36–37; Rücker 2012:70–71; Schottenius Cullhed 2016:98–99.

[47] Quintilian *Institutio Oratoria* 10.1.20.

[48] Formisano and Sogno 2010; Horster and Reitz 2010a. For more on ancient epitomes, see the various contributions in Horster and Reitz 2010b. For other late antique paraphrases, see Roberts 1985; Springer 1988; Dihle 1994:444, 461; MacDonald 1994; MacDonald 2001; Green 2006:44–46, 146–148; Johnson 2006a:98–99; Johnson 2016a; Müller 2016:16–17. Lamberton 1986:57 discusses an earlier, imperial example.

[49] Pucci 1986:240; Pucci 1998. Pucci's model complements other approaches to reading, particularly those of Barthes 1986:61; Nugent 1990:29; Hinds 1998; Pelttari 2014. For the depth of Ausonius' intertextual engagement with Proba, see Moretti 2008.

cento was redacted at least twice in the following centuries.[50] The Homeric cento manuscript tradition reflects these multiple redactions, resulting in at least three surviving versions.[51] The longest version is 2,354 lines and is attributed to Eudocia.[52] The second version is 1,948 lines, whereas the third version, itself revised three times, is 622, 653, and 738 lines.[53] Because Rocco Schembra carefully isolates these individual redaction moments, I use his editions.[54] In this section, I focus on Eudocia's surviving paratextual comments, which allow us to set her literary agenda and cento aesthetics against those of Proba and Ausonius. In the final section of this chapter, I provide a reading of one episode from her cento that illustrates how Eudocia exegetically paraphrases the biblical text with Homer's words.

As was popular in late antiquity, Eudocia introduces her cento with a preface, in this case a thirty-eight-line hexameter poem that contextualizes her project within the decision to revise Patricius' Christian cento. Eudocia also sketches her aesthetics for the ideal cento and apologizes for her own poetic deficiencies:[55]

> ἥδε μὲν ἱστορίη θεοτερπέος ἐστὶν ἀοιδῆς.
> Πατρίκιος δ᾽, ὃς τήνδε σοφῶς ἀνεγράψατο βίβλον,
> ἔστι μὲν ἀενάοιο διαμπερὲς ἄξιος αἴνου,
> οὕνεκα δὴ πάμπρωτος ἐμήσατο κύδιμον ἔργον.
> 5 ἀλλ᾽ ἔμπης οὐ πάγχυ ἐτήτυμα πάντ᾽ ἀγόρευεν·
> οὐδὲ μὲν ἁρμονίην ἐπέων ἐφύλαξεν ἅπασαν,
> οὐδὲ μόνων ἐπέων ἐμνήσατο κεῖνος ἀείδων,
> ὁππόσα χάλκεον ἦτορ ἀμεμφέος εἶπεν Ὁμήρου.
>
> ἀλλ᾽ ἐγὼ ἡμιτέλεστον ἀγακλεὲς ὡς ἴδον ἔργον
> 10 Πατρικίου, σελίδας ἱερὰς μετὰ χεῖρα λαβοῦσα,
> ὅσσα μὲν ἐν βίβλοισιν ἔπη πέλεν οὐ κατὰ κόσμον,

---

50 Recent work on Eudocia's cento includes Pignani 1985; Alfieri 1987; Pignani 1987; Alfieri 1988; Alfieri 1989; Schembra 1993; Schembra 1994; Salanitro 1995; Schembra 1995; Schembra 1996; Salanitro 1997; Schembra 1997; Usher 1997; Rey 1998; Schembra 1998; Usher 1999; Schembra 2000a; Schembra 2000b; Schembra 2001a; Schembra 2001b; Arbea 2002; Schembra 2002; Schembra 2003; Schembra 2006; Schembra 2007a; Schembra 2007b; Whitby 2007; Whitby 2009; Domínguez 2010; Sandnes 2011; Whitby 2013; Whitby 2016.

51 Schembra 2006; Schembra 2007a; Schembra 2007b.

52 Usher 1999; Schembra 2006; Schembra 2007b; Whitby 2007; Whitby 2009; Whitby 2016.

53 Schembra 2007b:clxxxi; Whitby 2016:230. These line numbers follow Schembra's editions; those found in Rey 1998 and Usher 1999 will differ.

54 Schembra 2006; Schembra 2007a; Schembra 2007b.

55 Schembra 2007b:cxxxiii–cxxxv follows Rey 1998, but he includes a discussion of the poetic quality of the preface (cxxxix–cxlii).

πάντ' ἄμυδις κείνοιο σοφῆς ἐξείρυσα βίβλου·
ὅσσα δ' ἐκεῖνος ἔλειπεν, ἐγὼ πάλιν ἐν σελίδεσσι
γράψα καὶ ἁρμονίην ἱεροῖς ἐπέεσσιν ἔδωκα.

15 εἰ δέ τις αἰτιόῳτο καὶ ἡμέας ἐς ψόγον ἕλκοι,
δοιάδες οὕνεκα πολλαὶ ἀρίζηλον κατὰ βίβλον
εἰσὶν Ὁμηρείων τ' ἐπέων πόλλ' οὐ θέμις ἐστίν,
ἴστω τοῦθ', ὅτι πάντες ὑποδρ' ἡστῆρες ἀνάγκης.

εἰ δέ τις ὑμνοπόλοιο σαόφρονα Τατιανοῖο
20 μολπὴν εἰσαΐων σφετέρην τέρψειεν ἀκουήν,
δοιάδας οὕνεκα κεῖνος Ὁμηρείων ἀπὸ βίβλων
οὔ ποτε συγχεύας σφετέρῃ ἐνεθήκατο δέλτῳ,
οὐ ξένον, οὕνεκα κεῖνος Ὁμηρείης ἀπὸ μολπῆς,
κείνων δ' ἐξ ἐπέων σφετέρην ποίησεν ἀοιδὴν
25 Τρώων τ' Ἀργείων τε κακὴν ἐνέπουσαν ἀϋτήν,
ὥς τε πόλιν Πριάμοιο διέπραθον υἷες Ἀχαιῶν,
αὐτὴν Τροίαν ἔχουσαν ἐν ἀργαλέῳ τε κυδοιμῷ
μαρναμένους αὐτούς τε θεούς, αὐτούς τε καὶ ἄνδρας,
οὕς ποτε χαλκεόφωνος ἀνὴρ ἀΰτησεν Ὅμηρος.

30 Πατρίκιος δ', ὃς τήνδε σοφὴν ἀνεγράψατο δέλτον,
ἀντὶ μὲν Ἀργείων στρατιῆς γένος εἶπεν Ἑβραίων,
ἀντὶ δὲ δαιμονίης τε καὶ ἀντιθέοιο φάλαγγος
ἀθανάτους ἤεισε καὶ υἱέα καὶ γενετῆρα.

ἀλλ' ἔμπης ξυνὸς μὲν ἔφυ πόνος ἀμφοτέροισι,
35 Πατρικίῳ κἀμοί καὶ θηλυτέρῃ περ ἐούσῃ·
κεῖνος δ' ἤρατο μοῦνος ἐν ἀνθρώποις μέγα κῦδος.
ὃς πάμπρωτος ἐπήξατο κλεινὸν ἔδος γε δόμοιο
καλὴν ἐξανάγων φήμην βροτέοιο γενέθλης.

This is the account of a God-honoring poem.
Patricius prudently authored this book
and is forever worthy of eternal praise,
because he first planned this glorious project.
5 But he did not tell everything truthfully—
neither did he preserve the complete harmony of the verses

nor, while singing, did he remember only verses
sung by the brazen heart of blameless Homer.

When I saw Patricius' glorious yet half-finished project,
10   I took his holy pages in hand and,
whatever verses were defective
I ripped out of his clever book,
and whatever he had neglected I
wrote back into the text and gave harmony to his holy verses.

15   But if someone were to blame or censure us,
because our remarkable book contains many double lines
and sequential Homeric verses are not customary,
know this—all humans are slaves to necessity.

But if one hears the poet Tatian's wise song
20   and his ears tingle with delight,
because Tatian never mingled double lines
from the Homeric texts into his book—
which is not remarkable, since, by picking up with the Homeric song,
Tatian made from those very verses his own ballad
25   that recounts the wretched cry of the Trojans and Argives,
when the sons of the Achaeans destroyed the city of Priam,
and contains Troy and, in a grievous din,
those fighting, both the very same gods and men,
of whom, once upon a time, the brazen-voiced man, Homer, sang...

30   But Patricius, who wrote this clever book,
recounted the race of Hebrews instead of the Argive army.
In lieu of the demonic and sacrilegious battle array,
he sang about the immortal Son and Father.

Nevertheless, this is a collaborative project by both
35   Patricius and me, despite the fact that I am a woman.
He alone received great honor among men,
because he first laid the illustrious foundation of the house
by spreading the good news for the mortal race.

Throughout the preface, Eudocia contrasts the oral and written qualities of
cento poetics. As a textual object, she claims to have seen (ἴδον, line 9) Patricius'

book (βίβλον, lines 2, 11, and 12; compare with lines 16 and 21), which warranted substantial revision in her estimation. Her equally textual editorial task was two-fold: to remove everything not in order and to add everything omitted. This decidedly bookish compositional and redactional process more closely resembles Ausonius' language than Proba's.[56] Even if Proba had composed her cento first, her paratextual remarks emphasize orality over textuality. Also similar to Ausonius, Eudocia competes with a predecessor whose work she surpasses or, at least, improves upon. To be fair, in the *PCN*, Valentinian orally performs his cento and Ausonius expresses anxiety over audience members present during his own recitation, whereas Eudocia competes with Patricius simply through the words on the page. From her self-perceived ability to outdo Patricius, Eudocia puts her mark on his incomplete (ἡμιτέλεστον, 9) text, which she, as redactor, has taken in hand (σελίδας ἱερὰς μετὰ χεῖρα λαβοῦσα, 10). This dependence on another poet, other than Homer and Vergil, further distinguishes Eudocia's cento from Ausonius and Proba's.

This final point leads to a rather remarkable rhetorical feature of Eudocia's preface: her concern over inadvertently depriving Patricius, as progenitor of the Homeric cento, of honor.[57] Because Patricius first undertook the project, he deserves credit or, in her words, eternal fame (line 3), which she partially secures by naming him four times (in lines 2, 10, 30, and 35) while never once naming herself.[58] This emphasis on Patricius' name is even more striking when we compare Eudocia's preface to a surviving prose summary of his cento, which only names him once.[59] Its deficiencies notwithstanding, Eudocia describes Patricius or his cento as σοφῶς or σοφός three times (lines 2, 12, and 30). In line 12, σοφός comes at the very moment she removes lines from his poem. Reading this σοφός proleptically only further complicates similar language elsewhere and conflicts with her complimentary and deferential posture. Even when she describes their "remixed" cento as a collaborative project and willingly shares the blame for its remaining deficiencies, she insists that Patricius alone should receive credit (line 36).

---

[56] I here differ from Usher 1998:20–23, who argues that Eudocia's cento is primarily orally composed. While Usher recognizes the multiple references to books, texts, pages, and reading, he emphasizes the presence of oral language (singing, hearing, songs).

[57] In addition to Patricius' Greek cento, Eudocia likely also had a copy of Proba's cento. See ILS 818.3; Clark and Hatch 1981:103; Cameron 1982:267; Usher 1997:315; McGill 2007; Whitby 2007:216–217; Curran 2012:328–329; Kelly 2013b:34–35; Schottenius Cullhed 2015:59; Whitby 2016:229–230.

[58] Eudocia is generally thought to be the author of the preface. See Usher 1997:310–315; Livrea 1998:70–72; Agosti 2001:74–85; Agosti 2004:70; Schembra 2007b:cxxxv; Whitby 2007:208–209; Whitby 2013:209.

[59] As a summary of Patricius' cento, that preface has been used to reconstruct Eudocia's editorial hand. See Rey 1998:516–518; Schembra 2007b:cxxxviii–cxlii.

Moreover, by emphasizing the performative qualities of Patricius and Tatian's centos, Eudocia implies that late antique centos were orally and aurally experienced. Beginning in the opening line of the preface, she describes Patricius' cento as a song (ἀοιδῆς, line 1) that he sings (ἀείδων, line 7) and orally delivers (ἀγόρευεν, line 5). His cento here mirrors the Homeric epics itself, explicitly sung by Homer (line 8), and parallels Proba's Vergilian duet and Valentinian's public recitation in the PCN. Additionally, Eudocia uses similar oral and textual language when she compares her cento to Tatian's. In a moment of self-critical anxiety, Eudocia fears that her audience will be more pleased by hearing Tatian's cento (σφετέρην τέρψειεν ἀκουήν, line 20), despite explicitly referring to his cento and the Homeric epics as textual objects (lines 21–22).

Compared to similar paratextual comments made by Ausonius and Proba, Eudocia's blend of oral and textual imagery suggests that centos were first composed and then performed to appreciative and learned audiences during fairly predictable "reading events."[60] Considering reading in antiquity was done aloud in certain (but not all) circumstances, Eudocia's references to singing centos and their positive (or negative) aural effects on listeners should be balanced with her visual and material language (seeing, book, pages) as evidence for multiple, complementary reading events.[61] Given this equal emphasis on the written and spoken word and on visual and oral perception, centos were likely read/composed in private and performed in public. Such public recitations varied from large gatherings to more intimate audiences of trusted friends, comparable to those advocated by Ausonius. Smaller reading events with select friends blurred the line between vocalized reading and public recitation; such hybrid events explain why Eudocia and Ausonius describe centos as performed textual poems. Therefore, after Eudocia likely read her cento to a trusted circle of literary friends, her cento was recited during subsequent events to literati beyond her circle. In this regard, the literary etiquette of Homeric and Vergilian centos, at least in terms of composition and circulation, generally is consistent with late antique intellectual habits.[62]

Eudocia provides additional information about her idealized reading community, when she worries that her audience will unfavorably compare her

---

[60] Johnson 2000:602. Compare Johnson and Parker 2009; Johnson 2010. Holum 1982:219–220 is probably correct when he suggests that Eudocia's literary circle also produced centos. For a parallel phenomenon five centuries later, see Bernard 2014:59–124.

[61] I will not here summarize the issue of oral reading in antiquity. The interested reader should consult Johnson 2000:594–600; Johnson 2009; Olson 2009; Johnson 2010:3–16. For poetic performance during late antiquity, see Cameron 1970:26; Livrea 2000; Cameron 2004:346–347; Agosti 2006:46; Cavallo 2006; McLynn 2006:228–233; Agosti 2012:277–280.

[62] On the circulation of early Christian literature, see Gamble 1995:82–143; Haines-Eitzen 2000:77–104; Hull 2010.

cento to Tatian's.[63] Although Tatian's Homeric cento no longer survives, it was widely appreciated in late antiquity, as demonstrated by its inclusion by Libanius in his classroom.[64] Through her reference to Tatian, Eudocia suggests that her idealized reader is familiar with the classical greats, especially Homer, and with more recent popular works.[65] That this recent work is also a secular poem—Tatian picks up where the *Iliad* ends—tells us about the contours of Eudocia's reading community and its interest in both classically and biblically themed poetry. Her engagement with Patricius' cento and her interest in preserving his reputation as the first Christian cento poet (at least in Greek) reinforces this image of a literary circle invested in the full range of Greek poetry.

Not only is Eudocia's ideal audience familiar with ancient and modern poets (from their perspective), classical and biblical alike, it is also familiar enough with Tatian's cento, written about half a century earlier, to critique her poem based on their reading of his. By suspecting that her ideal readership will compare her cento with his, Eudocia projects onto them a critical engagement indistinguishable from her own, in as much as she read, critiqued, and revised Patricius' cento. This argument assumes, of course, that Eudocia's circle, similar to Ausonius', shares well-defined expectations about literary criticism, including criticism of poetry composed and circulated within the coterie. Details within the preface support this image of a well-defined and critically engaged circle. For instance, when Eudocia defends her decision to revise Patricius' cento and preemptively apologizes for potential future criticisms leveled against her own cento, she advances four distinct yet interrelated literary concerns about cento poetics: its truthfulness (line 5), its harmony (lines 6 and 14), its adherence to a source text (lines 8–9), and its use of double lines (lines 16–17). Taken collectively, these concerns reveal critical aesthetics about early Christian poetry, particularly centos, assumed by Eudocia and likely shared by her ideal audience.

The distinction between truth and falsehood, developed quite early in Greek literary criticism, was expressed rather succinctly by Pindar in *Olympian 1* (lines 27–29): "Yes, wonders are many, but then too, I think, in men's talk, stories (μῦθοι) are embellished beyond the true account (ἀληθῆ λόγον) and deceive by means of elaborate lies (ψεύδεσι)."[66] According to Pindar, yet with obvious echoes in Plato and later critics of poetry, mythology is not intrinsically deceptive, but stories embellished (δεδαιδαλμένοι) beyond a true account

---

[63] On the identity of Tatian, as well as his role in Eudocia's literary circle and late antique education, see Livrea 1997a; Whitby 2007.

[64] Libanius *Epistle* 173.

[65] For this practice within Byzantine literary circles, see Cavallo 2006.

[66] Compare Pindar *Nemean* 7.20–27.

should be considered false.[67] In other words, poetic truth depends on carefully selecting (κρίνω) what material to include.[68] The Alexandrian librarians and ancient literary critics—named after the cognate κρίσις—exemplify this process by preserving those portions of texts that they decide are true and by omitting whatever does not pass muster.[69] Eudocia's concern with Patricius' honesty positions her as reader-redactor within this ancient critical tradition dating back at least to the Alexandrian library. Accordingly, she evaluates Patricius' cento based on the amount of unsuitable or false material contained within.[70] Similar to Pindar's esteem for unembellished μῦθοι, Eudocia takes an embellished cento and creates a more truthful account.[71]

Where exactly had Patricius gone astray? Had he included heresiological theology or episodes not found in the prose gospels available to her? While these are possibilities, Eudocia also might have simply considered certain missing episodes essential to any paraphrase of the Bible.[72] In fact, since she is thought to have modeled her cento on Proba's, Eudocia might have added the accounts of the Creation and the Fall of Man, as well as the (non-biblical) episode in which God decides to redeem humanity through the incarnation.[73] While Proba dedicates nearly half of her cento to Genesis, Eudocia's inclusion of some material from the Old Testament (Cento 1–205) may be a type of gesture to Proba. Interestingly, this added material likely influenced John Milton twelve centuries later.[74]

To further complicate matters, Eudocia's line ἐτήτυμα πάντ' ἀγόρευεν echoes Odyssey 1.174 (compare with Odyssey 1.179) where Athena, disguised as Mentes, visits the young Telemachus to encourage him to leave Ithaca in search of his father. After hosting the disguised Athena, Telemachus inquires about his/her identity and his/her relationship with Odysseus. Despite her fabricated

---

[67] Plato Republic 2.376–378; Plutarch Isis and Osiris 11. Kennedy 1989:22; Ledbetter 2003. For a summary on critical discussions of logos and mythos in poetry, see Trimpi 1971; Racionero 1998; Laird 2006; Richardson 2006:185–187.

[68] Compare Longinus 10. See also Nagy 1990:60–63.

[69] Cameron 1982:284; Usher 1997:310. Ausonius occasionally compares his fellow poets/critics to Alexandrian critics (Sowers 2016).

[70] Eudocia differs here from Augustine's argument (On the Trinity 15.11) in favor of enigmatic hidden truths (Malamud 2011:93–95).

[71] Compare Lucian True Stories, which contains nothing but lies and embellishments. In telling an entirely artificial story, Lucian risks many of the same charges as Patricius and Eudocia (Popescu 2014).

[72] Compare Paulinus of Nola Carmen 33–46.

[73] Green 1995:562; Agosti 2001:82; Agosti 2004:72; Whitby 2007:217.

[74] Milton had a copy of the Homeric centos, along with other early Greek and Latin Christian poetry (Harris 1898). There was precedent for rewriting the Genesis account; the Book of Jubilees had already done so. For more examples of Judeo-Christian paraphrases, see Harding 2003:147–153; Johnson 2006a:78–104.

background story, Athena provides some accurate information about Odysseus, specifically that he remains alive but is unwillingly delayed on Calypso's island. This complicated episode blends divine deception with the truth and, when read against Eudocia's critique of Patricius' cento, opens multiple interpretative possibilities. For instance, this allusion can undermine Eudocia's assessment or can be a playful gesture for a learned audience expected to recognize the line's Homeric context. On the other hand, its recognizably Homeric language may simply add rhetorical authority to Eudocia's critical assessment or may be a veiled criticism of the deceptive Homeric gods, in contrast to the truthful Christian God. If Eudocia is being playful or ironic here, her similarity to Ausonius should not be overlooked.

Her second critique, that Patricius failed to maintain (ἐφύλαξεν) harmony (ἁρμονίην) in his verses, has more direct parallels in Ausonius' *PCN*. The earliest known usages of ἁρμονία and its cognates refer to the process of combining multiple objects.[75] In the fourth century BCE, Aristotle defines ἁρμονία as a combination and composition of opposites (κρᾶσιν καὶ σύνθεσιν ἐναντίων).[76] Ausonius expresses a similar idea when he says that cento hemistiches should be seamlessly and undetectably conjoined, despite their diverse contexts (*sensus diversi ut congruant, adoptiva quae sunt ut cognata videantur*).[77] More than merely an aesthetic, this process of combining disparate and unrelated elements aptly describes cento composition. Even if Ausonius never uses the word harmony, his attempt to prevent his "densely packed pieces" from being seen suggests that harmony—κρᾶσις καὶ σύνθεσις ἐναντίων—is a constant concern.

Finally, Patricius did not limit himself to Homeric material. As mimetic songs that imitate through citation, centos are expected to use only Homer or Vergil—any elaboration or inclusion of original material deviates from its particular mode of composition. Admittedly, Ausonius never explicitly forbids the use of original lines but implies this when he describes centos as half-line or one-and-a-half-lines units. Based on the *Cento Nuptialis*, whose 131 lines contain no original material, Ausonius practices what Eudocia preaches.[78] Patricius, in contrast, had incorporated original material in his cento and perhaps had used biblical names. Adding biblical names would have been particularly tempting for Christian cento poets, who otherwise had to rely on Homeric/Vergilian

---

[75] Ilievski 1993; Lambropoulou 1996; Lambropoulou 1997; Lambropoulou 1998.
[76] *On the Soul* 407b30–32.
[77] Ausonius *PCN* 53–55 (Green 1999:147).
[78] Bright 1984:85. Proba also adheres to this rule: none of her 666 lines contains original material. On the other hand, numerous examples of centos do break this rule. The *De alea* (112 lines) and *De ecclesia* (111 lines) are the worst offenders, with each containing five original lines.

periphrases. In Eudocia's view, however, any non-Homeric material compromised the integrity of the entire project and needed to be removed.

Following her justification as cento critic and redactor, Eudocia apologizes for her role as cento poet. Seemingly more earnest than Ausonius with his self-deprecating dissimulations, Eudocia openly points out the flaws in her cento, particularly the presence of δοιάδες. The majority scholarly view, recently supported by Rocco Schembra, argues that δοιάδες refers to double meanings in the text.[79] Schembra even provides a few examples of such double meanings.[80] Mark Usher, in contrast, argues that δοιάδες likely refers to sequential lines, an interpretation supported by an apologetic epigraph for Eudocia's revision, preserved in the Neapolitanus manuscript:[81]

ἀπολογία Εὐδοκίας λαμπροτάτης τῆς καὶ τὸν παρόντα ὁμηροκεντρῶνα
τὸν συντεθέντα παρὰ Πατρικίου τινὸς ἐπισκόπου διορθωσαμένης, ὑπέρ
τε τοῦ αὐτὸν ταύτην διορθῶσαι, καὶ ὑπὲρ τοῦ ἐν μὲν τῷ ὁμηροκεντρῶνι,
ὃν Τατιανὸς ἐκ τοῦ Ὁμήρου τὰ μεθ᾽ Ὅμηρον ἔγραψε δύο στίχους ἐφεξῆς
κειμένους ὁμηρικοὺς μὴ εὑρίσκεσθαι· ἐν τούτῳ δὲ πολὺ τὸ τοιοῦτον
εἶναι.

This is the apology of Eudocia, the splendid woman who corrected the present Homeric cento composed by a certain bishop, Patricius; the apology is about her editing him, and about the fact that two successive Homeric lines are never found next to each other in the Homeric cento, which Tatian composed on a post-Homeric theme using verses taken from Homer; whereas, in this poem of hers, [she says] there is much of this sort of thing.[82]

According to this epigram, at least one reader of Eudocia's preface interpreted δοιάδες as sequential lines (δύο στίχους ἐφεξῆς), an interpretation that sets Eudocia in conversation with Ausonius. Even if Eudocia did not have a copy of Ausonius' Cento in hand, she shares his aesthetics about ideal centos. This suggests that the "rules" for composing centos found in the PCN were widely known within late antique literary circles from the Latin West to the Greek East. Of course, it is important to remember that Ausonius himself breaks his own rules on occasion. If the first recension of the Homeric centos is Eudocia's, then her anxiety about double lines is understandable. The first recension depends

---

[79] Ludwich 1897:84; Salvaneschi 1981:128–129; Alfieri 1988:154–155; Schembra 1994:328–331; Schembra 2007b:clxxxviii–cxci.

[80] Schembra 2007b:clxxxviii–cxci.

[81] *Neap.* II C 37. See also Pierleoni 1962:306; Mioni 1992:261; Usher 1997:314.

[82] Usher 1997:314.

heavily on sequential lines and strings together as many as seven lines in a row.[83] For modern readers more familiar with Latin centos, particularly those of Proba and Ausonius, Eudocia's use of sequential lines gives the effect that one is reading block quotes from Homer. This proliferation of block quotes also explains why Ludwich never completed his edition of the Homeric centos.[84] On the other hand, because Eudocia is aware of this feature in her cento and apologizes for it, modern readers can appreciate how this unique compositional style adds intertextual texture, depth, and complexity to her poem.

Despite this deficiency, Eudocia also describes her co-authored cento in positive terms—a poem pleasing to God (θεοτερπέος, line 1). Like Proba's Christianized improvement on Vergil and unlike Ausonius' ludic debasement of Vergil, Eudocia adopts an austere and reverent approach that she assumes is shared by her ideal audience. More than a poetic *tour de force* or parlor game to entertain fellow literary elites, her cento is godly entertainment, in that it both honors God and is inspired by God. Its Christian content makes the cento doubly deserving. Instead of rehashing the Trojan War—the very material that Tatian covered—Patricius selects honorable topics: the Hebrew people, God, and his Son. As a versified Bible, the cento becomes, at least partially, divinely inspired and its pages holy (ἱεράς, lines 10 and 14). Unlike Proba's preface and the wider tradition associated with her cento that foreground Vergil's active role, Eudocia emphasizes how biblical her cento is.[85] On the other hand, Eudocia and Proba distance their poems from the violence of war and heroic epic more generally. As a result, Homer recedes into the background of Eudocia's paratextual remarks, while a heavenly afterlife emerges to the foreground. That eternity is at stake is evident when she bestows everlasting praise on Patricius' poem (line 3). This claim further blurs the line between Bible and cento and more subtly secures Patricius' (and, by association, Eudocia's) place in heaven.[86] Undoubtedly hyperbolic, this eternal imagery underscores the stark contrast in the literary aims of biblical and secular cento poets, their shared aesthetics and methods of composition notwithstanding.

Eudocia's interest in paraphrasing the Bible with Homer's words has broader theological implications beyond her concern with Trinitarian-sounding topics (Son and Father, line 33). On the one hand, a versified Bible necessitates

---

[83] Schembra 2007b.

[84] Ludwich 1897.

[85] In addition to Proba's preface, there survives an anonymous dedication that further defends Proba's poetic contribution. See Clark and Hatch 1981:106; Shanzer 1986:233; Sivan 1993:144–145; Green 1997:548–549; Mastrandrea 2001; McGill 2007:173–174; Schottenius Culhed 2010:43; Formisano and Sogno 2010:388; Sandnes 2011:146.

[86] Compare the prefatory remarks of Juvencus and Prudentius, among others. See also Green 2006:18–19; Mastrangelo 2016:42–43.

some deviation from its biblical source, regardless of her claims as paraphrast. Homeric paraphrases, including biblical centos, are intertextually complex and exegetically rich poems; their intentional blending of biblical and Homeric ideas necessarily diverges from the rather strict vocabulary of fifth-century orthodox theology.[87] Moreover, considering its overabundance of sequential Homeric lines that further conflate biblical and epic passages, Eudocia's cento produces hybrid characters, first and foremost a Homeric Jesus.

In his treatment of the *Life and Miracles of Thecla*, a late antique paraphrastic expansion of the second-century *Acts of Paul and Thecla*, Scott Johnson suggests that rewriting and revising preexisting narratives was one early Christian strategy to alleviate potentially complicated theological issues and to curb rival, frequently heretical, theologies.[88] Although theological concerns are evident in the Homeric cento, particularly in those sections that emphasize Jesus' dual, divine-human nature, it is not explicitly or primarily anti-heretical. Rather, by retelling a pre-existing story in new and relevant ways, what Johnson calls a "backward looking forward," Eudocia "consolidates the past and reinterprets it for a contemporary culture and literary concerns."[89] The rigid poetic form inherent to centos makes them a unique method of "backward looking forward."[90] Each interpretation, rereading, and misreading—inevitable in any paraphrase—equally influences the new telling, as well as the original version. What sets centos apart from other late antique paraphrases, including *The Life and Miracles of Thecla*, *The Acts of Peter*, and the Codex Bezae manuscript of the *book of Acts*, is the role of ἀνάγκη (line 18). Its unique manner of composition compels the cento poet to engage both texts (Homer and the Bible) with a high degree of interpretational freedom. As a result, Homer or Vergil always lurks in the cento's shadows, eager to assist or hinder in countless ways.

This intertextual overload necessitates active readers who must make sense of a cento's two-fold Homeric and biblical allusiveness to understand not only the cento itself but also its source text(s).[91] In other words, Eudocia's Homeric Jesus has the allusive potential to simultaneously affect one's interpretation of her cento, the Homeric epics, and the Bible. This allusive double/triple duty takes on a proselytizing tone, implied when Patricius is described as the one who "brings forth good news for the mortal race" (line 38) but made more explicit in the cento's opening lines:

[87] Clark and Hatch 1981:123-135; Roberts 1985:58; Usher 1998:81-85; Arcidiacono 2011:9-54; Schottenius Cullhed 2015:137-138.

[88] Johnson 2006a:33-34.

[89] Johnson 2006a:15, 28.

[90] Johnson 2006a:95-104.

[91] Clark and Hatch 1981:137-159; Usher 1998:113-146; McGill 2007; Bažil 2009; Arcidiacono 2011:34-46; Sandnes 2011:181-228; Schottenius Cullhed 2015:138-188; McGill 2016b.

Κέκλυτε, μυρία φῦλα περικτιόνων ἀνθρώπων,
ὅσσοι νῦν βροτοί εἰσιν ἐπὶ χθονὶ σῖτον ἔδοντες,
ἠμὲν ὅσοι ναίουσι πρὸς ἠῶ τ' ἠέλιόν τε
ἠδ' ὅσσοι μετόπισθε ποτὶ ζόφον ἠερόεντα,
ὄφρ' εὖ γινώσκοιτ' ἠμὲν θεὸν ἠδὲ καὶ ἄνδρα,
ὃς πᾶσι θνητοῖσι καὶ ἀθανάτοισιν ἀνάσσων.

Listen, you countless races of world-wide humans,
as many mortals as are now eating grain upon the earth,
as many as dwell facing the dawn and sun,
and as many as dwell on the other side facing the western shade,
so that you may know him who is God and man,
who rules over all mortals and immortals.

The cento's persuasive aim is clear: proper engagement with it results in knowledge of the one who is God and man (θεὸν ἠδὲ καὶ ἄνδρα). A recurring circumlocution for Jesus in the cento, θεὸν ἠδὲ καὶ ἄνδρα, is the closest Homeric clause to express Jesus' dual nature, a theological matter of great concern in the fifth century. On the other hand, because it does not specify Jesus' humanity and divinity, θεὸν ἠδὲ καὶ ἄνδρα is equally ambiguous and can be reconciled in competing Trinitarian factions, without explicitly offending any. Eudocia carefully situates her cento within the context of late antique theology and emphasizes her explicitly didactic and proselytizing goals.

This focus on a receptive audience marks a shift in the epic proem tradition modeled on Homer and Hesiod and their emphasis on divine inspiration.[92] Unlike Proba's proem and its explicit engagement with her Vergilian original, Eudocia claims to speak entirely on her own authority. On the one hand, she speaks in the first person singular (εἴπω, με). On the other hand, her message comes from within her, whatever her heart (θυμός) bids. Such an internal inspiration, a veiled allusion to the Holy Spirit, provides an alternative poetic source to the classical Muse.[93] Since the Holy Spirit has inspired her story, Eudocia only requires a receptive audience.

Case Study: The Samaritan Woman at the Well

In this section, I examine the episode of the Samaritan woman as a representative example of how Eudocia simultaneously paraphrases and interprets the

---

[92] Green 2006:128–132, 244–247.
[93] Paulinus of Nola *Carmen* 10.19–32; Juvencus 1.25–27; Sulpicius Severus *Life of St. Martin* 4.245–50; Shorrock 2011:13–48.

biblical narrative, all while adding Homeric allusive potential.[94] Because this biblical episode comes only from the Johannine tradition (John 4:4–42) and is not found in the three synoptic Gospels, we can read Eudocia's version alongside a single source, without first reconciling multiple gospel accounts of the same episode. For that reason, Eudocia's engagement with the Bible is more apparent.

In John 4, while returning to Galilee from Judea on the shortest possible route, Jesus and his disciples stop at a well (originally dug by the patriarch Jacob) outside the Samaritan town of Sychar (4:5). The disciples leave Jesus at the well and continue on to the town to buy food. Shortly after they depart, Jesus meets a woman who has come to draw water from the well. Breaking with cultural norms, he asks this unnamed Samaritan woman for some water (4:7). She responds with shock, less at his specific request than his choice to speak with her at all. Ever mysterious, Jesus proceeds to engage the woman in a parabolic conversation about his own living water, characterized as a divine gift, which permanently quenches the thirst of all who drink it (4:10). Eager for this magical water, the Samaritan woman asks Jesus for some. Shifting the conversation again, Jesus tells the woman to call her husband and, upon hearing that she is not married, prophetically reveals than she has lived with multiple men out of wedlock (4:17–18). She responds to this by asking him about the religious sanctuary on Mount Gerizim and its rivalry with the Jerusalem Temple. Jesus explains to her that true worship is in spirit, not in a specific locale (4:23–24). Perhaps beginning to understand, she mentions the eventual coming of the Messiah, prompting Jesus' revelation that he is the Messiah (4:25–26). While the Samaritan women returns to proselytize the townspeople, Jesus has a parallel conversation with his disciples about the type of food he requires, which he equates with harvesting people (4:32–38). Prompted by the woman's insistence that Jesus predicted her sexual history, a crowd comes out to see Jesus for themselves (4:39–40). Impressed, they invite Jesus to stay with them, and many come to believe in him after a two-day visit (4:41–42).

A few salient themes emerge from this episode. First, despite its various digressions about Samaritan-Jewish religious practices and its metaphors of food and water, the episode is ultimately about Jesus' identity, his inclusion of religiously marginalized groups, and their eventual belief in him.[95] By the end of Jesus' brief stay in Sychar, his metaphors of food and water recede into the background, and the story focuses on the townspeople, who through the woman's testimony and their own experiences follow Jesus. In this way, the

---

[94] Schembra 2007b, lines 1053–1160 (Usher 1999, lines 1046–1152). See Usher 1998:113–126.

[95] Edwards 2015:148; Barnes 2016:274–275; Blessing 2016:132; Welzen 2016. Blessing 2016:133–135 compares the Samaritan woman to Nicodemus and argues that she emerges as the idealized disciple.

narrative culminates with an explicitly identified Messianic Jesus marked by his inclusivity, especially of those traditionally on the social fringes of first-century Judaism. As his first followers, these marginalized individuals become idealized disciple types, set in contrast to Jesus' religious rivals, especially the Pharisees.[96]

At 106 lines, Eudocia's version of the Samaritan woman episode is approximately the same length as her biblical model, although she makes a few substantial revisions—entire sections have been omitted, including the digression on Samaritan-Jewish worship, while other details have been added, such as the woman's evangelical speech to the townspeople.[97] In this way, the cento narrator presents a new version of a familiar story by emphasizing certain details while minimizing or omitting others. This narrative revision results in a more philosophically and theologically sophisticated account that actively expands the role of secondary characters and transforms them into primary agents. Compared to the account in the Gospel of John, the account of Eudocia's unnamed woman more persuasively convinces the townspeople about Jesus and directly leads to their conversion. Accordingly, she surpasses John's Samaritan woman as an ideal disciple type, not only through her eager conversion but also through her more eager conversion of others.

Equally striking is Eudocia's omission of the twelve disciples. Present in the previous episode (especially *Cento* 1047–1048) yet absent throughout Jesus' interaction with the unnamed woman, the disciples return in the following episode (*Cento* 1183) to help Jesus distribute his miraculous bread and fish. In some ways, this focus on Jesus at the exclusion of his disciples mirrors the gospel account. For instance, the disciples are never explicitly mentioned as traveling with Jesus (John 4:4–6), and all verbs are singular, although one can safely infer that they are with him. Since the disciples in Eudocia's version are not present to ask Jesus why he is talking with an unknown woman, he never tells them the story about his divine food, a parallel to the divine water offered to the woman. By removing the disciples and highlighting Jesus' interaction with the woman, Eudocia replaces their conversation about divine food with entirely new material: an evangelistic speech by the woman to the townspeople.

In addition to augmenting and minimizing the role each biblical character plays in her revised episode, Eudocia also changes the story's geographic setting in ways that profoundly alter its socio-cultural implications. For his part, the gospel narrator underscores exact Judean-Samaritan features of the story: Jesus

---

[96] Schneiders 2003:136–140; Welzen 2016; Bennema 2017.

[97] *Cento* 1053–1158. Eudocia's approach differs from that of Nonnus, who adheres closely to his biblical source (Agosti 2003:111). Nonnus' paraphrase of the Samaritan woman scene reflects the patristic readings of it (Caprara 2005; Simelidis 2016:290–291), a pattern throughout his epic (Livrea 1989:154; Agosti 2003:53, 295, 372; Simelidis 2016).

is traveling from one predominantly Jewish region to another and chooses to pass through Samaria. Sychar is explicitly marked as a Samaritan town and the unnamed woman explicitly Samaritan. These details have exegetical force useful for first-century Christians who define their communities' relationship with Judaism and other Mediterranean religious traditions.[98] While hotly contested in the first century, the religious distinctions between Samaritan and Jewish traditions were hardly relevant to late antique Christianity.[99]

Eudocia elides over these outdated Samaritan-Jewish details to make her content relevant to her late antique audience and, in the process, transforms a story originally about breaking down first-century socio-political boundaries into a more universal conversion narrative. Because the rhetorical force of Jesus' request for water depends on the now-omitted ethnic identity of the woman, Eudocia downplays the living water metaphor and focuses instead on sexual ethics. By structuring their conversation as a ring composition (A, B, A'), a common Homeric pattern, she gives Jesus' words epic authority but also underscores his concern with the woman's sexuality. For instance, when Jesus first addresses the woman, he begins by criticizing her for not speaking with him (1064–1065), then prophetically reveals her sexual history (1066–1068), and finally concludes with a second criticism about her unwillingness to talk (1069–1071). This structural pattern juxtaposes the woman's sexual ethics with her disinterest in speaking with Jesus.

Through this emphasis on sexuality, Eudocia's late antique Jesus deviates from his first-century archetype. In John 4, Jesus' words contain little criticism or shame, and whatever they imply is culturally dependent on Judeo-Samaritan sexual mores. In other words, the topic of marriage serves as a narrative pretext for Jesus' revelation as prophet. After this recognition scene, the woman's sexuality is forgotten until she narrates these same events to the townspeople, where she also emphasizes Jesus' identity, not her sexuality. Eudocia's construction of idealized sexual behavior, in contrast, reflects a more developed Christian theology of the body, one not found in early Christian literature (see *Didache* 2.2).[100] The sexual mores of the first two generations of Christianity generally are modeled on first-century Judaism, with which Christianity was still closely associated. As a result, the sexual ethics found in the Pauline epistles and the *Didache* focus on sexual acts, whereas second-century Christian communities evince a more complex sexual ethic focused on marital status.[101] As two

---

[98] Welzen 2016.

[99] By the fifth century, references to "Samaritans" were increasingly conflated within heresiological debates, perhaps deriving from Simon Magus' Samaritan origin. See Noethlichs 2007.

[100] Brown 1988; Cloke 1995:100–133; Nathan 2000:74–106, 130–132.

[101] Milavec 2003:4–5.

illustrative examples, women in the *Shepherd of Hermas* and the *Acts of Paul and Thecla* choose to remain virgins, an incipient form of ascetic sexuality developed more fully in the fourth and fifth centuries.[102]

In order to situate her idealized sexual behavior vis-à-vis marriage and to prevent any confusion, Eudocia interjects the following explanatory clause about the unnamed woman: ἡ δ' οὔτ' ἠρνεῖτο στυγερὸν γάμον οὔτε τελεύτα (but she neither rejected marriage as something disdainful nor brought it about).[103] Through this gloss, Eudocia advances two acceptable options for the woman: rejection of marriage (celibacy) or legal marriage, a choice that further distinguishes early Christianity from other ancient Mediterranean religions, including Judaism.[104] While celibacy and marriage were protected by late antique law, most early Church writers prioritize celibacy over marriage.[105] Because the woman at the well chose neither acceptable option, she finds herself in a sexually (and, by association, morally) liminal middle ground. That she has any choice reflects a decidedly late antique understanding of female virtue, one entirely foreign to the author of the Gospel of John.

Alongside these revised and updated sexual ethics, Eudocia offsets the omission of the Jewish-Samaritan religious controversy and the water metaphor by expanding other theological details. Without these elaborations, Jesus' interaction with the woman—what had been twenty-three biblical verses—would only comprise approximately ten Homeric lines. One such expanded detail is the metaphor of Jesus as divine gift (τὴν δωρεὰν τοῦ θεοῦ, John 4:10), which Eudocia conflates with the themes of celibacy and marriage. By interweaving imagery of sexuality and gift giving, particularly nuptial dowries, Eudocia subtly gestures toward the spiritual marriage between Jesus and the local townspeople. This conflation of sexuality and divine munificence thematically underpins the story and distinguishes it from its biblical template.[106]

The most straightforward interpretation about the gift of God (τὴν δωρεὰν τοῦ θεοῦ) in John 4:10 is that it represents the living water offered to the Samaritan woman. Shortly after this episode (John 7:37–38), Jesus implies that he is the water or its source.[107] The gospel narrator (John 7:39) clarifies

---

[102] Miller 2005:256–257; Moreschini and Norelli 2005:162; Trevett 2006:131.

[103] Schembra 2007b:73 prints ἡ δ' αὖ ἠρνεῖτο στυγερὸν γάμον οὔτε τελεύτα. I here follow the easier reading supported by the Homeric text itself (*Odyssey* 24.126).

[104] Nathan 2000:77, 130–131. Compare Hunter 1992; Shaw 2000; Foskett 2002:46; Deming 2004.

[105] Jovinian, the fourth-century heresiarch, quite famously attempted to place virgins on the same moral level as married women, which in turn provoked Jerome to write his *Adversus Jovinianum*. See Hunter 2007:30–35. On the legal protections for women to choose between chastity and marriage, see *Codex Theodosianus* 9.25.2; White 1982; Clark 1993; Nathan 2000:131.

[106] Usher 1998:113–126 examines the Homeric influence of this episode in detail.

[107] Bennema 2017.

this potentially confusing statement by explaining that Jesus is referring to the Holy Spirit, imparted on the disciples after his ascension. Influenced by these and other passages, early Christians symbolically described a convert's inclusion into their community with water and washing imagery, with the ritual of baptism the most obvious of these washing metaphors. In John 4, however, Jesus talks about drinking water, not bathing in it. Paired with the food that he mentions later to his disciples, this potable water has Eucharistic implications. While early Christian communities developed symbolic language for baptism and the Eucharist, they also used comparably symbolic language about Jesus' relationship with the Church, one of the most popular being that of a wedding.[108] This metaphor originates from nuptial imagery found in early Christian texts, including the Gospel of John.[109]

By omitting the water/baptism imagery from her version, Eudocia reworks Jesus' reference to the gift of God into an allusion about nuptial gifts and a dowry.[110] As a result, the characters within the episode, especially the unnamed woman, become part of a spiritual bridal party, although Eudocia reverses and bends their gender identities.[111] For instance, when the woman initiates gift giving (*Cento* 1094–1096) through the promise of civic generosity, food, drink, and gifts (δωτίνῃσι), her behavior is fairly unremarkable. She is simply being a good host. When she continues to bless the "man" who would lead Jesus into marriage and weigh him down with a dowry (*Cento* 1097–1098), her behavior becomes more exegetically and intertextually fertile. On the one hand, this reversal of expected gender roles situates Jesus as bride in search of a groom. More common in medieval than late antique literature, depictions of Jesus as a maternal woman are theological explanations about Jesus' own complex identities, including God, human, and Sophia (always a feminine personification).[112] Such gender blending, however, is less common in Christian nuptial imagery, where the Church or individual Christian is most often imagined as the bride of Christ. Moreover, by describing Jesus as a guest laden with gifts, possibly wedding gifts, Eudocia conflates the Christian imagery of Jesus as incarnate

---

[108] Compare Clement *Stromateis* and Tertullian *Ad Uxorem*.

[109] 2 Corinthians 11:2; Matthew 22:1–14; John 3:29; Ephesians 3:22–24.

[110] Eudocia here anticipates a trend in modern interpretations of this episode to view Jesus as wooing the Samaritan woman (Fehribach 1998:45–81; Brant 2004:247; Blessing 2016:135). This interpretation is not without its critics (Edwards 2015:126). For more context on Roman wedding practices into Late Antiquity, see Treggiari 1991:323–364; Clark 1993; Evans Grubbs 1994; Evans Grubbs 1995:156–171.

[111] Clark 1986a; Hunter 2000.

[112] Bynum 1982:110–169; Bynum 1991:35; Mathews 1999.

Savior of the World (John 4:42) with the Greek mythological trope of a god disguised as a human and hosted by unwitting people.[113]

Eudocia further complicates the marital and sexual undertones of this episode by drawing from Homeric hospitality scenes that are equally charged with sexual tension. Most line clusters (three or more sequential lines) and 60 of the 106 total lines come from *Odyssey* 6, 8, 17, and 23. In these books, the wayward Odysseus is hosted either in the palace of Alcinous by Nausicaa and the Phaeacians or in his own house by Telemachus and Penelope.[114] Since the words spoken by the unnamed woman depend so heavily on these Homeric contexts, her relationship with Jesus and her relationship with the townspeople become intertextually convoluted. For instance, when the woman blesses Jesus' future husband, her words come from Odysseus' blessing of Nausicaa, a story full of marital anxiety and sexual tension. Marital expectations burst at the seams, as Athena, Nausicaa, Odysseus, and Alcinous each allude to Nausicaa's eventual nuptials. In context, the sexual tensions between Odysseus and Nausicaa threaten to further delay Odysseus' nostos (homecoming)—he had just spent seven years as a type of husband to Calypso. Equally dangerous, Odysseus could decide to bring Nausicaa home with him as a rival spouse to Penelope, a type of decision that partly robs Agamemnon of his nostos. Both threats (delay or breakdown of marriages) are recurring themes in the *Odyssey*.

Although Eudocia opens these intertextual comparisons between the unnamed woman and Nausicaa or Penelope, modern readers must make sense of these allusions and their associated sexual tensions. In the *Odyssey*, Nausicaa and Penelope are subjected to intense scrutiny about their marital status and sexual availability, which potentially complicate Eudocia's use of them as female templates. For instance, Nausicaa's words: καὶ δ' ἄλλην νεμεσῶ ἥ τις τοιαῦτά γε ῥέζοι· ἥ τ' ἀέκητι φίλων πατρὸς καὶ μητρὸς ἐόντων, ἀνδράσι μίσγηται πρίν γ' ἀμφάδιον γάμον ἐλθεῖν (And I would disprove of another girl doing such a thing, namely, without the goodwill of her dear father and mother, associating with a man before publicly marrying, *Odyssey* 6.286–288) are themselves a projection of this type of sexual scrutiny. In context, Nausicaa has just imagined what her fellow Phaeacians would say if they saw her traveling with Odysseus into the city. She fears they will gossip about her sexual propriety and concludes by saying that she would criticize other women for doing the same. Eudocia creatively adapts Nausicaa's disapproval into the content of Jesus' criticism of the unnamed woman. On the one hand, this situates Jesus as a new Odysseus, displaced and wayward, suffering a type of death and resurrection on the path

---

[113] Usher 1998:114–115 argues that this episode replicates Homeric (i.e. Greek) ideas at the expense of its biblical context.

[114] Usher 1998:113–117.

toward his nostos.[115] The unnamed woman is not quite Nausicaa, however, but represents the object of Nausicaa's projected criticism, a "bizarro Nausicaa," the female type Nausicaa successfully avoids.

This revision of Nausicaa's character makes the nuptial imagery within the scene even more striking. Nausicaa's appeal as an ideal feminine type is defined by her social decorum: her willingness to do the family's laundry, her commitment to assist the naked Odysseus, her awareness of the scandals associated with public appearances with unknown men. This notion of familial duty, more similar to the Jesus in the Gospel of John (see John 4:34, 6:38) than to the Samaritan woman or to Eudocia's unnamed woman, is reflected in the cento, when the woman offers Jesus the dowry, thereby transforming him into Nausicaa or a Nausicaa-Odysseus hybrid. In this reading of Eudocia's allusion to *Odyssey* 6, she does not provide an epic model for the unnamed woman. Rather, she contrasts the woman's character with an imagined scenario conceptualized and vocalized by Nausicaa. At the same time, since the intertext is hypothetical or imagined, Eudocia underscores the unnamed woman's agency for change and the potential for conversion. In as much as Nausicaa can avoid the slanderous gossip of the Phaeacian townspeople, so can the unnamed woman turn to Jesus as the one true, ideal spouse.

To further complicate Jesus' criticism, Eudocia explains the unnamed woman's behavior with the aforementioned line: ἡ δ' οὔτ' ἠρνεῖτο στυγερὸν γάμον οὔτε τελεύτα (*Odyssey* 24.126). If we read this gloss through the biblical account, it makes perfect sense—the woman was sexually involved with men outside the confines of a legal marriage. When read in its Homeric context, however, it opens a variety of interpretive vectors. This line comes from a speech given by the ghost of Amphimedon to the ghost of Agamemnon about Penelope's strategic delay in choosing a suitor to replace Odysseus, including her plan to weave a burial shroud for Laertes during the day, only to unravel it at night. Her delay in choosing a husband both preserves her marriage with Odysseus, as seen in the test of the marriage bed in *Odyssey* 23, and saves Telemachus' life. On the other hand, from the perspective of the Homeric speaker, Amphimedon, Penelope's delay was decidedly negative and directly led to his death.

Like the Nausicaa material (*Odyssey* 6.286–288), this reference to Penelope only makes sense from a limited perspective, one predicated on a thorough familiarity with the Homeric epics. While subject to intense scrutiny over her marital status and sexuality, Penelope emerges as the prudent defender of the household, the female equivalent to Odysseus. Her deceptive weaving of

---

[115] Usher 1998:133–134; Louden 2011:258–282; Sandnes 2011:217–219. Odysseus is, of course, not the only Homeric hero compared to Jesus (MacDonald 2000:136–147).

the shroud reinforces her role as Odysseus' spouse. In other words, Penelope (and Nausicaa) are not like the unnamed woman in Eudocia's cento. When read against their Homeric contexts, these cento lines augment Eudocia's scene. From Amphimedon's perspective, Penelope's seeming ambivalence marks her as sexually and morally dubious, but, from the perspective of the entire *Odyssey*, Penelope is endowed with agency and the responsibility of defending her house from the arrogant suitors until Odysseus returns. This same potential is available to the unnamed woman. In other words, Jesus' Homeric words underscore the woman's current moral state but open the possibility for a different reality.

Conclusion

This chapter opens by contextualizing Eudocia's Homeric cento as one of nearly two dozen late antique centos, Greek and Latin, Christian and secular. The last few decades have seen an explosion of scholarship on these cento, including four critical editions and two commentaries dedicated only to Eudocia's Homeric cento and its tradition. My focus on this chapter has been to compare Eudocia's prefatory remarks to similar prefaces by Faltonia Betitia Proba and Decimus Magnus Ausonius. As the earliest surviving Christian cento poet in either Greek or Latin, Proba makes for a useful comparison for Eudocia. That Eudocia is thought to have had a copy of Proba's Vergilian cento and used it as a model for her own makes the comparison even more apt. Proba's preface, I argue, treats Vergil's content (violence, war, gods) as unsuitable to her new topic: the creation, fall, and redemption of humanity. As cento poet, Proba sings alongside Vergil, whose words she appropriates to tell a new message, one she implies was hidden within his epic but now requires divine inspiration to bring to light. For that reason, Proba recognizes that centos are intertextually complex poetic modes that conflate original authors/texts within new poems.

Ausonius assumes something similar in his light-hearted preface addressed to Paulus. In this preface, Ausonius apologizes, as is his habit when circulating poetry among friends, for debasing Vergil with such bankrupt metal, and he invites Paulus as learned friend and critic to assess whether his worthless cento passes muster. Within this epistle teeming with Ausonius' usual self-deprecations and dissimulations, he provides the best surviving theory for cento poetics. For that reason, his *PCN* has been treated as the standard for ancient centos, especially his rules that Vergilian lines can be divided and stitched together at all epic caesurae and that one must avoid using two or more sequential Vergilian lines, although he himself breaks this rule three times over the course of his *Cento Nuptialis*. Finally, Ausonius provides the metaphor of the game (*ludus*) for centos and provides as an analogy Archimedes' game, the *stomachion*.

Eudocia's thirty-eight-line preface reflects concerns expressed by both Proba and Ausonius. What sets Eudocia's cento apart from theirs is her revision of a previous cento written by Patricius. Like Proba, Eudocia treats biblical centos as divinely inspired texts and, in so doing, blurs the line between cento and Bible. For that reason, she criticizes Patricius for not telling the biblical story accurately and harmoniously, mistakes which force her to revise his cento by removing its deficiencies and adding new, more appropriate material. Even with her improvements, their new cento still contains sequential lines, a deficiency Eudocia admits and justifies as a product of their Christian content. By comparing her cento with Tatian's fourth-century cento, Eudocia suggests that her ideal audience would be familiar with it. In my view, we can infer from this that Eudocia's circle, similar to Ausonius', consists of fellow poets, familiar with the classics and more contemporary poems, which they use to critique poems written by members of their own coterie. As a result, the contours of Eudocia's poetic circle and their shared literary habits come into sharper focus.

The final section of this chapter analyzes Eudocia's version of the Samaritan woman at the well episode from John 4. In my view, Eudocia exegetically updates this story by first removing the Samaritan-Jewish material, which would have made little sense to a fifth-century audience, and by replacing this cultural context with a general conversion narrative. The unnamed woman, therefore, becomes the ideal type of female convert, one who not only believes in Jesus but also returns to her hometown to persuade others to believe in him. The speeches that she makes expand the biblical account, give the unnamed woman more agency, and center her as the main character in the story, arguably as a model for similar fifth-century Christians.

On the other hand, Eudocia's Homeric content opens intertextual vectors beyond her control and can only be interpreted by her readers, ancient or modern. In my reading, I focus on Eudocia's use of hospitality scenes from the *Odyssey*, scenes which conflate Jesus' metaphor of the gift of God into a type of wedding present or dowry. While still serving Christian ends and supporting the theology of the spiritual wedding between Christ as groom marrying his bride, the Church, the cento episode reverses gender roles and depicts Jesus as the bride. At the same time, Jesus' critique of the woman's sexual past uses Homeric lines said by or about Nausicaa and Penelope, characters in the *Odyssey* defined by their sexuality and their relationship with male characters. Eudocia's engagement with Nausicaa and Penelope is oblique and indirect, in that she uses lines that are either hypothetical or distorted by the limited perspective of characters within the story itself. In this way, despite her sexual past, the unnamed woman has the potential to emerge after her conversion as a redeemed Nausicaa or Penelope, the Homeric feminine ideal. Eudocia's engagement with the feminine ideal continues in her next poem and the subject of the next chapter: her *Martyrdom of Cyprian.*

3

The Conversion

Constructing the Feminine Ideal

Introduction

B Y THE MIDDLE of the fourth century, stories about a fictional Christian bishop and martyr, Cyprian of Antioch, began to circulate throughout the eastern half of the empire. According to these stories, a lovelorn Antiochene aristocrat, Aglaidas, hires a local magician, Cyprian, to seduce a young Christian woman, Justa, who had rejected his advances. Cyprian conjures three demons, whom he orders to fetch Justa for Aglaidas. Armed with the power of the cross, Justa repels each demon in turn. Their defeat convinces Cyprian of Christianity's supremacy and leads to his conversion. Cyprian rises through the ecclesiastical ranks and is eventually appointed bishop of Antioch. He changes Justa's name to Justina and charges her with overseeing Antioch's virgins. These events correspond to one set of stories about Cyprian, conventionally called the *Conversion of Cyprian* (hereafter *Conversion*).[1]

Written after the *Conversion* by a second anonymous author, the *Confession of Cyprian* (hereafter *Confession*), contains Cyprian's lengthy defense to the Antiochene Christians about the legitimacy of his conversion experience.[2] In this speech, he recalls the immediate events precipitating his conversion with some slight changes but also goes into great detail about his prior religious education. As a child, his Athenian family initiated him into all Greek mysteries, both those in Athens and across Greece. Because he excelled at participating in these rituals, he left Greece and traveled across the Mediterranean to Scythia, Egypt, and Babylon to formally study rituals of power or magic. Despite being a fictional account full of Christian embellishment about traditional Mediterranean religions and magic, the *Confession* remains a valuable document

---

[1] Zahn 1882:139–153 prints the prose version of the *Conversion*. See also Radermacher 1927, no. 3

[2] (A)AS(S) Sept. 7.204–223 and Gitlbauer 1879 print the prose versions of the *Confession*.

for religious history.[3] It also preserves the legend's most convoluted and impenetrable material—Cyprian's descriptions of Scythian, Egyptian, and Babylonian rituals.[4]

The final part of the Cyprian trilogy is the *Martyrdom of Cyprian* (hereafter *Martyrdom*), written by the same author who wrote the *Conversion*.[5] According to the *Martyrdom*, sometime after his appointment as bishop of Antioch and during the reign of Diocletian and Maximian, Cyprian is arrested and charged with being a Christian. Living in Damascus at the time, Justina is also arrested on similar charges and sent to Antioch to stand trial alongside Cyprian. When interrogation and torture fail to elicit their renunciations, Cyprian and Justina are thrown into a cauldron of burning pitch and wax. Similar to Daniel's friends, who survive Nebuchadnezzar's fiery furnace (Daniel 3), Cyprian and Justina remain unharmed, prompting Cyprian's former assistant, Athanasius, to jump into the cauldron as a demonstration of Satan's power. Predictably, Athanasius dies, so the Antiochene authorities decide to send Cyprian and Justina to Diocletian in Nicomedia, where they are beheaded. The subsequent removal of their remains to Rome gave rise to a cult of Saints Cyprian and Justina and a basilica for their relics.

Combining these fourth-century prose versions of the *Conversion, Confession,* and *Martyrdom*, Eudocia converted them into a three-book epic.[6] Until the eighteenth century, Eudocia's verse paraphrase of the *Martyrdom of Cyprian* was thought to be lost, surviving only in Photius' summary.[7] However, in 1760, while working through an eleventh-century manuscript of Nonnus' paraphrase of the Gospel of John (*Laurentiano* VII.10), Angelo Maria Bandini, director of the Bibliotheca Medicea, discovered an incomplete folio containing 801 lines of her epic, the final 322 lines of book 1 and first 479 lines of book 2.[8] A century later, Jacques-Paul Migne republished Bandini's edition for the *Patrologia Graeca* series, followed shortly by Theodor Zahn's edition of the fourth-century prose versions.[9] At the end of the nineteenth century, Arthur Ludwich published the only critical edition of Eudocia's *Martyrdom of Cyprian* in his volume on her poetry.[10] Sixty years later, while reading a few loose pages from an eleventh-

---

3   Nock 1927; Nilsson 1947; Festugière 1950; Nilsson 1950.
4   Jackson 1988:36 notes "not the least difficulty with our document is simply understanding what the text means."
5   (A)AS(S) Sept. 7.204; Zahn 1882:73–85; Delehaye 1921:320.
6   Livrea 1998 dates Eudocia's Cyprian epic to her visit to Jerusalem in 438–439 CE.
7   Photius *Bibliotheca* 184; Sabattini 1973:182–183.
8   Bandini 1761; Ludwich 1897:20; Bevegni 1982b:249–250.
9   Migne 1860; Zahn 1882; Radermacher 1927.
10   Ludwich 1897. Salvaneschi 1982b does not include a critical apparatus with his commentary and translation.

century manuscript (*BPG* 95) listed as *Fragmentum Homerocentonis*, the director of the Leiden University library, Karel Adriaan de Meyier, realized that this text was actually the first ninety-nine lines of Eudocia's *Martyrdom of Cyprian*.[11] In fact, the pages from the Leiden text had been removed from *Laurentiano* VII.10, the manuscript discovered two centuries earlier by Bandini.[12] Claudio Bevegni published these ninety-nine lines with a critical apparatus in 1982.[13]

Since Eudocia's epic paraphrase of the *Martyrdom of Cyprian* is her longest undisputed poem to survive, the next two chapters are dedicated to it. This chapter approaches her *Conversion*, especially its depiction of Justina, as a late antique verse continuation of early Christian prose fictions. The next chapter situates her *Confession* within late antique Christian polemics against traditional Mediterranean religions, which late antique Christian authors increasingly conflated with magic. A translation of Eudocia's epic, located in the appendix of this book, is the first complete English translation of her extant verses.[14] To avoid confusion, I refer to Eudocia's entire epic as the *Martyrdom of Cyprian* but the third part of the Cyprian legend simply as the *Martyrdom*.

Christian Prose Narratives

To speak of early Christian prose narratives as a unified category can be misleading, as "Christian prose narrative" includes a diverse range of texts: gospels (canonical and apocryphal), acts (canonical and apocryphal), saints' lives, and martyrologies.[15] As a result, within the scholarship on early Christian prose narratives, the question of genre or genres looms large, particularly the relationship between Christian narratives and the ancient novel.[16] Further complicating matters, classical scholars, who disagree about the categorization of the ancient novel, tend to fall into two schools. The first school limits the

---

[11] De Meyier 1956:93–94; Bevegni 1982b:251. This confusion with a cento underscores Eudocia's dependence on the Homeric epics.

[12] Bevegni 1982b:252–253. Apparently, the pages had been removed in the sixteenth century by the Dutch philologist P. Rulaeus, the first editor of the martyrdom of Cyprian of Carthage.

[13] Bevegni 1982b:258–261. See also Bevegni 1981; Bevegni 1982a; Bevegni 1990; Danesin 2001; Bevegni 2003.

[14] Bevegni 2006 contains an Italian translation. Plant 2004 translates part of the Conversion. Salvaneschi 1982b published his bilingual (Greek-Italian) edition/translation before the first lines of the *Conversion* were published by Bevegni 1982b.

[15] Delehaye 1961:4 calls the *Martyrdom of Cyprian* a hagiographic romance, a term that has not gained wide-spread acceptance.

[16] Consider the relevant sections in Hägg 1983; Aune 1987; Pervo 1987; Morard 1991; Reardon 1991; Schneemelcher 1991; Bowersock 1994; Dihle 1994; Bovon 1995; Bremmer 1995; Holzberg 1995; Bremmer 1996; Bremmer 1998a; Hock, Bradley, and Perkins 1998; Thomas 1998; Cooper 1999; Bremmer 2000; Bremmer 2001; Bovon 2003; Rhee 2005; Whitmarsh 2005; Mitchell 2006; Goldhill 2008.

canon to five Greek novels (those of Chariton, Xenophon of Ephesus, Achilles Tatius, Longus, and Heliodorus), separate from all other ancient prose fictions, despite their similarity to the canonical five.[17] The second school distinguishes between idealized and comic-realistic novels and considers the Latin prose fictions written by Apuleius and Petronius, as well as Pseudo-Lucian's *Ass*, examples of comic-realistic novels.[18] A third, more inclusive perspective views the ancient novel as emerging from a variety of generic conventions, including history, epic, tragedy, comedy, and oratory.[19]

By attenuating the modern divisions between genres, this third model provides space for generic influence and innovation in early Christian and late antique literature.[20] For example, since Christian prose authors situate their narratives within precise historical frameworks, including historical people, places, and events, their *acta* and *vitae* blend biographical and novelistic features.[21] It is tempting to wonder how an ancient reader would classify the *Acts of Paul and Thecla*, perhaps as a novel alongside her copy of *Chaereas and Callirhoe*.[22] Another reader, in contrast, might compare the *Acts of Paul and Thecla* to Plutarch's *Lives*.[23] Its fusion of generic features sets early Christian literature apart from its classical antecedents and paves the way for the wholesale literary hybridity characteristic of late antique prose and poetry. In fact, the third-century *Acts of Andrew* had already developed the novelistic plot of the evil magician who attempts to seduce a Christian virgin by (unsuccessfully) sending demons against her.[24] Eudocia's epic paraphrase of the *Martyrdom of Cyprian* epitomizes late antique generic hybridity by taking the prose expansion of this literary motif to the next level.[25] Indeed, not only is the prose version of the *Martyrdom of Cyprian* a literary bricolage, a spoliation of classical and early Christian texts, but its verse paraphrase by Eudocia also adds poetic features, with it simultaneously representing *acta*, *vita*, martyrology, and epic.

In addition to convoluted generic influences, early Christian prose narratives also have complex relationships with the Christian liturgy and cult of the

---

[17] Müller 1981; Reardon 1991; Morgan and Stoneman 1994.

[18] Wehrli 1965; Perry 1967; Holzberg 1995; Holzberg 1996.

[19] Ruiz-Montero 1996; Morales 2009.

[20] Bremmer 1998b:158–159; Lalleman 1998; Barrier 2009; Lipsett 2011:57–64; Futre Pinheiro, Schmeling, and Cueva 2014. For post-classical literature, Frye 1976; de Jong 1989; Elsom 1989; van der Paardt 1989; Huber 1990; Kortekaas 1990; Aerts 1997.

[21] Thomas 2003 sees this differently and situates the historical details of early Christian prose narratives within the novelistic tradition.

[22] Holzberg 1996; Pervo 1996; Bremmer 1998; Calef 2006; Schroeder 2006; Barrier 2009; Lipsett 2011.

[23] Karla 2009b.

[24] Quispel 1956:129–148; Quispel 1974:297; Bremmer 2000:25; Bailey 2009:10–11.

[25] Formisano 2007; Shanzer 2009; Lasek 2016; Mastrangelo 2016; Elsner and Lobato 2017b:11; Pollmann 2017:19–36.

saints.[26] Prose narratives, especially those incorporated into ritualized cultic spaces associated with local holy men or martyrs, became more geographically fixed than Greco-Roman novels and other early Christian gospels or acts (canonical and apocryphal).[27] During late antiquity, story, ritual, and place became inextricably fused together through annual public reading events, during which sacred text and sacred space educated visitors and, in some cases, even healed diseases or exorcised demons.[28] Such healing accounts suggest that the saints were conceived as present during their festivals and that readings of saints' lives ritually reenacted narrative events.[29] These public performances began as early as the second and third centuries. For instance, we hear about liturgical readings of apocryphal acts and martyrologies, such as the *Martyrdom Perpetuae et Felicitatis*.[30] In the fourth and fifth centuries, the Life of Martin was annually read in Tours, and, on the other side of the empire, John Chrysostom incorporated lessons from the lives of saints and martyrs into his homilies.[31] Prose narratives were so vital to the ideological landscape of late antique Christianity that one scholar aptly describes them as "scripture writ small."[32]

There is no direct evidence for late antique liturgical readings of the *Martyrdom of Cyprian*, although it was incorporated into Piacenza's liturgy in the Carolingian period.[33] Along with a few identified martyria for Cyprian and Justina, it is plausible that the *Martyrdom of Cyprian* was read each year on October 2, Cyprian and Justina's feast day.[34] Eudocia's epic paraphrase of the *Martyrdom of Cyprian* can be compared to narrative expansions or revisions of prose narratives, such the *Acts of Paul and Thecla* or the life of Martin, that were central to vibrant cult centers.[35] The parallel between Eudocia's Cyprian epic and Paulinus

[26] Compare Cyprian (of Carthage) *Epistle* 12.2.1, *Acts of the Abitinian Martyrs* 1, and the third council of Carthage (397 CE): *liceat etiam legi passiones martyrium, cum anniversarii dies eorum celebrantur*. See also de Gaiffier 1969; Yasin 2009:240–48.

[27] Konstan 1998 discusses the topic of regionalism in Greek prose narratives, and Merkelbach 1962 argues, likely based on details with the novels (e.g. Xenophon *Ephesiaca* 5.15.2), in favor of a cultic association, a view that is no longer accepted (Longo 1969; Vidman 1970; Engelmann 1975; Totti 1985). For the role of narrative in early Christian space/place, Brown 1981 remains essential. See also Salisbury 1997:169–176; Markus 1994; Mayer 2006b. For the role of late Latin poetry in the cult of the saints, see Roberts 1993:189–197.

[28] Van Dam 1993:90; Hägg 1994; Pervo 1996:691; Coon 1997:5–7; Mayer and Allen 1999:17–25; Mayer 2006b:209; Rapp 2007:194–222; Frankfurter 2010; Hershkowitz 2017:76–122; Sowers 2017.

[29] *De virtutibus sancti Martini episcopi* 2.29; Rose 2005; Rapp 2007:219–222; Rose 2008; Sowers 2017.

[30] Pervo 1996:691; Salisbury 1997:169–176; Misset-van de Weg 2006:146; Barnes 2010:74.

[31] Mayer and Allen 1999:17–25; Mayer 2006b:209; Rapp 2007:219–220; Barnes 2010:237; Roberts 2017a:389.

[32] Rapp 2007:222.

[33] Jensen 2012; Sowers 2017:444–445.

[34] Photius *Bibliotheca* 184; Bede *Martyrologium* (PL 94, 1055).

[35] Davis 2001; Johnson 2006a; Kraemer 2011:144–146.

of Périgeaux and Venantius Fortunatus' verse paraphrase of Martin's *vita* is particularly instructive, because Paulinus and Fortunatus augmented Martin's cult by transforming him into an epic hero.[36]

The uncertain relationship between the *Martyrdom of Cyprian* and the cult of Cyprian and Justina complicates our understanding of Eudocia's readership or audience. Measuring early Christian literacy rates is inherently different from quantifying literacy rates in the wider ancient world, with the possible exception of Jewish communities.[37] For instance, urban Christian communities responsible for composing, circulating, and publicly reading prose narratives functioned as a type of macro, pan-Mediterranean reading community.[38] Therefore, communities with deep ties to specific saints, such as Tours or Carthage, would have been intimately familiar with the *vitae* of their local saints and with other narratives that circulated across the pan-Mediterranean reading community and within more intimate coteries made up of the literary elite.[39] Since most Christians heard religious texts during ecclesiastical functions, their content primarily spread by word of mouth and was mediated by external interpreters. This further complicates the relationship between the written word and bookish religions. Moreover, the hyper-moralistic tone of these texts made them effective teaching tools, especially for audiences that only heard them piecemeal.[40] For every reader of Eudocia's *Martyrdom of Cyprian*, it is likely that countless others heard it read aloud.

Cyprian's *Conversion*

Since the events that comprise the *Conversion* are not widely known, this section provides a critical summary of the story.[41] The *Conversion* opens with an eight-line proem that situates the story within redemptive and theological history, beginning with the incarnation or, as Eudocia describes it, God's illumination of

---

[36] Roberts 1989b:136–144; George 1992; Roberts 2009; Roberts 2017b.
[37] In this regard, early Christian literature is different from the readership of the ancient novel (Hägg 1983; Wessling 1988; Bowie 1994; Hägg 1994; Stephens 1994). For literary rates and reading culture more generally, see Harris 1989; Johnson 2000; Johnson and Parker 2009; Johnson 2010; Fantham 2013.
[38] Cooper 1999:70–71; Barrier 2009:15–21.
[39] Coon 1997:5–7, 23.
[40] Shaw 2011; Frankfurter 2013:294–98.
[41] When referring to line numbers, I use the Roman numeral I. for Eudocia's *Conversion* and II. for her *Confession*. To distinguish Bevegni's line numbers (the first 99 lines of the *Conversion*) from Salvaneschi's line numbers (the final 322 lines), Bevegni's lines follow with an asterisk. For example, I.33* refers to *Conversion* line 33 in Bevegni's edition, whereas I.33 refers to *Conversion* line 33 in Salvaneschi's edition, technically the 132nd line of the book.

the earth and fulfillment of the prophets (I.1–2*).[42] In keeping with the times, Eudocia's God is explicitly Trinitarian (I.5–7*): one God (ἕνα θεόν) consisting of Father (πατέρα), Son (υἱέα), and Holy Spirit (πνεύματος ἠγαθέοιο). God illuminates the earth but receives assistance from the disciples (I.4*), whose diffusion of divine light throughout the world results in the conversion of humanity. Undoubtedly idealized, this global conversion recursively foreshadows events within the story itself, including Cyprian's conversion and his evangelical role in converting Antioch's citizens. Eudocia's proem, therefore, proleptically situates the *Conversion* within the past, an inevitable future outcome of redemptive history.[43]

Transitioning from proem to narrative, Eudocia introduces Justa with "there once was a certain" (ἦν δέ τις, I.9*), epic language that also places the *Conversion* within the literary world of early Christian prose fiction.[44] Through her marital status (single, virgin) and relationship with her Antiochene parents, Aedesius and Clidonia, Justa parallels Thecla in the second-century *Acts of Paul and Thecla* (hereafter, *APT*), although, unlike Thecla and other female protagonists in early Christian prose fictions, Justa is not engaged.[45] From her bedroom window (I.21*), she hears a local minister, Praulius, preaching the gospel.[46] His sermon (I.23–36*) spans the gospel, from messianic prophecies in the Old Testament to the annunciation, incarnation, crucifixion, resurrection, ascension, and glorification of Christ. After hearing this message, Justa burns with desire for Praulius, a further parallel to Thecla. Whereas Thecla breaks off her engagement and escapes her house to join Paul in prison, Justa speaks with her mother about the evils of idol worship.[47] Her language borrows heavily from Paul's speech to the Areopagites in *Acts* 17, lending apostolic authority to her words. Clidonia responds, her only words in the *Conversion*, "May your father never hear your opinions" (I.51–52*). Shifting the object of her desire, Justa insists that she loves God and is committed to searching for him (compare Gospel of Matthew 7:7–8). She closes by describing her "pagan" father as hostile to God (ἀντιθέῳ, I.53*), a

---

[42] Sc. Gospel of John 1:4–5.

[43] Van Minnen 2006 ascribes late antique hagiographies an etiological function to explain this newly emerged Christianized world. Compare Brandt 2000.

[44] Compare Homer *Iliad* 5.9 and Nonnus *Paraphrase of John* 5.3 with the *Acts of Paul and Thecla*, καί τις ἀνήρ (2.1) and Θέκλα τις παρθένος (7.2). See also Sowers 2012; Sowers 2017.

[45] The name Aedesius is attested in Syrian Antioch and its environs (Jones, Martindale, and Morris 1971; Martindale 1980), whereas Clidonia is unattested and should perhaps be read Cledonia, based on Cledonius (Martindale 1980).

[46] For more on the intertextual links between Justa and Thecla, see Sowers 2012; Sowers 2017.

[47] Compare Justin Martyr *Dialogue with Trypho* 7–8; Pagels 1995:117–123.

commonly used word about Cyprian and demons that intertextually and ideo-logically links Justa's unconverted family with demonic forces.[48]

After this brief conversation, Justa returns to her bedroom to spend the evening in prayer, and Clidonia tells Aedesius about Justa's desire to convert. That night, Aedesius and Clidonia see a vision of Christ, surrounded by angels, inviting them into heaven. His eyes opened, Aedesius leads Clidonia and Justa to the church to talk with the local priest, Optatus. Aedesius expresses his desire to be baptized by destroying his idols, an echo of Justa's response to Praulius (compare I.42–49*), but Optatus refuses until he first learns about Christ's prophetic fulfillment (compare I.2*, I.24*). Aedesius then cuts his hair (I.84–85*), a visual symbol of abandoning the pagan priesthood and embracing the Christian presbytery, a post he holds for eighteen months until his death (I.90*). Unmentioned until after Aedesius cuts his hair, Justa and Clidonia disappear into the background of the scene and become silent observers of their own conversions.[49] This positions Aedesius front and center, a strange detail considering Justa's prominence in the *Conversion*. The father/husband who brings his demon-attacked wife/daughter to church is a popular late antique motif but is reversed here, as Justa's routine journey between house and church exposes her to sexual assault and demonic attack.[50]

During one of these trips to church, Justa catches the attention of Aglaidas, a local pagan aristocrat who wants to marry her (I.97–99*). Choosing celibacy and a marriage to Christ alone, Justa rejects Aglaidas' proposal. In response, he twice attempts to rape her. His first attempt is public—in church, no less—and fails only after the local Christians fight off him and his supporters (I.3–7). He makes a second attempt while Justa is traveling to or from church, but he fails when she makes the sign of the cross, throws him to the ground, scratches his face, and tears his clothing. This episode explicitly echoes the *APT*, where Thecla fights off Alexander (I.14, compare *APT* 26). Aglaidas leaves utterly humiliated, (I.13), whereas Justa safely returns to church. In the *APT*, after Thecla fights off Alexander, he seeks legal retribution by bringing charges against her. Aglaidas, in contrast, looks for assistance in the local magician Cyprian (I.17), who, for two talents of gold and an undisclosed amount of silver, agrees to seduce Justa with the help of a trusted demon. Conjured by Cyprian, the demon demands to know why he has been called and what he is asked to do. Aglaidas express his desire for a "Galilean girl" and asks if the demon is powerful enough to seduce

---

[48] Lerza 1982.
[49] The verbs in lines 86 and 87 are plural.
[50] Palladius *Historia Lausiaca* 17.6; Cyril *Life of Euthymus* 57; Jerome *Life of Hilarion* 12; *Life of Symeon Stylites the Younger* 49. Dickie 1999; Frankfurter 2001.

her.[51] Spiritual power as a competitive dialectic becomes a key theme in the *Conversion*, as Justa repeatedly demonstrates God's superiority over Satan. To trust that the demon can seduce Justa, Cyprian asks him to narrate his prior accomplishments.[52]

Beginning with the cosmic struggle between God and Satan, the demon claims to have been the bravest angel to follow Satan against God (I.31), and, in the ensuing conflict, he shook heaven's foundations (I.34–35) and cast a host of rebellious angels from heaven (I.36).[53] After their departure from heaven, he single-handedly deceived Eve (1.37, compare Genesis 3:1–6), brought about Adam's exile from paradise (1.38, compare Genesis 3:23), and encouraged Cain to slay Abel (1.39–40, compare Genesis 4:8–9), which he vividly describes as "drenching the earth with blood," a complementary image to the curse he places on the land to grow weeds and thorns (1.40–41, compare Genesis 3:17–18).[54] The demon here revises the biblical narrative by taking credit for actions traditionally attributed to God. By casting his fellow demons out of heaven, expelling Adam from paradise, and cursing the land, he intertextually implies that he is either God or God's equal. The demon claims responsibility for adultery and idolatry, especially the fashioning of the golden calf during the Exodus journey out of Egypt (I.44–45, compare Exodus 32), as well as the crucifixion of Christ (I.46–47), the destruction of cities (I.48), and divorce (I.49). Convinced by this exhaustive catalogue, Cyprian gives the demon a magical herb that, when sprinkled in Justa's bedroom, will lead her to them.

While Cyprian and Aglaidas were conjuring this demon, Justa remains in her bedroom and sings songs during a nightly vigil. Perceiving the demon's presence, she protects herself with the sign of the cross and begins to pray. Her prayer focuses on God's accomplishments, which intertextually counteract the demon's claims and, through her words, ritually enact God's authority. For instance, while the demon actively expelled his fellow demons from heaven, Justa emphasizes how God expelled them from heaven, bound them in the underworld, and created the heavenly bodies and the earth (I.65–71).[55] The demon claims to have deceived Eve and driven Adam from paradise, whereas Justa's God created Adam and placed him within the garden (I.72–73). After the fall, God pursued humanity and redeemed it through the cross, a redemption

---

[51] "Galilean" was a common pejorative adjective for Christians. Compare Julian's *Against the Galileans* (Wilken 1984; Burr 2000; Hoffman 2004).

[52] For the role of competing curriculum vitae in the *Conversion*, see Sowers 2017.

[53] The agency claimed by the demon here is remarkable (Sowers 2017:434). Compare Tertullian *On the Shows* 16.

[54] Genesis 3:1–6; 3:23; 4:8–9.

[55] This episode is reminiscent of *Paradise Lost*, book 6. For more on Milton's manuscript collection, including other poems written by Eudocia, see Harris 1898.

which, in turn, re-stabilizes the cosmos—an intertextual nod back to the demon's claim earlier (I.76–81).[56] Therefore, heaven and earth resound with the salvation message and proclaim Christ as supreme ruler (I.81–82). The ongoing effects of salvation, reflected through present verbs, bring God's previous (aorist) actions into the here and now, specifically into Justa's conflict with Cyprian and Aglaidas. Within the competitive discourse of these speech acts, Justa gets in the last word, and, through her counter-revision of biblical stories, particularly the creation episode, she depicts God as omnipotent and rhetorically situates the demon in a position of weakness.

Justa praises Christ and asks him to preserve her chastity and keep her from evil, especially from sexual assault. Desiring to remain a virgin, she explicitly confesses her love for Christ (I.86), described as a burning desire (I.87–88). This erotic imagery juxtaposes her desire for Christ with Aglaidas' lust for her and echoes her conversion narrative (compare I.37–39*). She closes her prayer by asking God that she not transgress his laws by falling into Aglaidas' hands (I.91–92), a request that starkly implies her active culpability as potential rape victim. By crossing herself, she bookends her words with a ritualized sign of God's power and immediately sets the demon to flight.

In a scene repeated three times in the *Conversion* after Justa successfully defends herself, the demon returns to Cyprian to explain his failure. Demons, he informs Cyprian, must flee whenever they see the sign of the cross, which he calls a "scary sign" (φοβερὸν σῆμα, I.101). Undeterred, Cyprian summons a second, stronger demon, Beliar, sent directly by Satan himself. Similar to their first plan, Cyprian gives Beliar a potion with instructions to disperse it in Justa's house (I.107–108). At this point in the narrative, because Cyprian effectively replaces Aglaidas as the primary male protagonist, it now is unclear who wants to seduce/rape Justa (compare I.314–323). Cyprian's close association with Justa, described as an obsessive desire, anticipates his eventual conversion by mirroring the erotic imagery of Justa's own conversion. This eroticized association also anticipates their shared martyrdom and feast day.

Meanwhile, Justa remains vigilant in a prayer of repentance (I.110). After confessing her sins, she lists God's previous accomplishments that demonstrate his power: he accepted Abraham's sacrifice, he defeated Baal and the dragon, he revealed himself as God to the Persians, and he redeemed humanity (and the cosmos) through Christ's death (I.119–125). This list, like the one in Justa's first prayer (I.64–92), ritually guarantees her request, namely that Christ protect her body and preserve her chastity. Barely finished with this prayer, Justa immediately scares away the demon, whose presence is hardly mentioned in the

---

[56] Sowers 2017:435–440.

narrative. The rhetorical force of the demon's unvoiced entrance and rapid retreat is two-fold: demons attack without warning but are easily defeated.

Like the first demon, Beliar returns to report that the sign (σημήιον, I.137) of the cross was too much for him to withstand—an unbearable thing to behold, overwhelming and irresistible (ὑπέρβιον, οὐχ ὑποεικτόν, I.138). From a narratological perspective, the demon as secondary narrator adds information elided over by the primary narrator—this is the first time the reader hears that Justa performed the sign of the cross. Despite these setbacks, Cyprian conjures the ruler and father of demons, Satan. Questioning his authority, Cyprian calls Satan a coward and asks if he also will run away from Justa. To Satan's insistence that he has already started seducing her, Cyprian demands proof (σημήιον, I.144), which points back to the *signum crucis* in I.137 and anticipates Cyprian's own conversion, during which he crosses himself (compare I.285). Satan promises to torture Justa with a fever for six days and to bring her to Cyprian on the sixth night. This plan, never mentioned again in the *Conversion* and heavily influenced by the physical sufferings of the biblical character Job, may be an interpolation of a variant account alluded to in the *Confession* (compare II.372–398).

Satan then disguises himself as a young Christian woman and attempts to convince Justa to leave her bedroom.[57] The following morning, Satan (in disguise) enters Justa's bedroom, while she is still asleep, and asks her about celibacy. Satan claims that the Lord also called "her" to be celibate, but "she" wonders what rewards to expect in return, especially considering Justa's bone-dry, barren lifestyle and physical appearance, which Satan compares to a corpse.[58] This is the first time the reader hears about Justa's asceticism and her physical decrepitude, and the imagery Satan uses for her sun-scorched, bonedry life recalls the desert fathers.[59] If these ascetic details intertextually echo the demonic temptations experienced by the desert fathers in their *vitae*, they also situate Justa as an urban (and female) desert father and foreshadow her ultimate victory against Satan.

Satan's failed deception of Justa imitates the serpent's successful deception of Eve in Genesis 3; through her eventual defeat of Satan, Justa emerges as the superior exemplar, a celibate analog to Mary, the mother of Christ. At first, however, it seems as if Justa is going to fall for Satan's ruse. Her response to his question is innocent, even naïve. When she asserts that celibacy brings eternal

---

[57] This is similar to the motif of demons disguised as seductresses (*Life of Pachomius* 107; Pachomius *Instruction* 1.26), although Shenoute encounters a demon disguised as a government official (Shenoute *Because of You Too, O Prince of Evil*). Russell 1981:179–180; Brakke 2006:205–206.

[58] Compare Evagrius *Antirrheticus* 1.2 (Brakke 2009:69).

[59] Rousselle 1983:168–177; Brown 1988:213–240. Schroeder 2006 compares this early Christian motif to the ancient novel.

rather than earthly rewards (I.159–160), Satan compares her to Eve, whose children earned her the title "mother of children" and allowed her to learn "all good things" (I.164–165). He cleverly conflates the fruit from the tree of knowledge and its concomitant ability to know good (and evil) with Eve's sexuality (I.163). This symbolic exegesis of Genesis 3 is similar to other late antique allegorical readings that treat this episode as a metaphor for sexual discovery.[60] The narrative tension between Eve as mother of humanity and Justa is resolved by the end of the *Conversion*, when Justa becomes "mother of virgins" for the Antiochene church (I.318–319). Perhaps because Satan's words are so familiar, they nearly persuade Justa to leave the house. Just as she is about to follow Satan outside, she recognizes him, begins to pray, crosses herself, and commands him to leave (I.170–172). Justa plays a more active role in this exorcism than in the previous two. While still relying on the sign of the cross and prayer, she speaks directly to Satan and issues commands, which he obeys.[61] Her narrated prayer (I.175–178) occurs only after Satan departs and expresses thanks, rather than a request for protection. Justa's development into a more dominant character anticipates her leadership role in Antioch and eventual martyrdom alongside Cyprian.

The moment Satan returns empty-handed, Cyprian mocks him (I.181–182). Behind this contempt, which bookends their interaction (cf. I.141), is the hint that Cyprian wants to learn more about Justa's power, an interest with parallels in the archetypal magician of Christian literature, Simon Magus. In the earliest story about him, Simon converts, in order to acquire spiritual power (*Acts* 8:9–24). The Simon Magus legend proliferated in the first centuries of Christianity and even included accounts of magic competitions with Peter. By late antiquity, he was identified as the progenitor of all heresies.[62] Before explaining why he fears the sign of the cross, Satan forces Cyprian to swear an oath of loyalty on Satan's power (I.188–189), after which he admits that demons have no real power but deceive humans, so that they experience similar divine punishment. In response, Cyprian confesses his love for Christ (I.202–204) with erotic language that echoes Justa's conversion (I.37–39*, 54*). Reminded about his oath, Cyprian repudiates Satan as powerless and ineffectual, a claim that he proves by crossing himself, invoking the name of Christ, and commanding Satan to leave (I.213–218).

---

[60] Augustine *City of God* 14.21, *Literal Commentary on Genesis* 9.3.5–6, and a contrasting idea in Gregory of Nyssa *On the Origin of Man* (GNOS 46–47).

[61] Bastiaensen 2011:131–134.

[62] For a comprehensive treatment of Simon Magus, see Ferreiro 2005. Butler 1948:73–83 situates Simon Magus (and Cyprian) within the Faust legend. See also Butler 1949:208–209; Butler 1952:24. The next chapter explores the similarities between Cyprian and Simon Magus in more detail.

Cyprian gathers his books on magic (I.219) and brings them to the church, where he communicates his desire for conversion to the priest, Anthimus. Assuming that Cyprian is insincere or has ulterior motives, Anthimus rebukes him and sends him away (I.225–229). Instead of leaving, Cyprian acknowledges God's superior power, made evident when Justa easily defeated two demons and Satan with prayer and the sign of the cross. To communicate his sincerity and his commitment to God, Cyprian surrenders his magical texts to be burned (I.237–239; compare *Acts* 19:19).[63] Less suspicious because of this gesture, Anthimus instructs Cyprian to come back on Sunday. At home, Cyprian smashes his idols (cf. I.79–80*) and spends the night in prayer and self-flagellation (I.243–245).[64] He repents for the harm he inflicted on others, often with the assistance of demons, and he begs for God's mercy.

The next morning happened to be Easter Sunday, the day new converts were baptized into the church.[65] Cyprian joins the crowd on its way to the church, where he prays to be admitted and to hear some auspicious biblical passages. The readings, unusual for an Easter service, fortunately center around the themes of God's forgiveness and inclusivity, especially for those originally hostile to Him (I.259–275).[66] After a hymn and a message from the priest, the unbaptized are dismissed, presumably before the Eucharist. Seeing that Cyprian has remained seated, the deacon Asterius again asks him to leave. Admittedly not yet a full convert but still a servant of Christ, Cyprian refuses to leave until he is baptized (I.282–289). After speaking and praying with Cyprian, Anthimus agrees to baptize him (I.295). Cyprian rapidly rises through the ecclesiastical ranks. Eight days after his baptism, he is appointed lector; twenty-five days later, he is appointed deacon second-class, responsible for watching the church door during services.[67] After fifty days, he is promoted to deacon first-class and serves the community by performing exorcisms and healings, as well as

---

[63] Amirav 2011.

[64] Collas 1913; Torrance 2013:176–180.

[65] Duchesne 1904:292–293; Thompson 1914:19; Jungmann 1960:74–86; Bradshaw 1992:161–163. Kretschmar 1977 argues that baptisms were also performed on other Sundays. If this is Easter Sunday, the service described in the *Conversion* is unusual in a few respects. First, Easter services did not typically begin at sunrise but were evening vigils lasting from Saturday evening to Sunday morning. Second, the readings of an Easter service typically came from Exodus and the Gospel of John (Dix 1945:338–339).

[66] Psalm 51:11 (Ludwich identifies this as Psalm 35:22), Hosea 11:1 (or possibly Isaiah 52:13), Psalm 119:148, Isaiah 44:1–2, Galatians 3:13, and Psalm 106:2. This lectionary selection (two prophetic passages but none from the Gospels) is unusual for any service which read from a Psalm, a Gospel, and a Pauline epistle. See also Dix 1945:360–362.

[67] Eudocia's word for lector, αἰπυβόης, one who shouts forth, corresponds to the more common and prosaic ἀναγνώστης. She uses διακτορία for the position of διάκτορος. Explained variously in antiquity, deacons were ministers of some sort. Attested in Homer (*Iliad* 2.103; *Odyssey* 5.43; 12.390; 15.319), διάκτορος is also used by Nonnus (*Dionysiaca* 31.107; 30.250; 39.82). Sub-deacons

overseeing the conversion of Antioch's few remaining pagans (I.301–305). In this regard, his new Christian life is indistinguishable from his former one, except that he performs "miracles" rather than "magic." His exorcisms and healings, therefore, advance a competitive ideology in the *Conversion*: Cyprian now uses legitimate, godly power for good rather than evil. A year after his conversion, Cyprian becomes priest, a post he holds for sixteen years.

Nearing the end of his life, the bishop Anthimus names Cyprian as his successor.[68] As his first official act, Cyprian renames Justa Justina and appoints her deaconess, one of the highest roles available to urban Christian women. Although uncommon, people did change their names in late antiquity, but usually when their given name was associated with rival gods or, in the case of early Christianity, with demons.[69] This is obviously not the case with Justa/Justina. It is possible that late antique Christians referred to her as Justa and Justina and that this disagreement was resolved in the *Conversion* as a name change. This practice is attested elsewhere in early Christian literature, beginning with the first-century lists of Jesus' twelve disciples.

As deaconess, Justina oversees Antioch's community of virgins and is soon known as the "mother of maidens," an appellation that gestures back to her conversation with Satan (I.161–166), where Eve is described as the "mother of mankind." Since the early church allegorically interpreted Christ as a type of second Adam, Justina, as bride of Christ, adopts the role of second Eve. By juxtaposing Justina's position as overseer of fellow celibate women with Cyprian's miracles and mass conversions, the narrator advances strict gender roles that ultimately pervade the *Conversion*, despite moments when they are subtly suspended. These subversive moments notwithstanding, the *Conversion* ends with Cyprian firmly established as the male leader responsible for teaching, exorcizing, and healing the Antiochene community—actions that directly lead to the "Christianization" of the city. Justina, in contrast, is restricted to exclusively feminine activities—the superintendence and teaching of women—despite her previous ability to battle demons, which led to Cyprian's conversion.

---

were also responsible for guarding and protecting the church's sacred objects (Wipszycka 1996:234–248).

[68] This is a fictional account. The historical bishop of Antioch during this period was Cyril I (283–303). However, Anthimus was a common name in antiquity and in the ecclesiastical hierarchy. In the third century, we hear about an Anthimus, bishop of Rome, and an Anthimus, bishop of Nicomedia (where Cyprian and Justina eventually die). Both these historical Anthimi were killed under Diocletian and commemorated in their respective cities.

[69] Horsley 1987.

Social Drama: Justina's Literary Models

Justina's character, particularly the way she reinforces and challenges traditional ancient Mediterranean gender roles, warrants further attention. Beyond the *Martyrdom of Cyprian*'s unique place in the history of female authored texts, Eudocia's construction of a feminized heroine is doubly important, in that allows us to compare Justina and her gender identities against other late antique hagiographies.[70] Of special interest in this section is the way in which Eudocia's epic simultaneously depends on and deviates from popular literary exemplars, such as the *Acts of Paul and Thecla* (APT) and its use of gender ambiguity. Thecla's rejection of feminine paraphernalia and her adoption of masculine characteristics, especially regarding her hairstyles and clothing, become a gender bending common place in early Christian literature. Scholars have used these so-called "transvestite motifs" as evidence for female resistance to patriarchy (proto-feminism) or, alternatively, as evidence for the continued patriarchal control of women.[71] Since these gender bending tropes tend to cluster in anonymous and pseudepigraphic narratives, they have also been used as evidence for female authorship. Eudocia's epic—a text undisputedly written by a woman—challenges many of these assumptions.[72] In my view, Justina is a remarkable character, Thecla's literary heir but also a "free-agent," who deviates from other early Christian female characters and often challenges stereotypes by not engaging in gender bending tropes. Justina's deviation from the early Christian feminine ideal reflects Eudocia's agency in creating a traditional yet subversive female lead character.

This section compares depictions of the feminine ideal in the *Conversion* with two other early Christian narratives, the APT and the *Martyrdom of Perpetua and Felicitas*.[73] Reading these stories through the interpretive framework of Victor Turner's theory of social drama clarifies how Justa advances traditional (patriarchal) gender roles and simultaneously subverts that same traditionalism.[74] Briefly, Turner identifies four stages of social drama: (1) a character experiences a breach between social elements, (2) leading to a crisis that the character (3) addresses through adjustment or redress, (4) resulting in the character's reintegration within the same (or slightly altered) social structure.[75]

---

[70] Kazhdan 2001.
[71] Anson 1974; Burrus 1987; Castelli 1991; Cooper 1999; Davis 2002; Hylan 2015.
[72] For more on the connection between ancient prose fictions and female authors, see Johne 1996:156–164.
[73] Streete 2006.
[74] Turner 1974; Turner and Turner 1978; Turner 1979.
[75] Turner 1981:145. Turner 1979:249 advances a three-fold rite of passage: separation, margin or limen, and reaggregation.

Applying Turner's theories to late medieval hagiographies, medieval scholar Caroline Bynum concludes that Turner elucidates narrative structures of male authored stories but not those written by women. In Bynum's view, late medieval women's stories are accounts where "nothing happens."[76] For that reason, Turner's model maps quite well onto Thecla and Perpetua's experiences in the *APT* and the *Martyrdom of Perpetua and Felicitas*, but it fails to adequately explain Justina's experiences. Perpetua and Thecla's social drama differs from Justina's in a few essential ways. These differences in how Justina constructs her gender clarify her relationship to her social communities (both familial and religious ones) and explain her comparable lack of "social drama," despite facing sexual assault and demonic attack. At least in that regard, the *Conversion* is a story in which quite a bit happens.

Written in the third century to commemorate the execution of five Carthaginian catechumens in 203 CE, the *Passio Perpetuae et Felicitatis* (hereafter, *Martyrdom*) highlights the experiences of one martyr, Vibia Perpetua.[77] Most of the *Martyrdom* is written in the first person and is explicitly attributed to Perpetua who, the third person narrator claims, wrote down her prison experiences in the days before her execution. Alongside this Perpetuan material are a third-person introduction and conclusion, as well as a vision narrative allegedly written by Perpetua's co-martyr, Saturus.[78] Because these three distinct authorial voices (primary narrator, Perpetua, and Saturus) have been redacted to form a unified whole, the *Martyrdom*'s authorship is hotly contested.[79] If Perpetua had a hand in writing even some portion of it, the *Martyrdom* would be the earliest martyrology written by a woman. Because I have my doubts about Perpetua's authorial hand, I treat the *Martyrdom* as a narrative whole, redacted after her death by an unknown but likely male editor.[80] Turner's theory of social drama explains the narrative events of the *Martyrdom* quite well—Perpetua breaks from her immediate social community, overcomes the ensuing tensions, and joins a new, spiritual community that replaces her original, earthly one. For this reason, the *Martyrdom* explains how Christians relate to and can ultimately overcome the Roman world in which they live.

---

[76] Bynum 1991:39–40. The following section is influenced by Bynum's approach.

[77] Shewring 1931; van Beek 1936; van Beek 1938; Musurillo 1972:106–31; Amat 1996; Barnes 2010:66–74; Heffernan 2012; Farrell and Williams 2012.

[78] Cobb 2008:95 points out that Perpetua's portion of the narrative "is framed by his [the editor's] preface and conclusion; these additions inevitably shape the reader's impression."

[79] Perkins 2007:324 summarizes the argument against a Perpetuan authorship. The philological analyses of Heffernan 1995; Vierow 1999; Heffernan 2012 are central. For the opposing views, see Salisbury 1997:14–15; Bremmer 2002:83–86; Plant 2004; Bremmer and Formisano 2012. See also Shaw 1993; Bremmer 2004; Bremmer 2006.

[80] For more on my approach, see Sowers 2015.

Perpetua breaks from her social community after multiple altercations with her father, an aristocratic pagan, who visits her in jail to persuade her to renounce Christianity.[81] His arguments imply that her conversion and arrest have ruined the family's honor and are estranging them. Failing to convince her, he resorts to violence, then to begging. As a final demonstration of their growing rift, Perpetua's father abducts her infant son, who had been with her in jail. This familial estrangement symbolizes Perpetua's rejection of earthly concerns and readiness for martyrdom. Early Christian prose narratives frequently contain similar episodes, in which young women overthrow patriarchal authority as a symbol of Christianity's social reversal.[82] The ensuing tension is eventually attenuated as the women substitute their earthly relationships for heavenly ones, frequently addressed with familial language.[83] Perpetua's rejection of human patriarchy is set against her use of familial language for other Christians and God's increased role as her surrogate father. Once Perpetua is securely re-established within a patriarchal context as a daughter of heaven, the social drama is resolved, resolution that paves the way for her death.

Moreover, Perpetua experiences a series of visions that presage her execution and resolve the social tensions she experiences in prison. For instance, immediately following her father's abduction of her child, Perpetua sees two visions of her brother Dinocrates (*Martyrdom* 7–8). Having died in childhood from a face lesion, Dinocrates represents the narrative conflict between Perpetua's earthly and spiritual families. At first, he appears dirty and thirsty, unable to drink from a nearby pool of water, and still suffering from his face lesion—a vestige of his earthly disease and visual symbol of his hardships in the afterlife. Perpetua prays for his relief and sees a second vision, in which Dinocrates is dressed in white (a common image of baptism and salvation) and splashes around in the pool. Unable to care for her earthly son, Perpetua meets Dinocrates' spiritual needs. From a narrative perspective, he serves as a heavenly surrogate for Perpetua's earthly son, who no longer appears in the story.

In terms of gender identity and authority, Perpetua guides the story's pace and direction. Her fellow prisoners speak to her as their leader, often with the honorific *domina*, and she advocates for them on a few occasions.[84] Even her father stops calling her daughter and adopts the term *domina*. This image of Perpetua as the one in charge is frequently paired with the image of Perpetua as *matrona*. In this way, her character blends various gender markers, simultaneously an authoritative leader for her fellow martyrs (and for the audience

---

[81] Rossi 1984; Sigismund-Nielsen 2012:108–109; Sowers 2015:373–382.
[82] Coon 1997; Castelli 1991.
[83] Perkins 1994:838; Sowers 2015:373–378.
[84] Compare Cobb 2008:72–76; Sigismund-Nielsen 2012:103–105.

hearing/reading the *Martyrdom*) and a nurturing, maternal figure who cares for the needs of her earthly child and, when he is removed from the scene, for her fellow prisoners and Dinocrates, her heavenly "son."

This balance between Perpetua's masculine and feminine roles culminates in her fourth vision, arguably one of the most memorable, discussed, and controversial parts of the *Martyrdom*.[85] In this final premonition of her death, Perpetua enters an arena, where her attendants prepare her to fight an Egyptian gladiator. When they remove her clothing, she proclaims, "I became masculine" (*facta sum masculus*, *Martyrdom* 10). Although it can be argued that Perpetua became a man in her vision, Perkins and Williams provide more philologically nuanced readings in favor of her continued femininity.[86] For example, in *facta sum masculus*, the doubly masculine, *masculus*, depends on the explicitly feminine verb (*facta sum*). Since Perpetua's visions serve as psychological/spiritual parallels to her physical experiences, between father and God or between her son and Dinocrates, "becoming masculine" likely alludes to the physical and rhetorical control she maintains throughout the *Martyrdom* but especially in the story's final scene, where she directs the novice gladiator's trembling sword toward her own throat.[87] From a Roman rhetorical perspective, this type of control and authority corresponds to the masculine ideal and is described as masculine when carried out by women.[88]

About a half-century before Perpetua was executed in Carthage, an anonymous author penned the fictional story of Paul and Thecla, with the latter's exceptional rejection of traditional feminine roles, symbolized by cutting her hair and wearing men's clothing.[89] Behind this gender bending is a desire to join Paul's apostolic mission and to travel around the Mediterranean preaching the gospel. This desire, paired with Thecla's ambiguous gender, distances her from her original social community and makes her susceptible to sexual assault. Therefore, the *APT* corresponds well with Turner's theory of social drama. In the ensuing centuries, the spread of the *APT* across the Mediterranean made Thecla one of the most popular women in late antique Christianity, second only to Mary, the mother of Christ. Its gender ambiguity and social drama became literary commonplaces in later Christian prose narratives, such as the *Martyrdom of Cyprian*, that found inspiration in the *APT*, which itself was updated and revised to make Thecla's character, particularly her sexuality, relevant to

---

[85] Cobb 2008:105–107; Williams 2012.

[86] Perkins 2007:326; Williams 2012.

[87] Sowers 2015.

[88] Perkins 1995:104–113; Rodman 1997:38; Burrus 2004:58; Knust 2006:108–109; Schroeder 2006:58.

[89] Burrus 1987; Cooper 1999; Vorster 2006:99. For a different perspective, see Hylan 2015:73–81.

subsequent generations.[90] Although other women in early Christian literature break from their social communities in gender ambiguous ways, Thecla's influence on late antique women, especially late antique literary women, makes her essentially relevant for our reading of Justina.

To summarize the narrative briefly, during a missionary journey through Asia Minor, Paul stops at Iconium, where he preaches an ascetic revision of Jesus' sermon on the mount (*APT* 5).[91] The young Thecla hears Paul's sermon from her bedroom window and falls in love with him, a love expressed through her desire to hear him in person.[92] Concerned, Thecla's mother, Theoclea, asks her fiancé, Thamyris, to speak with her. During this conversation, Thecla refuses to change her mind but, instead, breaks off her engagement. The household, in turn, mourns her as if she were dead (*APT* 10). This funerary imagery positions Thecla outside the immediate family structure and underscores how socially transgressive her actions are. Meanwhile, Thamyris convinces the civic authorities to arrest Paul under the charges of propagating subversive sexual ethics (celibacy). Still committed to seeing him in person, Thecla barters her possessions, traditional feminine objects (bracelets and a mirror), to escape her house and enter the jail, where she lies at Paul's feet. Finding them in this compromising position the next morning, the Iconian authorities whip Paul and expel him from the city, but they condemn Thecla to death as a lesson for other women tempted to choose celibacy. Stripped naked, Thecla mounts a burning pyre but is saved by a providential rainstorm.

Still committed to joining Paul's apostolic team, Thecla cuts her hair into a masculine style and leaves Iconium to look for him. Her adoption of a masculinized appearance convinces Paul about her dedication, although he suspects she will face some greater trial. Shortly thereafter, Paul and Thecla arrive in Antioch, where a local aristocrat, Alexander, sees her. When Paul denies knowing her (compare Genesis 12:10–20), Alexander attempts to rape her. At first, she begs for him to stop and invokes her status as a well-born Iconian citizen. When he persists, Thecla fights him off, tears his cloak, and throws his crown to the ground, which effeminizes him by making him a public spectacle.[93] Humiliated, Alexander seeks revenge in court, where Thecla is condemned to the beasts.

---

[90] Davis 2002:15–16 discusses transvestism in late antique narratives, including the influence of the *APT*. See also Johnson 2006a; Haines-Eitzen 2007.

[91] Paul's sermon in the *APT* was likely constructed from details in the Pauline epistles, such as 1 Corinthians 7 (Knust 2006:79–81; Knust 2011:107–110; Hylan 2015:85–87).

[92] Cooper 1999:50–53 characterizes this as an "apostolic love triangle." See also Miller 1993; Lipsett 2011; Cooper 2013:82. Compare Justin Martyr *Dialogue with Trypho* 7–8.

[93] Hawley 1998 discusses the role of the male body as object of the gaze in Attic drama. Salient here are his "man in pain" and "sexual humiliation" (86–88). See also Duncan 2006:188–217.

Gender markers become more explicitly pronounced in the second half of the *APT*, as women and female animals side with Thecla, while male characters are hostile to her.[94] Acting as a tragic chorus, the Antiochene women lament the injustice of Thecla's death, and a local aristocrat, Tryphaena, hosts Thecla and accompanies her to the arena. At first, Alexander sends out a lioness, but she licks Thecla's feet and defends her against a bear and lion. When the lioness dies of her wounds and more beasts are sent into the arena, Thecla baptizes herself in a pool full of man-eating seals providentially killed by a bolt of lightning. A cloud sent from heaven, by covering Thecla, preserves her modesty and discourages what beasts remain in the arena from attacking her. In a final attempt, Alexander orders Thecla to be tied to a pair of bulls. By burning their genitals, Alexander hopes to tear Thecla in two. Once again, a providential fire burns these ropes.

Overwhelmed by these ordeals, Tryphaena faints and is presumed dead; her assumed death scares the city magistrates and prompts them to free Thecla.[95] After converting the women in Tryphaena's house, Thecla dresses like a man and leaves Antioch in search of Paul, who welcomes Thecla into his entourage and gives her the authority to preach the gospel, starting with her hometown.[96] Over time, multiple endings have been appended to the *APT*. In one version, Thecla sets up an ascetic community for Christian virgins in nearby Seleucia, where she performs miracles and heals the sick. Jealous of her success, some local physicians hire criminals to rape her. God saves her from these male assailants by opening a fissure in her mountain retreat. When Thecla climbs into this crevice, it closes, thus saving her from sexual assault but ending her life.

Above all, Thecla's story is one of displacement, tension, and reintegration. Not only does she experience familial displacement, through her rejection of marriage and her family's subsequent rejection of her. She also experiences civic displacement as the Iconian officials convict her, because she had chosen celibacy over marriage.[97] Whereas Perpetua finds immediate support in the Christian community, Thecla's relationship with Paul's Christian community is strained until the end, when she has already baptized herself, survived an assortment

---

[94] Misset-van de Weg 2006:154–156.

[95] Johnson 2006a:59–60 compares this episode to Nonnus' resurrection of Lazarus.

[96] The authorization of women to preach by Paul is inconsistent with the pastoral epistles, written around the same time as the *APT*. See MacDonald 1983:86–98; Kraemer 1992:153–155, 175; Ruether 1998:38–43; Castelli 1999; MacDonald 1999:245–251; Wire 2004. Women served as apostles in the first century, but, as proto-orthodox Christianity adopted a patriarchal structure during the early second century, it suppressed female leadership and even associated the evangelizing woman with heretical groups. See also Trevett 1999; Cloke 2000:432–433; Kraemer 2011:117–152.

[97] Cooper 1999:36–40.

of attacks, and converted entire households to Christianity. Thecla finds more support in Tryphaena's pagan house than in Paul's circle. One way by which Thecla physically manifests this displacement and reintegration is through her adoption of male physical characteristics (short hair, men's clothing). Similar to Perpetua's vision of "becoming male," Thecla's adoption of male features physically represents her spiritual exceptionalism, frequently marked in Greco-Roman literature by attributing male characteristics to female characters.[98] Late antique Christian exegetes frequently interpreted the commonplace of women cutting their hair as a way to avoid the sexual advances of strangers, an explanation that only partially works for Thecla, who also barters away her beautification accessories and dresses in men's clothing.[99] As argued by Marie Delcourt, these changes in Thecla's physical appearance symbolize the rupture of her former existence.[100] Unlike Perpetua, whose death reintegrates her within her heavenly family, Thecla's reintegration is disrupted through subsequent adventures. Despite having a home in late antique Christianity, Thecla's life and miracles situate her always on the threshold of communities (from windows to mountains).

Inversion of Social Drama in the *Conversion*

Compared to Thecla and Perpetua, whose displacement is a central theme of their stories, Justina, in contrast, experiences considerably little social anxiety, despite being the victim of two rape attempts and three demonic attacks. In this regard, the *Conversion* is a story in which "nothing happens." Whereas Thecla and Perpetua are geographically liminal, Justina remains safely within the confines of her house and under her father's authority. Her conversion is delayed until Aedesius and Clidonia join her, or, more accurately, lead her to the church. This is a remarkable difference from Thecla and Perpetua, who convert despite intense familial opposition. While their conversions set in motion serious civic consequences, Justina's conversion occurs without any significant familial or civic tension. In fact, her conversion is so unremarkable that it is subsumed within Aedesius' conversion and receives no civic response whatsoever. Finally, Thecla and Perpetua adopt masculine traits, but Justina does not, despite her ability to fight off rapists and demons. Turner's theory of social drama, therefore, elucidates Thecla and Perpetua but fails to explain Justina's narrative arc or Eudocia's development of female characters. Moreover, Eudocia inverts three literary motifs (hairstyle, clothing, and the body) that further complicate her

---

[98] Söder 1932:127–128.
[99] Anson 1974:3.
[100] Delcourt 1961.

depiction of gender identity and the feminine ideal. This section compares these motifs to the central themes of celibacy and asceticism.

After hearing Paul preach, Thecla explicitly equates her desire to join his entourage with her decision to cut her hair: περικαροῦμαι καὶ ἀκολουθήσω σοι ὅπου δ' ἂν πορεύῃ (I will cut my hair and follow you wherever you go, *APT* 25). This assertion suggests that, for Thecla, the act of cutting her hair marks a social transition from domestic duty and prospective marriage to apostolic preaching and celibacy.[101] For that reason, it also symbolizes a holiness that further distinguishes Thecla from other potential converts.[102] By physically marking herself as androgynously exceptional, Thecla can join the men during their Asian mission, although her androgyny also metaphorically anticipates her physical assault in Antioch. If Thecla's conversion depends on sexual renunciation and is predicated on Paul's ascetic revision of Jesus' Sermon on the Mount, those threats against her religious identity, in as much as her religious identity is conflated with her sexuality, take the form of sexual assaults or sexualized attacks. Because Justina's conversion intertextually depends on Thecla's (they both hear the gospel from their bedroom windows and desire to convert), the *Conversion* explicitly invites a comparison between Justina and Thecla.

That Justina never cuts her hair is itself a type of intertextual engagement with the *APT*, especially considering the prominent role hair plays in episodes that heavily rely on the *APT*. For instance, following his nocturnal vision of heaven, Aedesius brings Clidonia and Justina to church to convert as a family. Before being baptized, Aedesius cuts his hair because (the narrator tells us) he was a pagan priest: αὐτίκα δ' Αἰδέσιος περικείρατο βόστρυχον ἀμφὶς ἐκ κεφαλῆς γενυός τ' ἱερεὺς γὰρ ἔην ἀμενηνῶν εἰδώλων (And Aedesius immediately cut his hair on both sides from his head and chin–for he was a priest of powerless idols, I.84–86*). Because the verb, περικείρατο, is the same verb (περικαροῦμαι) that Thecla uses in the *APT*, Aedesius' haircut has more intertextual complexity than the narrator's gloss suggests. The intertextual engagement between Thecla and Aedesius' hair is doubly important, because it comes directly from Eudocia's authorial hand. The verb 'to cut' in the prose accounts of the *Conversion* is ἀπεθρίξατο/ἀπεθρήξατο, a more common word.[103] By using περικείρατο, Eudocia simultaneously deepens and demarcates the pre-existing intertextual relationship between Thecla and Justina. Unlike Thecla, whose conversion marks the beginning of her social displacement, Justina remains secure in her house with her parents.[104] If Thecla's adoption of an androgynous appearance symbolizes

---

[101] Compare 1 Corinthians 11:5–14; Knust 2006:81–85; Kraemer 2011:137.
[102] Castelli 1991:43.
[103] Zahn 1882.
[104] Cooper 1999:34.

her rejection of earthly patriarchy, Justina's preservation of her femininity underscores her familial continuity, facilitated by Aedesius and Clidonia's conversion.

Moreover, when Justina fights off Aglaidas, the narrator compares her to Thecla: Θέκλης ἀντιθέης τὸν ὁμὸν δρόμον ἐκτελέουσα (she ran the same course as glorious Thecla, I.14). Yet this is a very different fight. Thecla tears Alexander's clothing and throws down his crown, whereas Justina throws Aglaidas to the ground, scratches his cheeks, pulls out his hair/beard, and tears his clothes. Alexander and Aglaidas suffer a similar shame, although their choice of retribution differs. Equally different is the degree to which Justina's victory over Aglaidas emphasizes how utterly she defeats him. By throwing Aglaidas onto his back, a submissive and sexually vulnerable posture, Justina reverses their roles.[105] She also disfigures him and strips him of his clothing. This is more than a scene where a potential rape victim gives her assailant a taste of his own medicine. Rather, Justina fully emasculates Aglaidas, leaving him physically and sexually androgynous.[106] In terms of social drama, Aglaidas' androgyny displaces him and anticipates his use of magic to seduce Justina, who, in contrast, never adopts masculine imagery, despite her exceptional ability and intertextual connection with Thecla. Instead, Eudocia's Justina expresses her exceptionalism by maintaining control of her femininity while robbing Aglaidas of his masculinity.

In early Christian literature, clothing metaphorically represents social control and spiritual reintegration.[107] For example, Thecla changes into masculine attire (*APT* 40) as a symbol of her apostolic authority and eventual inclusion into Paul's apostolic circle. Wearing men's clothing becomes the visual indication of her ability to do "men's work," which Tertullian understood as the authority to conduct baptisms.[108] In other words, Thecla overcomes social displacement by breaking from Greco-Roman feminine ideals of domestic duty and submissiveness and reintegrates into Christian society by claiming masculine ideals of religious authority and sexual control.

Clothing also represents the ability to exert control over others or to maintain control over one's own body. When the Antiochene magistrates force Thecla to change her clothes before entering the arena (*APT* 33), she loses control over her body.[109] Shortly thereafter, she requires providential assistance in the form of a cloud from heaven to cover her body, now exposed after diving in the

---

[105] Knust 2011:88–89.
[106] Knust 2006:107.
[107] Coon 1997:52–70.
[108] Tertullian *On Baptism* 17; Kraemer 2011:144.
[109] Barrier 2009:158 provides other comparable examples.

pool of man-eating seals. A comparable event, without the seals, occurs in the *Martyrdom* (6.3), when the female prisoners are expected to dress as priestesses of Ceres and the male prisoners as priests of Saturn before they enter the arena. At Perpetua's behest, they collectively refuse to put on these costumes, thereby maintaining control over their bodies. Perpetua and her fellow martyrs also exert control over their captors, who are powerless over their captives. As the eponymous martyr of the story, Perpetua exerts the most control, both when she covers her exposed body while facing the beasts and when she guides the executioner's hand to her throat.[110]

Similarly, the removal or tearing of another person's clothes represents physical control over them, as when Thecla tears Alexander's clothes, a scene explicitly imitated in the *Conversion*. In both cases, Alexander and Aglaidas are physically and (perhaps) symbolically exposed. The roles are reversed, as Thecla and Justina overwhelm their assailants and humiliate them by emasculating them or, said differently, by raping them of their masculinity. Humiliated and violated, Alexander leverages his social standing to bring legal charges against Thecla that further displaces her. Aglaidas, in contrast, responds to this humiliation by situating himself at the periphery of Antiochene society after hiring Cyprian. Here, Aglaidas is the one who experiences social displacement, while Justina remains securely established within her religious and domestic communities.

In late antique descriptions of male and female ascetics, the neglected body is a popular and recurring symbol of their rejection of earthly concerns and an intentional return to paradise (Eden/Heaven).[111] For women, the first step in joining a monastery is to sell off their property, including their cosmetics, jewelry, and fine clothing, which, according to these monastic communities, symbolize vanity and pride.[112] Because they reject feminine concerns and eat meager diets, late antique female ascetics are frequently mistaken for men and even join male monasteries.[113] The *vitae* of female ascetics emphasize their physical appearances, especially as feminine virtue was frequently linked to the body. As a result, wearing fine jewelry or clothing was increasingly attributed to specific sins, especially pride, and rejecting finery became a visual indicator of humility. Because late antique asceticism advanced an explicit renunciation of

---

[110] Perkins 1994:844–845; Sowers 2015:387.

[111] Shaw 1998:161–219.

[112] Evagrius *Antirrheticus* 3.50; Shaw 1998:149–150. Compare Hylan 2015, who does not discuss *APT* 18 in her treatment of Thecla as a model of early Christian female modesty. For a parallel in the classical period, see Xenophon *Oeconomicus* 10.1–6.

[113] *Life of Pelagia* 43–49; Shaw 1998:222–253; Miller 2003; Burrus 2004:141–145. Moreover, male ascetics, Shenoute in particular, frequently described demon-fighting female ascetics with masculine language (Brakke 2006:195–196).

wealth, political influence, and status, most ascetics also eschewed urban centers in favor of isolated regions, including (when available) the desert. Removed from urban temptations, wilderness ascetics dressed in camelhair clothing, fasted, and prayed throughout the day. Some practiced self-flagellation as a form of penance. In this regard, late antique literary depictions of asceticism, particularly representations of the bound, pierced, and starved female body, served didactic purposes.[114]

Despite living in one of the largest urban centers in the late antique Mediterranean, Justina adopts an asceticism more frequently seen in the wilderness retreats of the desert fathers/mothers. She remains in a constant stage of prayer, which prepares her to fight off demonic attack. When Satan disguises himself as a young woman to seduce her, his description of her is similar to other late antique descriptions of desert mothers, with their characteristic emaciated, disfigured bodies, their overexposure to the sun, and their meager diets.[115] Justina's self-abnegation parallels but surpasses Thecla's rejection of finery symbolized when she barters her bracelets and mirror to escape her house and visit Paul in prison (*APT* 18). Through her more exacting asceticism, Justina emerges as the superior disciple, one intertextually modeled on Thecla but one who also adopts a more rigid lifestyle and faces more perilous attacks.

Elsewhere in the *Conversion*, however, Justina is a typical urban Christian virgin who travels between her house and church, complicating her anchoretic etiquette. Satan's attempt to draw her outside her bedroom has its origin in comparable demonic attacks in the writings of the desert fathers, in which demons attempt to draw monks out of their anchoretic sanctuaries, likely because these spaces were thought to be particularly sacred, impervious to demonic trickery.[116] Satan's interest in leading Justina outside, however, also points back to Aglaidas' second attempted rape while Justina was traveling to church. The *domus*, therefore, represents the *locus* of masculine and feminine power and the security of civic conformity.[117] Being outside the house is intrinsically threatening, both physically, as Thecla and Justina face sexual assault, and spiritually, as Satan's power seemingly increases if Justina were to leave. Restraining domestic women requires one to restrain their *domus* first. For that reason, two demonic attacks include rituals (magic herbs or potions) to control her domestic space and break the power of its safety. Of course, potential threats to patriarchy can also enter the *domus*, such as Paul and Praulios' subversive

---

[114] Coon 1997:36–41; Gorman 2006.

[115] On the temptation to break one's fast and/or engage in gluttony, see Evagrius *Antirrheticus* 1; Shaw 1998:139–158; Brakke 2006:58; Brakke 2009:53–68.

[116] Frankfurter 2006:13–21.

[117] Coon 1997:76; Jacobs 2006; Osiek and MacDonald 2006:144–152.

messages, which Thecla and Justina hear from their windows. A domestic limen, the window connects the inside and the outside and provides an entryway for multidirectional transgression.

This power dynamic between inside and outside spaces also pertains to Cyprian's conversion. Although never explicitly stated in the *Conversion*, it is likely that Cyprian issues the three demonic attacks from his house. The demons are described as "returning to Cyprian," and his eventual rejection of Satan imitates Justina's exorcism of Satan from her bedroom (I.216–218). Immediately thereafter, Cyprian orders servants to carry his books to the church to be destroyed. After speaking with Anthimus, Cyprian returns home to destroy his idols and spend a prayerful night whipping himself and asking for God's forgiveness, before returning to the church the next day. In this regard, Cyprian emulates Justina in few essential ways. His initial conversion moment requires a spiritual housecleaning, symbolized first by exorcizing Satan, followed by burning his magic texts and destroying his idols. Once his domestic space is appropriately free from demonic contagion, Cyprian adopts an ascetic version of Christianity, marked by nocturnal vigils and corporal punishment, a second parallel to Justina. Finally, his conversion involves repeated journeys between his house and church. Whereas these excursions expose Justina to sexual assault and demonic attack, they (re)integrate Cyprian into Antiochene Christian society and anticipate his conversion of Antioch's remaining pagan population.

This contrast between sacred, inside spaces (havens from sexual/demonic attack) and liminal, outside spaces (perils to chastity) underscores how the *Conversion* adapts common literary tropes to advance its own feminine ideal. Interpreted variously as liberation or oppression literature, early Christian stories about exceptional women seem particularly interested in feminine and masculine spaces.[118] Those written before Constantine and the legalization of Christianity depict exceptional women, such as Thecla and Perpetua, as breaking from civic or patriarchal authority in favor of liminal identities and spaces. These liminal identities and spaces represent Christianity's rejection of Roman social norms. After Constantine, however, as Christianity became increasingly institutionalized through imperial support and increasingly authoritarian through ecumenical councils and imperial legislation, opposing civic institutions was tantamount to challenging ecclesiastical authority. As a result, exceptional women in fourth- through sixth-century narratives are more exceptionally domestic, even if that *domus* is a house in the desert.[119] For instance, after her conversion, Pelagia remains within domestic spaces: her

---

[118] Coon 1997:72–73, 93–105; Aubin 1998.
[119] Compare the life of Pelagia and Macrina (Ruether 1998:64–69; Miller 2005).

own house, Romana's house, eventually a monastic cell on the Mount of Olives, where she lives out her life disguised as a man. Despite her gender bending and battles with Satan, Pelagia's domestication distinguishes her from anchoretic men, who inhabit outside spaces, where they frequently encounter demons.[120]

Like that of Pelagia and unlike those of Thecla and Perpetua, Justina's narrative arc is decidedly domestic, beginning with her conversion that stresses a continued existence within Aedesius' house. Not only does she have to wait for her father to convert, her own baptism is embedded within his. Domestic spaces, therefore, symbolize social, spiritual, and sexual safety, havens from the dangers of the outside world, where Justina, as everywoman, is vulnerable to sexual assault and demonic attack. If Thecla and Perpetua's social displacement and search for reintegration force them outside the house, where they similarly face threats, Justina, in contrast, experiences little social displacement. Instead, her daily routine of prayer (I.58*; I.63–92; I.110–131; I.170; I.174–178; I.211; I.235), church attendance (I.91*; I.95–96*; I.4; I.15), songs (I.56–57), vigils (I.110), and celibacy (I.1–2; I.85–90; I.127–129; I.159–160; I.316–319) are rather unremarkable yet consistent with other fourth- and fifth-century remarkable women.

Paradoxically, these unremarkable activities, particularly daily church attendance, expose Justina to sexual assault and demonic attack but also equip her to withstand them. For instance, Aglaidas only notices her during her regular trip to church, and her defense against him is predicated on her Christian community and commitment to celibacy. From an intertextual perspective, Justina's emulation of Thecla empowers her, not only to defend off Aglaidas but also to physically overpower him.[121] Similarly, by remaining in a constant state of prayer, Justina perceives imminent demonic attacks, and her prayers preemptively ward off unknown attacks. This emphasis on Justina's vigilance makes Satan's final attack doubly clever: he wears a disguise and enters her room while she is sleeping and not in prayer.

In this section, I have argued that Eudocia's Justina is built on literary commonplaces that intertextually complicate her character, especially as she adheres to and rejects early Christian feminine ideals. Deviating from Thecla, Justina does not cut her hair as a marker of her conversion; Aedesius does, however, with language that further contrasts Justina from Thecla. Moreover, by tearing out Aglaidas' hair and ripping off his clothes, Justina effeminizes him in a hyper-sexual manner that effectively makes Aglaidas Justina's rape victim. That this scene explicitly alludes to the now androgynous Thecla's victory over

---

[120] For example, in the *Life of Antony* 8–10, Antony battles demons in a cemetery (Brakke 2006:30–33; Vos 2011:161–162). For more on Pelagia, see Coon 1997:74–80; Burrus 2004:128–129.

[121] I argue elsewhere (Sowers 2017) that Justina's intertextual connection with Thecla guarantees her protection and was thought to protect later Christian women from sexual assault.

Alexander only underscores Justina's adherence to spatial and physical feminine ideals.[122] Nevertheless, these physical ideals are decidedly post-Constantinian ones, similar to those of the desert mothers. For that reason, Justina remains within Aedesius' house, which becomes contested space, assaulted by Cyprian and his demons and defended by Justina and God.

Conclusion

This chapter situates the *Conversion*—book one of Eudocia's epic paraphrase of the *Martyrdom of Cyprian*—within the context of early Christian prose narratives and, by association, the ancient novel. As a narrative written concurrently with the rise of the cult of the saints, the *Martyrdom of Cyprian* is inextricably connected to ecclesiastical readings in honor of the martyrs, comparable to public reading of the *Acts of Paul and Thecla*, the *Martyrdom Perpetuae et Felicitatis*, and the life of Saint Martin. Liturgical readings of the *Martyrdom of Cyprian* are attested as early as the medieval period, although they likely began earlier.

After providing a detailed, interpretive summary of the *Conversion*, the remainder of the chapter focuses on Justina as the primary character in the episode who overshadows and overpowers all other, typically male, characters. This emphasis on Justina here also contrasts nicely with the following chapter, which focuses on Cyprian's magical education. My approach has been to read Justina alongside other exceptional women in early Christian prose narratives, especially Thecla and Perpetua. By applying Victor Turner's theory of social drama to early Christian literature, I argue that Justina experiences comparatively less social displacement than her female models, who communicate their rejection of traditional Greco-Roman norms by adopting male characteristics and by traveling outside their houses. Justina, in contrast, does not adopt explicitly masculine traits but remains safely within Aedesius' house, despite being able to battle demons and fight off rapists. Her adherence to civic and familial structures, I contend, reflects an evolution in post-Constantinian Christianity away from socially transgressive female characters. As holders of social authority, fourth- and fifth-century Christian communities had more at stake when civic and domestic mores were challenged. Instead, exceptional female characters, including Justina, more frequently remain within domestic spaces, even when, as in the case of Pelagia, they cross-dress and leave their hometowns.

By the end of the *Conversion*, Justina has taken on the position of mother of virgins for the Antiochene community. This is an internal reflection, not

---

[122] Compare Prudentius *The Origin of Sin* 258–297 (Dykes 2011:211–220).

only of her exceptionalism, but also her didactic function for future readers and listeners. In as much as Justina combats demons and fights off assailants by regularly attending church and remaining in a constant state of prayer, subsequent Christian women can do the same, if they follow Justina's model. As an intertextual heir to second- and third-century exceptional women, Justina becomes a model in her own right.

4

The Confession

Competing with Magic

Introduction

IN THE PREVIOUS CHAPTER, I argue that the *Conversion* depends on early Christian prose narratives, especially martyrologies and *acta* that depict exceptional women. My approach in that chapter focuses on how Justa intertextually engages these exceptional female characters, particularly Thecla and Perpetua. In fact, despite the *Conversion*'s ostensible interest in Cyprian, Justa receives far more attention and emerges as the story's main character. She is allotted far more "screen time" than Cyprian, and we learn more about Antioch's Christian community from her. Because the second book of Eudocia's epic, the *Confession*, has a different focus and uses sources differently than the *Conversion*, it demands a distinct approach. This new approach is doubly necessary, because the narrative shifts from Justina to Cyprian.

As main character of the *Confession*, Cyprian outlines for the Antiochene Christians his life story, beginning with his initiation into various Greek religious cults and eastern magic rites, culminating in his failed attempt to seduce Justina, which precipitates his conversion.[1] Nearly three-quarters of the *Confession*, therefore, is a frequently perplexing list of religious and occult arcana. Because this list contains some information about pagan (classical) religious cults and magic rituals, especially how late antique Christian communities understood them, it has received attention from scholars interested in the history of ancient religions.[2] The first part of this chapter traces Cyprian's mystical journey throughout the Mediterranean and his mastery of various rituals. When possible, I situate these details within their wider religious contexts.

It is important to note, however, that Eudocia and her prose sources are not ideologically neutral to these ancient religious/magic practices. Rather,

---

[1] My translation of Eudocia's *Confession* can be found in the appendix.
[2] Nock 1927; Nilsson 1947; Festugière 1950.

in keeping with the competitive rhetoric of the time, her tone is decidedly polemical. After Constantine, late antique Christianity adopted a more aggressive stance against their religious competitors, which resulted in a heightened and increasingly intolerant legal and rhetorical posture against traditional ancient Mediterranean religions.[3] As part of this rhetoric, rituals of power were equated with demonology, and their effects were repudiated as deceptive schemes of demons working to undermine God's redemptive plan (see the opening of the *Conversion*). Written within this tradition, Eudocia's *Confession* (like the *Conversion*) categorically rejects demonic power by conflating Cyprian's "demonic" magic with ancient Mediterranean religions, including those of Greece, Egypt, and Babylon.[4] Eudocia's anti-pagan rhetoric, therefore, stands at odds with her religiously moderate or ambiguous stance at Hammat Gader. Because the *Confession* fits within a tradition, culminating in the Faust legend, of fictional magicians who make deals with the devil, it is valuable for the history of western literature.[5] This chapter advances the research previously published on the *Confession* by providing a reading of Cyprian's travels across the late antique Mediterranean world.[6]

The second part of this chapter examines the narrative relationship between the *Confession* and the *Conversion*. Since the original prose versions were written independently of each other but had been incorporated into a single narrative before their versification into an epic by Eudocia, I treat the *Conversion* and *Confession* as two episodes of one unified story, however disjointed they may be at times. This approach is not without challenges, as the *Confession*'s version of the Justina-Aglaidas episode differs from the longer version found in the *Conversion* in a few essential ways. My aim here is not to resolve all textual and narrative discrepancies between the two accounts but to argue that Eudocia subtly situates the *Confession* against the *Conversion*, particularly the *Conversion*'s intertextual engagement with the *Acts of Paul and Thecla* (*APT*). This approach creates a unified way of reading Eudocia as she reads Justina as a new, even more idealized Thecla.

In the final section of this chapter, I conclude with an examination of the literary models behind Cyprian's character. By the fourth century, when the *Confession* was first written, and certainly by the time Eudocia turned it into an epic a century later, itinerant wonderworkers were a well-established literary

---

3   McLynn 1992; Gaddis 2005:68–102; Kahlos 2009; Shaw 2011. For the contours of late antique religious competition, see the excellent essays in Engels and van Nuffelen 2014; Rosenblum, Vuong, and DesRosiers 2014; DesRosiers and Vuong 2016.

4   Compare Kazhdan 1995; Addey 2014:171–213.

5   Zahn 1882; Radermacher 1927; Butler 1948; Butler 1949; Butler 1952; Salvaneschi 1982a.

6   Salvaneschi 1982a; Jackson 1988a; Graf 1997:96–97; Livrea 1998; Livrea 2000; Martin 2005:126–129; Bevegni 2006; Bailey 2009; Jensen 2012.

trope. This trope, I argue, influenced the wider Cyprian legend, which, through a series of narrative reversals, exploits and critiques this trope. By contrasting Cyprian with Pythagoras and Apollonius, among others, the contours of his character come into sharper focus.

Cyprian's Confession

The *Conversion* ends with Cyprian fully integrated into the Antiochene church, rising to the rank of bishop, and using his (now God's) power to heal the sick, exorcize demons, and convert the city's remaining pagan population to Christianity. For her part, Justa, now renamed Justina, has been appointed deaconess and Mother Superior for Antioch's young Christian women. The *Conversion* anticipates the final portion of the legend: Cyprian and Justina's arrest, torture, trial, and execution during the Diocletianic persecution. As a narrative whole, however, the *Conversion* contains a neatly packaged story about Christianity's triumph over traditional Mediterranean religions, including magic, and God's triumph over Satan, which results in mass conversions and rapid growth. In other words, the *Conversion* is a type of etiological myth about Christianity's rise and spread, circulated by subsequent generations unaware of its gradual, consistent growth.[7]

The *Confession*, however, does not pick up where the *Conversion* ends but begins with Cyprian addressing an Antiochene audience about his desire to convert. Its start *in medias res* most likely gestures to Apuleius' *Apology* and ultimately back to Plato's *Apology* and the wider genre of legal defense literature, which frequently begin with carefully devised requests for sympathetic judges/juries (compare Cicero *On Invention* 1.20).[8] Unlike Apuleius, who argues that his actions have been mistakenly misrepresented as magic, Cyprian readily admits that he learned magic, yet asks for forgiveness.[9] Here, his *Confession* fits within an emerging tradition of literary *poenitentiae* and anticipates Augustine's *Confessions*, written a few decades later.[10]

Eudocia's *Confession* is incomplete and ends at the moment when the presbyter Eusebius would have granted Cyprian forgiveness and welcomed him into the Antiochene church. As it survives, however, her version is bookended with two direct addresses to the Christian community—Cyprian begins by pointing

---

7   Stark 1996; van Minnen 2006.

8   Apuleius *Apology* 1; Plato *Apology* 17a. See also Hunink 1997; Bradley 2014; Noreña 2014; Moreschini 2015.

9   Moreschini 2015:34–39. Compare the *apologia* within Philostratus' *Life of Apollonius of Tyana* (Robiano 2016).

10   Courcelle 1957:27–28; Courcelle 1963:101–103; Quinn 2002:3–6; Burton 2007:35–43; Mann 2006; Fox 2015.

out his tears (II.1–4) and concludes by asking if God can forgive him (II.475–479). This suggests that Cyprian's primary audience is the Christian leadership or, perhaps, the church as a whole. For that reason, the *Confession* can be read as a narrative expansion of Cyprian's mini-confessions found in the *Conversion* (I.230–239, 285–289). Through this rhetorical *tour de force* and literal tour across the Mediterranean, Cyprian successfully convinces the Antiochene Christians that he has turned from his previous life, marked by an insatiable curiosity for ritual power, toward a new life marked by a commitment to God's power.

Nevertheless, despite the *Confession's* overtly Christian context, including Cyprian's admission into the Antiochene church, his defense addresses two different audiences—Christians, potentially skeptical about his sincerity but hopefully moved by his tears (II.1–4), and traditionalists (meaning "pagans"), still committed to idol worship but potentially persuaded by his story about the ineffectiveness of demons (II.5–6). This two-fold audience may reflect the story's ultimate ideological agenda. As a result of this opening, the *Confession* has been interpreted as targeted toward a non-Christian readership.[11] If so, then the *Confession* complements Eudocia's Homeric cento (*Cento* 1–6), which similarly begins by addressing a diverse audience, especially those outside the Christian faith.[12] Eudocia's poem at Hammat Gader also directs its reader toward God, although ambiguously and only at the end. Her surviving poetic corpus, therefore, has a clear proselytizing tone and is speaking, at least partially, to a secular audience.

As literary model of the converted pagan, Cyprian represents Eudocia's ideal audience. Previously committed to demon worship but now convinced of their weakness, his conversion guides the tone and content of his speech. Moreover, his emerging Christian ideology pervades the story, for instance, when he conflates demons and idol worship into a single, indistinguishable whole or when he describes demons as worthless (μαψιδίων, II.9), unseemly (ἀεικέσιν, II.5), and full of deception (ἀπατήλια, II.6). As secondary narrator, Cyprian consistently uses pejorative language when speaking of demons and traditional religious rituals. These anachronistic moments reflect his eventual realization that demons cannot withstand the sign of the cross and are, therefore, unable to seduce Justina, a failing that directly and explicitly motivates his conversion.[13]

Similar to Simon Magus, the archetypal magician turned Christian (compare *Acts* 8:9–25), Cyprian converts after realizing God's superior power. The

---

[11] Bailey 2009:4–5.

[12] See my discussion of this passage in chapter 2.

[13] For the sign of the cross in the early church, especially as a mark of conversion, see Cyril of Jerusalem *Catecheses* 13.36; Augustine *Tractates on the Gospel of John* 118.5; Dinkler 1967.

conversions of Simon and Cyprian presume a zero-sum competitive discourse used throughout the ancient Mediterranean, especially by Judeo-Christian communities as they distinguished themselves from each other and from their religious competitors. Unlike Simon Magus, however, whose misappropriation of divine power elicited apostolic disapproval and solidified his reputation as ideological enemy of Peter and the Church, Cyprian is not motivated by a desire to use the power of the cross for self-serving ends but for the advancement of the faith (I.301–305).[14] In this regard, Cyprian's two-fold audience (Christian and pagan) corresponds to his own transformation over the course of the narrative. As a newly converted Christian eventually responsible for mass conversions and miracles, Cyprian's first public address reflects this desire to advance the faith. In other words, rather than simply seeing Cyprian's pagan audience as a reflection of the *Confession*'s ideological agenda, his speech is equally consistent within the narrative arc of the Cyprian legend itself.

Cyprian in Greece

To mark the transition from his programmatic introduction to the account of his early life, Cyprian names himself, "I am that famous Cyprian (οὗτος ἐκεῖνος ἔφυν Κυπριανός, II.11)." His ensuing journey spans thirty years, during which he travels from Greece through Asia Minor to north of the Black Sea, south to Egyptian Memphis, and east to Babylon, and ends with his settling in Syrian Antioch, where the Aglaidas-Justina story takes place. His use of οὗτος ἐκεῖνος implies notoriety, someone with a reputation for supernatural power, eventually appointed Satan's right-hand man and granted unusual honors by Satan and his followers (II.220–230). Not entirely a literary conceit, Cyprian was immensely popular in late antique magic lore beyond the Christianized story, and he continues to be invoked in rituals throughout the world. For instance, the late antique Cyprian love spell is written from his perspective and contains a narrative version of Cyprian's conversion to Christianity before invoking Gabriel to seduce a young woman.[15] Cyprian currently remains the primary

---

[14] The earliest stage of the Simon Magus legend (*Acts* 8:18-24) is fairly innocuous, as Simon repents for the desire to have the ability to bestow the Holy Spirit, which is seemingly under the auspices of the apostles and their immediate entourage. A century later, the Simon legend culminates in the *Acts of Peter*, where Simon and Peter face off in a battle of supernatural forces. Although absent in *Acts* and *the Acts of Peter*, early Christians associated Simon's name with early heresies, especially Gnosticism. Compare Justin Martyr (*First Apology* 26), Irenaeus (*Against the Heresies* 1.23.1–4; 1.26; 1.56), Hippolytus (*The Refutation of all Heresies* 6.11.1–19), and Clement (*Recognitions* 2.5.26–29). See also Hultgren and Haggmark 1996:15–27; Tuzlak 2002; Ferreiro 2005.

[15] Jackson 1999:153–158

authority invoked in South American rituals that require practitioners to bind or control Satan.[16]

As part of the ancient biographical tradition that projects the virtues and vices of its adult subjects onto their younger selves, Cyprian's exceptional religious ability begins while just a young child (κοῦρος) in Athens, where his parents dedicate him to Apollo (II.12).[17] As an initiate, the young Cyprian participates in a serpent-based ritual, presumably the Delphic Stepterion.[18] According to Plutarch, the Stepterion was a purification ritual celebrated every eighth year that required the participation of a young boy with living parents. This boy processed with torches and attendants into a hut, which was specifically built for the occasion and which symbolized a serpent's lair. The boy and his attendants ritually destroyed the hut, set it on fire, and fled into the temple precinct. Shortly thereafter, he would fast in Tempe and would return to Delphi, crowned in laurel and hailed as the serpent's killer.

Cyprian transforms this popular Greek festival into a Satanic one in a few essential ways. By equating the Stepterion with a beast (θηρός, II.13) and a stomach-traveling serpent (νηδυπόροιο δράκοντος, II.14), he replaces the ritual's historical and religious features with biblical reference about Satan. The θηρός (II.13) echoes the two beasts (θηρία) found in Revelation 13:1 and 13:11, which, if not directly about Satan, certainly symbolize Satanic forces hostile to God and humanity. The stomach-traveling serpent (νηδυπόροιο δράκοντος, II.14) alludes to God's curse on the deceptive serpent in Genesis 3:14. By late antiquity, the serpent from the Genesis account was widely assumed to be Satan in disguise.

This association between Cyprian's early religious occupations and Satan is hardly accidental. On the one hand, his participation in demonic activity and his allegiance to Satan parallel those in Revelation who adopt the mark of the beast and ally themselves against God. On the other hand, through his allusion to Genesis 3, Cyprian equates his early religious upbringing with Satan's deception of Eve. From a biblical perspective, these allusions bookend world history, from Eden to the Apocalypse. Moreover, as I argue in the previous chapter, Satan models his attempted deception of Justina on his earlier, successful deception of Eve (I.149–172). By using language that explicitly invokes Genesis 3, Cyprian simultaneously admits that he, like Adam and Eve, was deceived by Satan, but he also anticipates Justina's defeat of Satan and his own conversion.

---

[16]   Leitao 2014; Cummins, Diaz, and Zahrt 2016; Leitao 2017.

[17]   Typically, a *kouros* is an adolescent teen, although some examples of this word are used for very young children, including those *in utero* (*Iliad* 6.59). In context, Cyprian is not yet seven.

[18]   Plutarch *Greek Questions* 12; *Moralia* 418 A–B; Aelian *Various Histories* 3.1; Philostratus *Imagines* 2.24. See also Harrison 1903:113–114; Nilsson 1947:170.

Apollo and his serpentine ritual are the first of many traditional Greek cults in which Cyprian is initiated, perhaps because Python is a convenient classical proxy for Satan. In fact, the name Apollo may also allude to the demonic leader in charge of the beasts released in Revelation 9:1–11 and may underscore this association between Apollo/Python and the devil. Although such an anticlassical polemic is consistent with the ideological agenda of the *Confession*, it is equally possible to see a parallel between Cyprian and Apollo through their shared interest in oracular divination, a skill Cyprian repeatedly claims throughout his apology. At the same time, his participation in Greek cults, his connection to Apollo, and his interest in divination have strong resonances in the biographies of Apollonius of Tyana and Pythagoras.[19] These Apollonian and Pythagorean influences on the Cyprian legend are the focus of the final section of this chapter.

While in Athens, the seven-year old Cyprian is initiated into the cult of Phaethon Mithras.[20] Because he excelled at these rituals, his parents encourage him to become an Athenian citizen (II.17). This detail suggests that they were not originally from Athens but want him to have access to positions only open to citizens. From what we know about ancient Mithraism, it was a common practice for parents to dedicate their sons to Mithras.[21] Cyprian's early training with Apollo and Mithras reflects the extent to which mystery cults, traditional Greco-Roman religions, and rituals of power magic had been conflated by late antique Christian polemicists.[22] In fact, ritual initiations found in the Greek Magic Papyri and elsewhere reflect a similar conflation, often by borrowing language from the mysteries.[23]

Cyprian goes to great lengths to communicate his parents' involvement in these initiations. Regarding the Stepterion, their involvement is essential, because the child participant needs to have living parents. The other rituals Cyprian mentions do not require direct parental involvement, although their involvement makes sense due to his young age at the time. Moreover, by the second century, magicians beginning their education at very young ages had become a type of literary trope, and we know that parents could and did enroll their children in local religious offices.[24] On the other hand, considering their

---

[19] Nock 1927:411; Dzielska 1986:65–70.
[20] Phaethon was commonly conflated with Mithras (Cumont 1927:122–126; Claus 1990:160–162), although Eudocia's wording here is strange. For more on the form Μιθραῖος, see *P.Gurob.* 22.10; Callander 1927:239.
[21] *CIL* 6.751b; Cumont 1899:2.93; Nock 1927:411; Liebeschuetz 1994:197–198.
[22] Dickie 2001:116–117, 140; Martin 2005:128; Addey 2014:43–82.
[23] *PGM* 4.733–747; 12.315–322, 403–408; Apuleius *Metamorphoses* 11. See also Graf 1997:97–117; Dickie 2001:28–29, 73–74, 116–117.
[24] Compare Lucian *Alexander* 5; Clinton 1974:113; Dickie 2001:220–222.

rather insignificant role in the story as a whole, Cyprian's parents may serve a didactic purpose, especially when they are compared to Justina's parents, Aedesius and Cledonia. Both sets of parents begin as committed pagans involved in the religious lives of Athens and Antioch. Whereas Cyprian's parents encourage his participation in Greek cults leading to his apprenticeship under Satan, Aedesius and Cledonia convert to Christianity, a conversion that, as I argue in the previous chapter, sets in motion Justina's conversion, her participation in the Antiochene church, and (ultimately) Cyprian's conversion. The contrasting role that Cyprian and Justina's parents play in the *Conversion* and *Confession* underscores the influence parents have on the religious lives of their children. Therefore, Cyprian's parents appear as literary warnings for late antique adults against encouraging their children to participate in traditional religious festivals.

In addition to participating in the Stepterion and cult of Mithras, Cyprian serves as torch bearer (δᾳδοῦχος) of a god (II.18–19), likely Demeter at Eleusis. Because only adults from ancient, aristocratic Athenian families served as δᾳδοῦχος, it is extremely improbable that Cyprian held this position at any point in his life, let alone as a young child. This detail is likely a historical error on the part of the original prose author. Perhaps aware that the young Cyprian could not have served as δᾳδοῦχος to Demeter, Eudocia replaces the original τῇ Δημήτρᾳ with the slightly more ambiguous Δηοῖ. Nock also attempts to resolve this error by suggesting that Cyprian served in some comparable position open to children, perhaps as hearth initiate (ὁ παῖς ἀφ᾽ ἑστίας) to Zeus.[25] Because the παῖς ἀφ᾽ ἑστίας was chosen through a lottery system, it was technically open to all Athenian adolescents, although most came from the same old, aristocratic families.[26] Shortly thereafter, Cyprian is initiated as one of the *epheboi* in the Eleusinian mysteries (II.19–20) and serves in the serpent cult to Athena (II.20–21), where he likely feeds honey cakes to the sacred snake on the Acropolis.[27] Therefore, while still a child, Cyprian participates in the cults of Apollo, Mithras, Demeter/Zeus, Persephone, and Athena.

After rising to the position of temple servant (ζάκορος), Cyprian leaves Athens for Olympus (II.22), where he sees and hears various, confusing supernatural things. For instance, he hears echoes and sounds (II.24–25), which have been interpreted as an allusion to the belief that demons could be born

---

[25] Nock 1927:411. For more on the position of δᾳδοῦχος, see IG 1413; IG 1414; Toepffer 1889:49, 87n4; Nilsson 1947:170; Clinton 1974:67; Lalonde 2006:118.

[26] Esdaile 1909:3; Foucart 1914:277–281; Clinton 1974:113, 98–114.

[27] Compare Herodotus 8.41. The white robe worn by *epheboi* during the procession had been discontinued but was eventually reinstated by Herodes Atticus (Münscher 1912:942; Nock 1927:411).

out of echoes from God's voice.[28] Cyprian also observes basic pharmacology, an essential part of ancient magic, which he describes as plants and roots used by demons (II.25–26).[29] He learns about the seasons, winds, and days of the year, and he watches a choir sing songs and other people perform violent acts (II.27–31).[30] During his forty-eight-day stay on Olympus (II.34–35), Cyprian witnesses a demonic army travel throughout the world deceiving humans (II.36–38) and, one evening, ritually fasts on a diet of freshly picked berries (II.39–40).[31]

At the age of fifteen, under the tutelage of seven hierophants, he advances from observing to performing these rituals (II.40–42). Although the number seven may be symbolic, hierophants were Athenian priests, frequently from aristocratic families, who served in the Eleusinian Mysteries. During late antiquity, the term hierophant could be used for any ritual expert.[32] These seven hierophants teach Cyprian about demons, spirits, and divination, a skill closely associated with at least one well-known late antique Athenian hierophant.[33] Because his parents are still eager that he receive a complete education, he learns everything about the earth, sky, and sea (II.45), including human destruction (II.46), pharmacology (II.47-48), human oppression (II.48)—everything discovered by Satan (II.49–51). By attributing his education to Satan, Cyprian admits his own aberrance and, in so doing, transforms Satan into a type of biblical Prometheus. Like Prometheus, Satan teach humans those practices and skills he had developed.[34] Whereas Prometheus opposes Zeus through assisting humanity and teaching them various arts, Satan opposes God by teaching humanity intentionally harmful arts. By calling Satan the ruler of the earth (ὁ τῆσδε γύης ἀρχός, II.50), Cyprian echoes eschatologically rich biblical passages (John 12:31, 16:11, 2 Corinthians 4:4) that mark Satan's authority over the earth, sky, and sea as provisional and limited.

When he departs Olympus for Argos, Cyprian augments his cosmological curriculum by becoming initiate of air, water, and earth at a festival for Dawn ('Ηώς, II.52–57). In the prose version, he claims to have been initiated into the mysteries of Hera, whose marriage to Zeus has been interpreted allegorically

---

[28] Jackson 1988b:32–37; Jackson 1996:1–20; Bailey 2009:35, based on *Testament of Solomon* 4:8; Pseudo-Philo *Liber Antiquitatum Biblicarum* 53.3–4, 60.3; *PGM* 13.192-204, 522-546.
[29] Scarborough 1990; Gordon 1999:244–252; Graf 2014:390–394; Rücker 2014:86–89.
[30] For Ares in later Greek cults, see Farnell 1909:5.396–414.
[31] Compare Lucian *Menippus* 7.
[32] IG I² 76.24; Lysias Against Andocides 1; Isocrates Panegyricus 28; Plutarch *Alcibiades* 33; Hierocles Platonicus *In Carmen Aureum* 20; Clinton 1974:8–47. On the use of seven as allegory, see Nock 1927:413.
[33] Clinton 1974; Kaldellis 2005.
[34] Compare Werblowsky 1973.

as the marriage of the ether and air.[35] He continues on to Sparta to see the cult image of Artemis (Keladeine) Tauropolos and to study destructive natural forces, engraved stones (ψήφους γραφίδας), cosmic symbols (χαρακτῆρας), and ancient myths (II.60–62).[36] It is tempting to compare these stones and symbols with those found in the Greek Magic Papyri (*PGM*) and elsewhere.[37] Rituals of power frequently mention inscribed stones and occasionally require practitioners to inscribe words of power onto stones that then were worn or carried to guarantee or enact their efficacy.[38] Some of these words of power are incomprehensible symbols (χαρακτῆρας) representing secret names of deities or commands to deities.[39] Through the act of knowing/writing these secret names and commands, each ritual becomes imbued with power.[40] Sparta, however, is not usually associated with these practices. Considering the ambiguity of Eudocia's wording and its departure from her prose models, one should not read too much into this section.

From the Peloponnese, Cyprian travels to Phrygia (II.62) in central Asia Minor, where, under divine inspiration, he learns hepatoscopy (divination by inspecting livers). It may strike us as odd that Cyprian makes no direct references to Magna Mater or the Phrygian goddess Cybele, the region's most popular and wide-spreading cult,[41] although there is nothing explicitly Phrygian about Cyprian's Phrygian education. What is striking is his use of μαντιπόλος ("frenzied" or "inspired") to describe his mental state in Phrygia. Beyond mere intoxication, μαντιπόλος implies a mantic experience, what Burkert calls an "intensified mental power," frequently in reference to Dionysus, who also had deep roots in Phrygia.[42] By late antiquity, μαντιπόλος can simply mean a diviner.[43] Therefore, despite the rather un-Phrygian content of his Phrygian visit, Cyprian describes his mental state with language that has deep roots in eastern mantic traditions.

---

[35] Nilsson 1947:174–175.

[36] On the epithet Tauropolos, compare Euripides *Iphigenia among the Taurians* 1457; Sophocles *Ajax* 172. For Keladeine, see *Iliad* 16.183; 20.70; 21.511; *Hymn to Aphrodite* 118; *Hymn to Artemis* 1. This cult is likely to Artemis Orthia, whose temple and the image within served an important cultic function during late antiquity. Some connections between the sanctuary of Artemis Orthia and fourth-century Spartan philosophical seers survive (Julian *Oration* 2.119b–c; Cartledge and Spawforth 2002:183, 190–211; Whitby 2002:23–24).

[37] *PGM* 3.303; 4.937; 7.391; 7.927; 12.201–269. Delatte and Derchain 1964:329; Betz 1992:58n126; Muñoz 2001:144; Ogden 2002:261–274.

[38] *PGM* 12.201–269.

[39] Van Rengen 1984:213–233; Martin 2015:265.

[40] Janowitz 2002:33–43.

[41] Lane 1996; Roller 1999:108–109.

[42] Burkert 1985:162–163. Euripides *Hecuba* 121; Euripides *Bacchae* 13–14.

[43] Manetho Astrologus 6.306.

Cyprian in Scythia

After spending his childhood years in Attica, the Peloponnese, and Asia Minor, the adult Cyprian continues his journey to Scythia (II.65). While there, he learns ornithomancy (divination by tracking the flights or sounds of birds) and divination by analyzing the paths of animals.[44] In addition to these, he learns the sound of wood and stone, voices of the dead, creaking of doors, human anatomy (especially how to make bodies twitch and suffer), and, finally, oaths and other powerful words. Although this seems like a disconnected and disjointed list, some patterns emerge. Located near the borders of the Roman Empire beyond the confines of the Mediterranean, the Scythians, especially their culture and religion, were greatly mischaracterized by classical authors.[45] The *Confession* operates within this tradition.

In the ancient Mediterranean ideological landscape, divination was contested territory.[46] For instance, despite there being a well-established Italian tradition of bird divination, Cicero (*On Divination* 1.92) repudiates ornithomancy as an example of eastern influence and identifies *oionistes* (those who practice ornithomancy) with Phrygia, Pisidia, Cilicia, and Arabia, not his native Italia.[47] Cicero here participates in a well-established Roman practice of projecting potentially threatening religious customs onto foreign or distant people. Within the more general Greco-Roman literary tradition, practitioners of rituals of power frequently hail from "distant" cultures (Thessaly, Egypt, Babylon, etc.).[48] A similar practice is at play here in the *Confession*. After Cyprian leaves Greece for Phrygia and Scythia, he studies hepatoscopy and ornithomancy, although both forms of divination are equally attested in Greece and Rome.[49] As he travels further from Greece, Cyprian characterizes his studies as increasingly transgressive. This suggests that the *Confession* operates on two ideological registers: a Greco-Roman register that treats eastern religious traditions—even very ancient ones—with suspicion or hostility and a Christian register that repudiates all other religious practices.

Cyprian's Scythian education contains a great deal of sounds: bird chirping, the utterances of diviners, noises made by wood and stone, voices of the dead,

---

[44] Compare Homer *Iliad* 1.71–72; Aeschylus *Agamemnon* 104–204. See also Luck 2006:308–309; Augustine *The Divination of Demons* 3.7, 4.8.

[45] Herodotus 1.1–144; Thucydides 2.97; Lucian *The Scythian or the Consul*; Lucian *On Mourning* 21; Rice 1957; Cartledge 2002:69–71; Braund 2004a; Braund 2004b.

[46] Janowitz 2001; Flower 2008.

[47] Compare *On Divination* 2.80.

[48] Dickie 2001; Spaeth 2014.

[49] Aeschylus *Prometheus Bound* 484–499; Flower 2008:69. Greek mantic practices tend to borrow from eastern ones (Flower 2008:32–37).

and creaking of doors. Such sounds play a crucial role in prescriptive magic.[50] Some sounds were to be emulated in the form of hissing, clucking, sighing, groaning, and lip smacking to make rituals more efficacious.[51] Other sounds were to be avoided for rituals to work.[52] Hearing, listening, speaking, and replicating sounds were an essential part of the ritual process, one found in countless prescriptive sources.

Despite the proliferation of sounds and hearing in the *PGM*, the rhetorical force of Cyprian's list of sounds is not to elaborate on them or their ritual function but to conflate them into a single catch-all category of divination, idolatry, and necromancy. This bundling of Christianity's ideological competitors is accomplished by balancing well-known and quite popular methods of divination (necromancy and ornithomancy) with vague descriptions that make the list more "spooky," such as Cyprian's multiple references to bodily harm.[53] The inclusion of sounds from stone and wood further conflates cult practices with divination and is consistent with the biblical tradition of describing idolatry as the worship of objects fashioned from wood and stone (Jeremiah 2:27, Jeremiah 3:9, Ezekiel 20:32).

Cyprian also learns divination from songs and texts (II.73). The prose version of the *Confession* more explicitly indicates that this divination comes through identifying the numerical values of words. This is consistent with ancient gematria or isopsephy, a practice found in ancient theurgy and the Greek Magical Papyri but also commonly employed in Judeo-Christian allegorical exegesis.[54] Despite its varied permutations, gematria emerges from a competitive discourse about sacred or celebrated texts, especially those that contain potentially embarrassing myths and legends. By interpreting these myths as the medium for hidden codes, their historical or ethical problems can be elided over. In fact, of the multiple occasions when Cyprian learns songs, verses, and words of power during his journey, this is the only time he calls them *mythoi*, which may be an allusion to the ritualized use of literature, particularly classical epics and biblical passages, to predict the future.[55] The prevalence of numerology within the Christian allegorical tradition throughout late antiquity makes Cyprian's negative depiction of gematria here particularly strange. Instead of a

---

[50] Janowitz 2002:45–61.

[51] *PGM* 13.946; Plotinus *Enneads* 4.4; Luck 2006:6, 55; Brisson 2013:450–452.

[52] *PGM* 36.134–160.

[53] The role of cemeteries and the dead in magic rituals is well-attested: Plato *Laws* 933a–e; Philostratus *Life of Apollonius* 4.16; Plutarch *Moralia* 585E–F; Iamblichus *Pythagorean Life* 148; Gager 1992:214–215; Ogden 2001:3–16; Wilburn 2012:238–246.

[54] Stambursky 1976; Fideler 1993:25–36; Janowitz 2002:50–52; Ast and Lougovaya 2015. For Pythagorean numerology, see Guthrie 1988:41, 53; Afonasin 2016; Izdebska 2016.

[55] *PGM* 1.328–331; Schwendner 2002; Struck 2002; Sandnes 2009:45–47.

general criticism of numerology, it is most likely a targeted criticism of gematria in non-Christian contexts with non-Christian texts.

These disparate ritual practices are unified under a more general understanding of the limits of nature (στήλας φύσιος, II.74). By invoking φύσις, Cyprian gestures to two over-arching themes found within his *Confession*. First, he reiterates how his education comprehensively includes all of nature—land, sea, and air. With this proficiency of all three cosmic spheres, he effectively controls all of nature or influences those demons appointed over each sphere. Before running into Justina, he is, at least in his own mind, master of the universe. Second, by alluding to nature's limits, he highlights the boundary between the acceptable and the unacceptable and, in so doing, subtly situates magic outside the appropriate natural order.[56] Cyprian certainly uses a recurring trope from competitive rhetoric that discredits one's competitors by insisting they transgress nature or what is natural. Related to this is the popular assumption, both in antiquity and modernity, that magic is an intrinsically transgressive system, the antithesis of nature.

According to this view, magic is transgressive, because its practitioners intentionally undermine socially accepted norms about spiritual and religious traditions.[57] As a result of this social breach, magic practitioners find themselves alienated from their communities and from society as a whole.[58] This model, however, is prescriptive, not descriptive, and prioritizes "religion" as the only acceptable way to engage the spiritual world or the cosmic order. Positioning religion as the antithesis of magic simply employs competitive terminology (religion = natural; magic = unnatural) and ignores the obvious fact that many socially acceptable religious traditions contain rituals that, from an ideologically neutral position, are indistinguishable from those in rival traditions stigmatized as unnatural or transgressive.[59] By late antiquity, early Christianity had already coopted this competitive rhetoric from the Greco-Roman rhetorical tradition and had directed its proscriptive attack not only against magic but also against traditional Greco-Roman religions more generally. As a typical late antique Christian convert, Cyprian operates within this competitive mode by repeatedly insisting that his studies overstep human limits. At the same time, by claiming to have earned a reputation among his neighbors and friends in Antioch, he does not give the impression that, prior to attacking Justina, he lurked at the margins of Antiochene society.

---

[56] For more on φύσις, see Heinimann 1945; Naddaf 1992; Patzer 1993; Vergnières 1995; Naddaf 2005; Müller 2006.

[57] Frazer 1907; Luck 1962; Aune 1980; Thomassen 1999; Luck 2006.

[58] Graf 1991a; Graf 1997; Ogden 2001:xviii–xix.

[59] Styers 2004; Naddaf 2005:86–87.

Cyprian in Egypt

Now twenty years old, Cyprian leaves Scythia and travels south to Egypt. Late antique Egypt and Persia (Babylon) were the stereotypical places where curious students went to study magic.[60] The *Confession* here builds on this literary trope when Cyprian arrives in Memphis (II.84).[61] His admittedly vague description of this part of his training focuses on attempting (πειρήθην) things inappropriate for humans and, therefore, builds on his experiences in Scythia. Over the course of the *Confession*, Cyprian progresses from child novice to adult expert by using a fairly consistent "order of operations." As a child in Olympus, he simply observes rituals and uses language of visual and auditory perception (ἤχον καὶ ἄκουον, II.24; λεῦσα, II.25; κάτιδον, II.27; εἰσιδόμην, II.30; and εἶδον, II.32). Starting at the age of fifteen, however, he begins to learn various skills (ἤα διδασκόμενος, II.42; μάθοιμι, II.44; δαείην, II.59; and ἐδάην, II.64). Now twenty, he advances from learning to doing (πειρήθην).

Cyprian's Egyptian studies concentrate on demonology (II.86–97), including their origins, names, astrological positions, and ways to invoke or dispel them.[62] Knowing a demon's name and its astrological position has parallels in prescriptive magical sources, including the *PGM*, and was a common method of influencing spirits.[63] Assumed here is the belief that secret information could be ritually used to control others, even humans.[64] To further augment his demonic power, Cyprian learns which spirits oppose which demons. These spirits could either be angels or more powerful demons. He then catalogues a somewhat strange list of demonic activity, including swift movement, knowledge, memory, terror, deception, footprints, and forgetfulness.

One practical application of these demonic pursuits is the ability to control nature and cause earthquakes, rainstorms, and other comparable disturbances (II.97–99). The manipulation and control of these elements rhetorically situates Cyprian as preternaturally disposed and part of a long-standing tradition of eastern holy men and magicians.[65] For instance, Pythagoras was said to have been able to predict earthquakes, avert hail storms, and calm rough waters.[66]

---

[60] Ogden 2001:203. For more on Egyptian religion and magic, see Hornung 2001; Lopez 2001; Taylor 2001; Ciraolo and Seidel 2002; David 2002; Mirecki and Meyer 2002; Ogden 2002; Kaper 2003; Maravelia 2003; Noegel, Walker, and Wheeler 2003; Dieleman 2005; Martin 2005; Szpakowska 2006; Bricault, Versluys, and Meyboom 2007.

[61] Thessalus of Tralles *De virtutibus herbarum* 1–12; Lucian *Philopseudes* 33–36. Ogden 2006:123–127.

[62] Compare Porphyry *On Abstinence* 2.37–39. For Egyptian demonology, Quack 2015 contains a good discussion and recent bibliography.

[63] PGM 4.261–274; 7.505–528; 13.213–224; 61.24–31; PDM 61.28. See also Janowitz 2002:33–43.

[64] Compare Catullus 5.11–13.

[65] Herodotus 7.191; Tibullus 1.2; Ovid *Heroides* 6; Ovid *Amores* 1.8; Apuleius *Metamorphoses* 1.9.

[66] Porphyry *Life of Pythagoras* 28–29.

In the early Christian literary tradition, Jesus, another eastern wonderworker with ties to Egypt and Babylon, also controls the weather.[67] Because Jesus' calming of the storm is used in his first-century biographies as evidence of his divinity, Cyprian contrasts their ability to control nature by insisting that he merely imitates God's power.[68] This distinction between appearance and reality is a recurring way through which Cyprian acknowledges Satan's power but dismisses it as inferior to God's.

In keeping with the hero's decent into the underworld, Cyprian experiences an epically inspired vision of hell.[69] There he sees the Titans (II.102), confused here with Giants, imprisoned under the earth and the Titan Atlas (II.104–105) bearing the earth on his shoulders.[70] In addition to figures from classical mythology, he sees a variety of demons, some of which appear like snakes, while others take the form of winds. All of these demons attack humans and inflict harm on the earth. Hard pressed, the earth remains securely on its foundation, a cosmological position reiterated throughout the *Confession*.[71] The demons are more successful against their human targets, some of whom they possess and use to wage war against those Cyprian describes as holy and righteous, presumably Christians.[72]

This conflict between humans and demons is characterized as an allegorical battle between demonic vices and human (divine) virtues (II.122–164). The *Confession* here follows a tradition of personification epic begun by Prudentius.[73] If the personifications in Prudentius' *Psychomachia* are somewhat theologically simplistic, a view challenged in recent years, those in the *Confession* are even yet more simplistic, little more than a catalogue with few explanations and no mention of their virtuous opponents until the end.[74] Nevertheless, the *Confession*'s personifications overlap with those in the *Psychomachia*: Idolatry, Lust, Anger, Pride, and Greed are all represented.

Cyprian describes seeing Falsehood (II.122), joyless and full of embellishment; Lust (II.123–124), covered in blood and singed by fire; Wrath (II.125–126), a winged feral creature; Deceit (II.126–127), relentless, secretive, and full of

---

[67] Mark 4:35–41; Matthew 8:23–27; Luke 8:22–25. Compare Matthew 27:51–53. See also Berenson Maclean 2004; Busch 2015.
[68] Compare IG 3.1403 and Wisdom 17:3 from the Septuagint.
[69] Hardie 2004. The vision of the underworld becomes a fairly central part of late antique theurgy (Proclus *Commentary on Plato's Republic* 1.37, 2.153). Copeland 2014.
[70] Compare Hesiod *Theogony* 711–745.
[71] On this cosmological debate in antiquity, see Aristotle *On the Heavens* 294a.
[72] Late antique Christian authors commonly depict their earthly opponents, particularly pagans and heretics, as demon-possessed (compare Ephesians 6:12–13). See Pagels 1995; Juergensmeyer 2000:182–185; Gaddis 2005:180.
[73] Haworth 1980; Mastrangelo 2008.
[74] Nugent 1985:11–14 traces the history of this criticism. Compare now Stabryła 2005.

trickery; Hatred (II.128–133), gruesome, blind in the front but with four eyes on the back of his head. Hatred prefers darkness over light, has multiple feet sticking out from his head, and has no stomach, since he is without emotion. Jealousy and Envy are next (II.134–135), nearly identical in appearance except for Envy's mouth, which is shaped like a shovel. Emaciated to death, Morosity (II.136–138) has many eyes, all set on revenge. Cyprian dedicates five lines to Greed (II.139–143), who has a narrow head and two mouths: one in his midriff, the other on his back. Greed's diet consists of rocks and solid earth, which he consumes insatiably. Next is Cupidity (II.144–146), attractive and keen—her eyes are always open. She is followed by Commerce (II.147–148), ever on the move and carrying on her shoulders the hope for wealth. Then comes Vanity (II.149–150), noble and attractive, but whose beauty is skin deep. Soaring high on her four wings is Idolatry (II.151–154), seemingly able to guard others but unable to protect even herself. Cyprian sees Hypocrisy (II.155–157), full of terror, yet powerless and with a hollow chest. Delirium (II.158–160) appears as half man and half woman, nude, guileless in her evil. Then appears Recklessness (II.161–162), who has a tongue larger than any other part of his body. The final image seen by Cyprian is Insanity (II.163–164), recognized by his nut-shaped head and empty soul.

In addition to these personified vices, Cyprian sees three hundred and sixty-five other demons—one for every day of the week (II.165–170). They spread throughout the cosmos battling against Virtue, Wisdom, and Justice. Unlike in the *Psychomachia*, where Prudentius emphasizes the victory of each virtue over its corresponding vice, Cyprian implies that his demonic vices successfully defeat virtue and deceive humanity (II.172–173).[75] Their success, however, is limited to the Hellenes (Ἑλλήνων, II.172), namely those who remain beyond the reach of Christianity. Since Christians are armed with the power of the cross, these daily demonic attacks are rendered powerless and ineffectual against them (II.174). Through this, Cyprian foreshadows his own realization of the powerlessness of demons against the cross and anticipates his subsequent conversion.

Cyprian in Babylon

Ten years after arriving in Egypt, the now thirty-year-old Cyprian leaves Memphis for Babylon, where he finishes his training and rises through the ranks, eventually appointed Satan's right-hand man. Unfortunately, because this section of Cyprian's account is corrupt or, at least, confused, the reconstruction

---

[75] Compare James 1999:71–72.

of many details remains difficult. He begins by emphasizing the antiquity of the Babylonians and their interest in cosmology, with particular expertise in the relationship between *aether* and fire.[76] According to Cyprian, most Chaldeans think *aether* rests on flaming fire (ἐπὶ φλογεροῦ πυρός, II.183), but their scholars know that it actually rests on light (ἐπὶ φάεος, II.184).[77] From such experts he learns the nature of *aether*-based stars, their positions in the sky, the constellations to which they belong, what nourishes them, and their dependence on light (II.185–190). Similar to his catalogue of demons, the *aether*-cosmos is divided into 365 parts, each of which he studies (II.191–192).

These cosmic forces obey orders issued by their leader, the so-called demiurge (II.193–194). In late antique Gnosticism, the demiurge is the creator of the cosmos, responsible for the formation of the cosmos and actively opposed to the good god.[78] In Christian-influenced Gnostic texts, the demiurge is a conflated with the god of the Old Testament and contrasted with God the Father and the devil.[79] Here in the *Confession*, the demiurge is a cosmic authority distinct from and possibly subservient to Satan. While the cosmic powers obey him, they have unique interests and can be controlled in various ways (II.195–199). Some, for instance, prefer sacrifices, while others reject them. Some desire the light, while others are bound by oaths and words of power. By learning each spirit's defining features, Cyprian influences them all. During his study of these cosmic powers, he observes that, despite their individual preferences, they collectively work to deceive humanity, cause them to forget God, and perform all sorts of evils (II.214–217).[80]

Noticing Cyprian's rise in power, Satan takes a liking to him and compares his beauty and magical aptitude to Jambres (II.222–223). Jambres and Jannes were Pharaoh's magicians from the Exodus account (Exodus 7:11–12, 7:22, 8:7, 8:18). Not named in Exodus, their reputation and accompanying legend grew in the following centuries, so that they were known and named by first- and second-century Roman authors.[81] Of the various accounts about Jannes and Jambres, one maintains that they were originally entrusted with Moses' education while he grew up in Pharaoh's court. Within the classical and Jewish literary traditions, they emerge as the Egyptian magicians par excellence,

---

[76] Aether was the fifth element, which made up celestial bodies at the furthest issue of the cosmos (Guthrie 1981:270) and was the home of the celestial gods (Apuleius *On the god of Socrates* 7.137; Moreschini 2015:124).

[77] Compare Plotinus *Enneads* 4.5.7; Sam-bursky 1958.

[78] Williams 2000; Pearson 2007:276.

[79] Pearson 2007:160–161.

[80] Contrast this depiction of the demiurge and his cosmic powers with that found in the *Poimandres* (Pearson 2007:277–281; Lewis 2013:113–114).

[81] Pliny *Natural History* 20.2.11; Apuleius *Apology* 90.

despite originally serving in the Hebrew Bible as negative foils for Moses and God's superior power.[82]

The reasons for Satan's comparison of Cyprian to Jambres and not Jannes are clarified by reading the *Confession* alongside another late antique pseudepigraphic *poenitentia, Jannes and Jambres* (alternatively entitled *Poenitentia Iamne et Mambre*).[83] Generically comparable, *Jannes and Jambres* may have influenced the form and content of the *Confession*.[84] Throughout this story, Jambres is depicted as the superior magician to Jannes, and he even repents at the end.[85] While a possible allusion to *Jannes and Jambres*, Satan's comparison between Cyprian and Jambres also ironically foreshadows Cyprian's inability to seduce Justina, a narrative parallel to Moses' victory over Jannes and Jambres in Exodus. For the time being, however, Satan predicts that Cyprian will become a cosmic leader and entrusts him with a cohort of demons (II.224–229). These public recognitions from Satan encourage his priests to honor Cyprian as Satan's equal (II.230). In claiming equality with Satan, Cyprian imitates Satan's rebellion against God, which rhetorically underscores their similarities and alludes, at least obliquely, to Cyprian's eventual defection from Satan's faction to God's camp.

Cyprian proceeds to describe Satan's appearance: he has a golden sheen, flashing eyes, and long hair (II.231–232). As a type of monarch, he wears a crown decorated with jewels that, together with his clothing, illuminates the underworld (II.232–235). When he moves, the earth shakes (II.235). He sits on a throne surrounded by a demonic host with their eyes fixed to the ground yet prepared for battle (II.236–237). This description of Satan mirrors biblical descriptions of the glorified Jesus, especially those found in Revelation (see Revelation 1:12–16, Revelation 7–8). Cyprian further compares Satan to an Olympian god who illuminates the earth by making the stars shine and plants grow (II.238–239). An angel of light (2 Corinthians 11:14) desirous of equality with or, perhaps, superiority over God, Satan imitates God's appearance and actions (II.240–241). By describing hell as a mirror image of heaven, where Satan sits enthroned as supreme ruler, Cyprian confesses that Satan's mimetic strategy lacks substance and is intentionally deceptive, a type of cosmic smoke and mirror show.

As an imitator of God, Satan encourages humans to participate in animal sacrifice, a practice early Christian polemicists equated with demonic activity.[86] Accordingly, demons sit next to sacrificants and fashion smoke-based illusions

---

[82] Pietersma 1994.

[83] von Dobschütz 1912:84; James 1920:34; Schneemelcher 1991:1.38–40.

[84] Bailey 2009:13–16.

[85] For a different reading of this section, see Bailey 2009:14–15.

[86] Compare Augustine *The City of God* 18.51, *Epistle* 17 (Kahlos 2009:124, 128–129). Themistius (*Oration* 5) attempts to distinguish between magic arts and sacrifice (Kahlos 2009:85–86).

to delude them into believing that their idols are alive (II.248–253). In order to reach as many people as possible, Satan demands countless sacrifices of every species (II.254–257), a further illusion or mirror image of the type of worship given to God. To illustrate Satan's deception, Cyprian contends that he is like fire that is actually ice, or like catching an inedible fish, or like poverty-inducing gold (II.264–266). Because humans fall for these illusions, Satan constructs all sorts of objects: cities, bedrooms, plains, fields, glens, all of which require a precise sacrifice (II.267–274).

Perhaps these references to cities and bedrooms remind Cyprian of events immediately preceding his conversion. Wanting to fear God but paralyzed by fear, Cyprian's rejection of Satan only comes after Justina proves how powerless Satan and his demons truly are. In a miniature retelling of the *Conversion*, Cyprian describes how his demons, one by one, flee from Justina and how his monstrous serpent has the strength of a fly (II.278–283). Reducing Satan's boasts to empty words, Justina tramples his head with her feet (II.286). This action obviously refers to Eve and the Eden story, a central text in the *Confession*, especially in the construction of Justina as idealized Christian woman. Cyprian realizes his error when he sees demons unable to enter her house and Satan fleeing from her (II.287–293). Instead of a ferocious lion, Satan has become little more than Justina's plaything, a domesticated cat (II.294–296).

Cyprian in Antioch

Backtracking slightly, Cyprian returns to his arrival in Antioch, where he experiences success in curing people of love, jealousy, rivalry, and other physical desires (II.296–300).[87] When compared to ancient binding spells, Cyprian's offerings for his Antiochene clientele are fairly predictable and anticipate his eventual seduction of Justina.[88] Because of Cyprian's growing reputation, a desperate Aglaidas hires him to alleviate his desire for Justina. This event, Cyprian confesses, marks the moment he fully realizes how truly powerless demons are. The *Confession*'s version of the Justina-Aglaidas episode differs from the version found in the *Conversion* and reflects not only Cyprian's now Christian perspective but also a more developed cult of Cyprian and Justina.

Cyprian initially sends his legion of demons against her, but they return unsuccessful (II.305–306). After ten weeks of combining his magic with their attacks (II.310–311), Cyprian asks Satan for help, but he also fails (II.312–317). In the face of these repeated setbacks, Cyprian asks Beliar to make him no longer

---

[87] Compare Lucian *Philopseudes* 12–14.
[88] Gager 1992.

love Justina. This request suggests that Cyprian has fallen in love with Justina or that his character has been slowly conflated with Aglaidas. A similar conflation between Cyprian and Aglaidas emerges in the *Conversion*. Beliar, however, is not able to help him, an inability that prompts Cyprian to compare demons to a weak and disabled cavalryman, who foolishly takes credit for his horse's speed (II.332–334). This realization that demons claim power that is not theirs leads to three conflicts: between Cyprian and his demons, between rivaling factions of demons, and between Cyprian and Satan. These arguments end when Cyprian casts out Satan.

Unfazed, Satan attempts to deceive Aglaidas by passing off a different girl as Justina (II.344–346). Since this girl looks nothing like Justina, Satan's trick is immediately obvious. He next transforms a demon into Justina (II.348–349).[89] When Aglaidas excitedly says Justina's name, the demon runs away (II.351). This implies a transfer of power from the sign of the cross and the name of Christ to Justina, whose name, by the story's end, has ritual power over demons.[90] This scene is also a reversal of the episode found in the *Conversion*, where Satan disguises himself as a young girl to persuade Justina to leave her bedroom. The *Confession* replaces an episode that emphasizes Justina's humanity and near deception with an account of her increased power. This change likely reflects a later stage in the Cyprian and Justina cult when Justina was invoked to protect others.

Distraught, Cyprian experiences insomnia and eventually transforms himself, first into a woman, then into a bird (II.358–359). Although slightly conflated, these metamorphoses ostensibly give Cyprian access to Justina's bedroom. Yet, even this strategy fails. Upon entering her house, he returns to normal form (II.359–361). Cyprian then transforms Aglaidas into a bird (II.362). Landing on Justina's roof, he catches her attention but is immediately transformed back into a human. Cyprian insists that Aglaidas would likely have fallen to his death had Justina not kindly helped him down and sent him on his way (II.368–371). She is described as looking out her light-bearing window (ἀπὸ φωτοφόροιο θύρης, II.364), a gesture back to her conversion in the *Conversion* (I.20–22*) that rhetorically underscores how Justina's window makes her susceptible to outside influence. It also situates Aglaidas' winged sexual assault alongside Praulius' message of the Gospel, both of which are described in erotic terms. As I suggest in the previous chapter, Justina's eroticized reception of Praulius' message leads to her repeated trips to church and makes her susceptible to Aglaidas' eroticized attacks.

---

[89] In the prose version, this demon is Beliar.
[90] Sowers 2017.

At this point in the *Confession*, Aglaidas recedes into the background of the narrative, while Cyprian and Satan continue to attack Justina's health, an expansion on *Conversion* I.146, where Satan plans to wear down Justina with fevers. This sickness is incapable of breaking her spirits. In fact, when the doctors predict that she will die, Justina encourages her parents by insisting that she will not die, because she only has a light fever. In addition to this disease, Cyprian and Satan send many others against her, but she defeats them each with the sign of the cross (II.382). Here, the *Confession* anticipates Justina's role as healer of various sicknesses in the medieval church.[91]

In a scene that reverses Satan's strategic attack against Job (Job 1-2), after illness fails to persuade Justina, Cyprian targets her parents' flocks, herds, and mules. Justina encourages them by reminding them that those who follow Christ are rich in possessions (Matthew 5:12, 6:19-20). When Justina's neighbors advise her parents to compel her to marry, she strengthens their resolve with the sign of the cross. As a final act of desperation, Satan sends a plague against Antioch with an oracular message that the plague will continue until Justina marries Aglaidas. Justina responds by dispelling the plague from the city. As a result, Antioch's citizens and those in its environs praise God and blame Cyprian as a local nuisance. The *Confession* here anticipates the Christianization of Antioch but credits Justina as an active agent in the process. Unlike the Justina found in the *Conversion*, who serves as Mother Superior for Antioch's virgins while Cyprian performs miracles and converts the city's remaining pagans, the *Confession*'s Justina performs miracles of her own and convinces the city to honor Christ.

Now despised by the Antiochenes, Cyprian realizes the power of the cross and confronts Satan. Whereas, in the *Conversion*, Satan admits his weakness after Cyprian swears an oath of loyalty, in the *Confession*, Cyprian preemptively lectures Satan in a prolonged speech that takes up nearly ten percent of the *Confession* (II.406-447). In this speech, Cyprian condemns Satan as powerless, evil, and incapable of standing against Christ. Because he was deceived by promises of Satan's power, Cyprian also stands condemned. He instead wishes that he had used the money that funded his magic studies to feed the poor (II.431-435). Worn out, exhausted, nearly a corpse, Cyprian tells Satan that he will beg for mercy from Christ and his servants. He ends his speech by commanding Satan to leave.

Rather than admit defeat, Satan attempts to choke Cyprian to death (II.448-450). With Justina in mind, Cyprian prays for God's protection and crosses himself, which causes Satan to depart. Before leaving, Satan predicts that God

[91] Jensen 2012; Sowers 2017.

will never forgive Cyprian but will use and abandon him. Unnerved by Satan's threats, Cyprian ends his story here and asks his Antiochene audience if it is possible for him to receive God's forgiveness. The crowd remains silent for some time, but someone eventually begins to speak. This is where the manuscript cuts off, thus ending Eudocia's *Confession* before Cyprian can be admitted into the Antiochene church.

Origins and Influences

At the beginning of this chapter, I suggested that the *Confession*, as a literary form, borrows from other apologetic texts, especially Plato and Apuleius' apologies. Unlike the apologetic tradition, in which the speaker maintains his innocence, Cyprian readily admits his guilt and asks for mercy from God and the Church. In this regard, Cyprian's *Confession* anticipates Augustine's *Confessions*. These generic influences, however, do not clarify the literary models behind the fictional magician Cyprian.

This section analyzes Cyprian's fictional or quasi-historical literary influences, comparable to the section in the previous chapter that examines how Justina's character is intertextually constructed from pre-existing exceptional Christian women, particularly Thecla. Cyprian is more complicated than Justina in a few essential ways. To begin with, the Antiochene portion of the Cyprian legend, namely the story about a magician who sends demons to seduce a young woman, borrows from a primarily Christian tradition, most evident in the *Acts of Andrew*, although there are also echoes to Lucian's *Philopseudes*.[92] This material lays the foundation on which the rest of the story, including Justina's character, is built. By intertextually engaging with the *APT* and basing Justina's character on Thecla, the Cyprian legend adds to the stock story (found in the *Philopseudes* and *Acts of Andrew*) a sub-plot about the late antique feminine ideal.

The non-Antiochene material, in contrast, borrows from stories about itinerant wonderworkers, especially those who travel to or from Egypt and Babylon. These include Pythagoras, Apollonius of Tyana, multiple characters from Lucian's *Philopseudes*, and (to a lesser extent) Jesus.[93] Of course, a rich scholarly tradition also situates Jesus as literary heir of these itinerant wonderworkers.[94] Unlike Justina's intertextually explicit imitation of Thecla, Cyprian does not directly point to any one of these literary figures or their stories. Instead, his

---

[92] I discuss the relationship between the Cyprian legend and the *Acts of Andrew* in the previous chapter.

[93] Nock 1927; Berenson Maclean 2004; Paschalis 2011.

[94] Rather than summarize the history of this debate, which began in antiquity, see the summary and bibliography in Martin 2005:119–126.

legend blends these various sources and turns him into a type of intertextual bricolage, a stock character of the itinerant wonderworker, initially hostile to Christianity but eventually won over through its superior power. As intertextual and ideological foil to these multiple classical characters, the literary Cyprian advances a late antique Christian polemic.

The life and legend of the first-century Pythagorean wonderworker, Apollonius of Tyana, survives primarily in his third-century *vita* written by Philostratus (hereafter *VA*), although some details are preserved in Iamblichus' *Pythagorean Life* and Lucian's *Alexander*.[95] Born into a typical aristocratic family, Apollonius receives his early education in his hometown of Tyana. At fourteen, he leaves Tyana for Tarsus to begin his formal training in rhetoric.[96] Realizing that he has no interest in oratory, he moves to Aegae to study philosophy. His claim to have studied every philosophical tradition is a commonplace coopted by Judeo-Christian intellectuals, especially Josephus and Justin Martyr.[97] At twenty, Apollonius returns to Tyana to administer his father's estate and give away his inherited wealth. Shortly thereafter, he travels across Cilicia, Pamphylia, Syria, and Arabia and participates in their local cults. According to Philostratus, Apollonius next visits (in order) Nineveh, Babylon, India, Babylon, Nineveh, Antioch, Seleucia, Cyprus, Asia Minor, Lesbos, Athens, Crete, Rome, Spain, Africa, Sicily, Greece, Chios, Rhodes, Alexandria, Ethiopia, Alexandria, Tarsus, Egypt, Corinth, Rome, Greece, Ionia, and Rome. While some of these destinations, such as India, Ethiopia, and Egypt, warrant extended stays, his visits are typically brief and spent participating in local festivals or revitalizing abandoned cults.

The occasional overlap of Apollonius and Cyprian's itineraries affords a fruitful contrast between them. For instance, during his first visit to Athens (*VA* 4.17–19), the Eleusinian hierophant forbids Apollonius' initiation by insisting that a sorcerer (γόης) would defile the sanctuary. He must wait until a later visit to be initiated into the Eleusinian Mysteries (*VA* 5.19). Like Cyprian, Apollonius visits Sparta (*VA* 4.27), where he perceives that the legendary Spartan lifestyle had been neglected. Under his supervision, the ephors purge effeminizing influences from the community and return Sparta to their traditional austere lifestyle (compare *VA* 4.31–34). Whereas Cyprian spends a decade in Egypt, Apollonius spends twenty years in Egypt (*VA* 6) studying under the Gymnosophists in

---

[95] For more on Apollonius, see Harris 1969; Dzielska 1986; Aitken and Berenson Maclean 2004; Jones 2006a; Bowie and Elsner 2009; Paschalis 2011; Robiano 2016. For the material preserved by Iamblichus and Lucian, see Gorman 1985.

[96] Marrou 1964:381–390; Morgan 1998:190–239; Cribiore 2001:220–244; Watts 2006:31; Reydams-Schils 2015.

[97] Josephus *Life* 1–12; Justin Martyr *Dialogue with Trypho* 2. See also Lamberton 2001.

Upper Egypt and Ethiopia. Since Philostratus goes to great lengths to distinguish Apollonius' activity from Greco-Roman magic, his *vita* contains few details about Egyptian rituals of power and, instead, emphasizes the wisdom and asceticism of Apollonius' Egyptian, Babylonian, and Brahman teachers. On the other hand, he includes episodes of Apollonius' extraordinary wonders that evoke the "miracles" accounts found in Jesus' biographies. When we compare the *VA* to the pseudepigraphic collection of epistles attributed to Apollonius, the competing images about him come into sharper focus.[98] For instance, in these epistles, Apollonius boasts a special relationship with gods and demons (*Epistle* 52, compare *VA* 4.44) and claims to be their equal or otherwise unique (*Epistle* 44, 48). This uniqueness allows him to perform those wonders one reads about in Philostratus' biography.

Despite Philostratus' efforts to depict Apollonius as a philosophical "do-gooder," the wonder-worker is always at hand: his Apollonius exerts control over disease/death (*VA* 4.45), demons (*VA* 4.20, 4.25, 4.43, 5.42, 6.27, 6.29, 6.43), and nature (*VA* 2.4, 2.14, 2.15, 2.33, 3.27, 4.13, 5.11, 5.35, 6.32). He also engages in necromancy (*VA* 4.11), performs incantations (*VA* 4.4), interprets visions (*VA* 1.23, 4.34), and demonstrates prophetic foreknowledge (*VA* 1.22, 1.34, 4.4, 4.6, 4.18, 4.24, 4.43, 5.7, 5.11, 5.13, 5.30, 5.37, 6.32, 8.26).[99] The similarities between these actions and those claimed by Cyprian bring Apollonius' biographies and the *Confession* into conversation. Like Apollonius, Cyprian is initiated into a series of mysteries and uses his skills to predict the future and alter reality. On the other hand, their narrative structures are markedly different. The *VA* is primarily an episodic account, whereby the reader learns about each of Apollonius' powers as the need arises; the *Confession*, in contrast, catalogues Cyprian's abilities in list form, organized geographically, without providing supporting episodes or narrative content, with the sole exception of the Justina episode.

Despite traveling to some of the same places as Apollonius, Cyprian's itinerary is not based on Philostratus' account. For example, the order of their destinations is different in at least one essential way: Cyprian begins in Greece before heading east, whereas Apollonius visits Greece only after traveling east to India. Pythagoras' eastern journey effectively authorizes his participation in Greek cults, especially when he revitalizes those in abeyance. Cyprian's childhood participation in Greek cults, in contrast, foreshadows his later participation in eastern magic. For Cyprian, traditional Mediterranean religions serve as a "gateway drug" to more powerful and nefarious rituals of power. Moreover, Cyprian visits Scythia, a destination not mentioned in Philostratus' *vita*, and he

---

98 Penella 1979; Jones 2006b.
99 Mead 1980:110–118; Dzielska 1986:85–127.

never travels to India. Studying under the Brahmans is arguably the most important part of Apollonius' world tour and a *sine qua non* for itinerant Pythagorean wonderworkers.

From a narrative level, Cyprian's *Confession* more closely parallels the life of Pythagoras, at least as it is depicted in his later biographies.[100] According to Iamblichus and Diogenes Laertius, Pythagoras is born in Samos, where his earthly father names him in honor of Apollo, his putative divine father. Cyprian, we remember, is similarly dedicated to Apollo as a young child. While Pythagoras' biographers present contradictory accounts about his early life and education, they agree that, as an adolescent, he is initiated into various mysteries, a further parallel to Cyprian's *Confession*. According to Iamblichus, Pythagoras leaves Greece/Asia, first for Syria, where he studies under the priest of Moses and is initiated into other Phoenician mysteries (*Pythagorean Life* 3). From there, he continues south to Egypt and studies astronomy, geometry, and various religious rituals from the Egyptian priests in Memphis (*Pythagorean Life* 4). From Egypt, he goes to Babylon, where he studies for twelve years under Chaldean Magi. When his studies are complete, he first returns to Samos and later travels throughout Greece to be initiated into local cults.

Pythagoras' itinerary (Greece/Asia, Syria, Egypt, Persia) is nearly identical to Cyprian's, with the exception of Cyprian's journey north to Scythia. Despite having never traveled to Scythia, Pythagoras learns Scythian culture and rituals of power from a Scythian "Hyperborean," Aberis, who gives him a magic arrow that allows him to fly and perform purification rites (*Pythagorean Life* 19). Aberis is depicted as a magician, skilled in *hieroskopia* (divination through examining entrails) but lacking *paideia*, which Pythagoras teaches him. For that reason, Cyprian's journey roughly follows a Pythagorean itinerary.

In addition to having similar destinations, Cyprian and Pythagoras master similar skills, albeit to different ends. During his eastern travels, Pythagoras learns prophecy, science, mathematics, astronomy and nature, and, in the Aberis episode, he learns to fly and to ritually cleanse cities. With these skills, he performs a number of wonders and can even control wild animals (*Pythagorean Life* 13). Like Philostratus, Pythagoras' biographers make a concerted effort to depict him as an exceptional and exceptionally powerful Greek philosopher. For that reason, his powers are frequently muted, at least in comparison to the *Confession*. That said, the legend of Cyprian's education depends, at least in part, on Pythagoras and Apollonius. As a gesture to Pythagoras, Cyprian learns astronomy, biology, numerology, and nature–essential skills of the Pythagorean

---

[100] For more on Pythagoras, see Carcopino 1968; Guthrie 1989; Riedweg 2005; Cardini 2010; Mele 2013.

philosopher. But like Apollonius, Cyprian also masters diverse arcana, including demonology, magic stones, and incantations. If Philostratus suppresses Apollonius' ability as a magician, the *Confession* underscores Cyprian's magical/demonic education.

Lucian's *Philopseudes*, or *Lover of Lies*, a satirical essay written as a philosophical dialogue about gullible people who place their trust in the supernatural, further clarifies Cyprian's literary influences.[101] The *Lover of Lies* is a treasure trove of Greco-Roman tropes about ancient magicians and witches, dating back to classical Athens. Many of these tropes can also be found within the *Confession*. For instance, Cleodemus, one of Eucrates' guests, regales his fellow diners with an account about a Chaldean wonderworker who once arrived in his town and performed various services for the community. These include curing a servant of a poisonous snakebite and ritually cleansing the farm of its snakes (*Lover of Lies* 12). This he accomplishes by drawing all the farm's snakes to him and blasting them with his breath. In addition to ridding farms of their reptile problem, he also helps lovelorn men seduce women (what Cleodemus calls "sending cupids after people"), engages in divination (invoking daemons), and reanimates corpses.

One of these services, that of erotic seduction, parallels the Cyprian legend in a few essential ways.[102] According to Cleodemus, while serving as tutor for Glaucias, a young aristocratic man, he learns that Glaucias was in love with Chrysis, a married woman (*Lover of Lies* 14). At his wits end, Glaucias, through Cleodemus' encouragement, hires the Chaldean wonderworker to procure Chrysis for him. The Chaldean magician accomplishes this with a series of necromantic rituals, including invoking Glaucias' father, Alexicles, to give his blessing and invoking Hecate to draw down the moon. He next makes a clay Cupid, animates it, and sends it to find Chrysis, which it does. When the sun begins to rise, Hecate and the other spirits (φάσματα) return to Hades, and Chrysis returns to her husband.

Elsewhere in the *Lover of Lies*, Eucrates tells an autobiographical tale about his trip to Egypt (33–36), where he studies in Memphis under a temple scribe. This narrative, one ancient source for the sorcerer's apprentice motif, also parallels Cyprian's journey.[103] As is to be expected in Lucian, Eucrates' account is hardly serious. He relates how his Egyptian teacher ritually animates objects to perform various domestic duties. By replicating the ritual, Eucrates successfully animates a pestle to draw water for him, only to discover that he does not know the second half of the ritual to un-animate it. Chopping the pestle in half

[101] Ogden 2007:105–114.
[102] Ogden 2007:109–111.
[103] Ogden 2007:231–270.

only makes matters worse and results in two animated water-drawing pestles. What follows is a comedic scene of a nearly flooded house and a distraught Eucrates that culminates with the arrival of the Egyptian priest and his refusal to continue Eucrates' education. The punchline of the story is that Eucrates still remembers only the first half of the animation ritual and, as a result, cannot prove the veracity of his account.

In the previous chapter, I argue that the *Conversion* borrows from early Christian prose narratives and their depictions of the feminine ideal to present Justina as the ideal, urban woman, superior to her literary models. Rhetorically, Justina out-Thecla's Thecla, and emerges as a remixed version of the ideal late antique Christian woman. By intertextually contrasting Cyprian with Pythagoras, Apollonius, Cleodemus' Chaldean, and Eucrates, the *Confession* has the opposite effect. As a former itinerant wonderworker, Cyprian critiques his models and their reliance on spiritual arcana, which he characterizes as demon worship. This sets the convert Cyprian against his intertextual competitors, who, by association with their shared educations and participation in religious rituals, are discredited as equally deceived. In this regard, the rhetorical force of Cyprian's language is similar to Lucian's, although the *Confession* generally eschews parody and satire.

Part of the rhetorical force of the *Confession* is the central role of space and place in Cyprian's account. In Greco-Roman literature, the itinerant wonderworker trope depends on their foreignness, their otherness. For that reason, ritual experts originate or study from cultures known for magic and other mystical skills, such as astrology and divination. By studying under Egyptian priests in Memphis, Chaldean Magi in Babylon, or Indian Brahmans, these wonder-workers legitimate their power and master skills unknown and inaccessible to those in Greece or Antioch. This trope influences the biographies of Jesus, who, as a child, travels to Egypt and meets itinerant Magi. Like Jesus, Cyprian undermines this tradition through the act of alluding to it. Initially effective, Egypt and Babylon magic are shown to be illusionary and ultimately ineffective. By repeatedly calling his studies demonic, Cyprian, as narrator, situates them as transgressive and harmful.

If magicians travel the world to study demonic smoke and mirrors, Justina, by contrast, possesses a superior power without leaving her house. This is emphasized repeatedly in both the *Conversion* and *Confession*. She controls, thwarts, and undermines the learned Cyprian, his legion of demons, and even Satan himself simply by performing the sign of the cross from the safety of her bedroom. Without studying from experts, she heals the sick and saves Antioch from the plague. By invoking Justina as his new model, Cyprian adopts a new approach toward spiritual power, one available to all individuals, even young virgins who only leave their house to attend church. As a Christian, Cyprian performs wonders that help the Christian community and convert Antioch's remaining pagan population, but these wonders are accomplished through God's power, not Cyprian's pan-Mediterranean studies. This polemic against Greek cults and foreign cultures, even very ancient ones, underscores Cyprian's embrace of Christianity and its increasing hostility to other religious traditions.

Conclusion

WHEN JUDY CHICAGO'S installation piece, *The Dinner Party*, debuted in 1979, it was rightly hailed as a tour de force of feminist art. Choosing which women to represent at the thirty-nine settings around the table must have been so difficult that the names of another 999 women were written on porcelain tiles and displayed on the ground under the table. For someone to be considered for the Heritage Floor, Chicago stated that she must have made a significant contribution to society, must have attempted to improve conditions for other women, and could serve as a role model for future generations. Found among these 999 exceptional women is the name of Aelia Eudocia.

It is not entirely clear what information about Eudocia had been made available to Chicago and her research team. In fact, one wonders if Eudocia might have been considered for one of the thirty-nine table settings, had more scholarly research been produced about her and her poetry when Chicago was creating *The Dinner Party*. The first major wave of critical studies on Eudocia and her late antique milieu emerged shortly after the art world read her name on the Heritage Floor. These critical studies only underscore what Chicago and her team already recognized: Eudocia's significant contributions to fifth-century society, her attempts to improve conditions for other women, and her service as a role model for future generations. Housed now in the Brooklyn Museum just down the street from my Brooklyn apartment and the CUNY campus where I teach, *The Dinner Party* has served as an inspiration for this project. Each time I visit the installation, I am drawn back to Eudocia's name, where I can reflect on her life and poetry in the context of 1037 other exceptional women.

It is my hope that this book has contributed in some small way to our understanding about Eudocia and her impact on late antique society. As I stated at the outset, my aim here has been intentionally selective, to focus on Eudocia's surviving works and to allow her words to guide the organization and content of each chapter. In this final section, I would like to highlight a few salient features of Eudocia's poetry that have emerged over the course of this book.

Eudocia's Antiochene speech and her verse panegyric at Hammat Gader reveal her active role and creative agency in urban and rural euergetism. She took the opportunity during her brief visit to Antioch to praise the city. This was no empty gesture on her way to Jerusalem. She communicated through this speech her interest to serve as a local *euergete*, a financier of building projects and a sponsor of alimentary programs. That Eudocia inaugurated her social activity in Antioch with a complex Homeric allusion underscores both how deeply she had internalized her classical education and the central place that the Homeric epics still held in the public life of the late antique East. Her allusion to *Iliad* 6.211 and the wider conversation between Glaucus and Diomedes imply the creative blending of an *euergesia-xenia* relationship. Eudocia's audience was equally familiar with Homer and responded by commissioning two honorific statues for her, one gold, the other bronze, a veiled reference to the exchange of armor that inaugurates Glaucus and Diomedes' *xenia*. For her part in this reciprocal relationship, Eudocia helped support the physical needs of the city.

Eudocia's seventeen-line epigraphic panegyric at Hammat Gader is equally informative and provides a complementary picture of her Antioch speech. In my reading, this poem reveals Eudocia's religious sensitivities when interacting within religiously diverse spaces. By structuring her panegyric as an ekphrastic tour of the bath, she highlights its multiple pools and furnaces and, in so doing, commemorates its traditional patrons, healing divinities, or associated religious figures, Antoninus Pius, an unnamed patriarch, a nun, Elijah, Galatea, and Hygieia, among others. Each of these figures represents some part of the late antique world, unified by their role at Hammat Gader, where they support or provide rest, relaxation, and physical healing. Eudocia opens this list with an allusion to the Catalogue of Ships in *Iliad* 2, which gives her entire poem an epic quality and the figures in her list epic significance. At the same time, when honoring the bath's furnace, Eudocia compares it to an ocean, language that, by late antiquity, was commonly used to honor local *euergetes*.

After praising the furnace's euergetistic aptitude and commemorating key social, spiritual, and political figures associated with the space, Eudocia directs her attention to a euergetistic god who, as benefactor par excellence, addresses human cares and needs. The language used for this unnamed deity is explicitly monotheistic yet without Judeo-Christian theological or Christological terminology. In fact, her words evoke classical and social origins by simultaneously gesturing to the *Homeric Hymn to Hephaestus* and honorific speeches for late antique *euergetes*. This inherent ambiguity allows each reader to see her own ideology represented or valued in Eudocia's words, even if the god she refers to is a Christian one. Although therapeutic springs, along with countless other sacred spaces, were heavily contested during late antiquity, especially as Christianity grew in power and influence, this poem represents a subtle, less heavy-handed moment in that process. Eudocia's approach here at Hammat

Gader stands in contrast to her language in the *Confession*, where she advances an explicitly competitive rhetoric against traditional Greco-Roman religions, especially mystery cults and magic.

If Eudocia's pilgrim poetry evinces her socio-political milieu, her Homeric cento typifies her literary agenda. As one of approximately two dozen centos or biblical paraphrases written during late antiquity, Eudocia's cento straddles these two poetic modes. Although most ancient centos survive with little historical context or information about their authors, the prefatory material accompanying the centos of Ausonius, Proba, and Eudocia—introductions written by each poet—allows us to situate Eudocia's cento more precisely within this established tradition. Following Proba and the Christian Latin cento she had available to her, Eudocia describes her poem as a holy product, a sacred text comparable to the Bible. Proba positions her cento against its Vergilian source-text and legitimizes the Holy Spirit as voice of poetic inspiration, a late antique vestige of the prophetic tradition from the Hebrew Bible. Eudocia, in contrast, defends her credentials as cento poet, with a particular focus on her meticulous adherence to the Bible. That both Eudocia and Proba prioritize Christian over classical content, despite overtly borrowing from this classical material to paraphrase the Bible, underscores the complementary nature of both their poetic agenda and poetic mode.

Eudocia's explicit reflections on cento aesthetics make it particularly instructive to compare her preface with Ausonius' preface to the *Cento Nuptialis* (*PCN*). Although the *PCN* is widely viewed as outlining a guide for cento poetics, in my view, Ausonius uses his prefatory epistles, first and foremost, to advance a carefully curated literary etiquette. By reading the *PCN* as another paratextual reflection by Ausonius about the process of writing and circulating ludic poetry, the ludic language he uses about cento poetry complements his wider literary program and does not characterize centos per se. Additionally, when the performative background that Ausonius attributes to the cento, a poetic competition between the emperor Valentinian and himself, is interpreted against his poetic etiquette, it becomes little more than another self-deprecation, common in Ausonius' prefaces, not a straightforward, historically reliable account.

That said, Ausonius does elaborate on the "rules" for composing an acceptable cento, rules that he himself violates multiple times. For that reason, these didactic metaliterary reflections may better fit within his light-hearted manner of communicating with friends. According to Ausonius, centos should avoid using two whole sequential Vergilian lines; three whole sequential lines were considered ridiculous (*nugae*), language found whenever Ausonius describes his poetry. He compares the process of composing a cento to the *stomachion*, a game played by configuring fourteen bones into various images. Taking Ausonius' analogy to its inevitable conclusion, the accomplished cento poet so successfully positions lines or hemistichs of Homer or Vergil that her readers are unable to see the original context of each piece. This model for reading centos explicitly differs from that advanced by Proba and her community.

Despite having radically divergent ideas about the literary value of centos, Ausonius and Eudocia do share a few assumptions about what constitutes a good cento. First, like Ausonius, Eudocia knows that she should avoid using sequential Homeric lines, and she goes to great lengths to explain why she violated this rule. Concerned that readers familiar with Tatian's cento would fault hers because it contains double lines (while Tatian avoided them), Eudocia defends herself by pointing out that, unlike Tatian, who simply continued narrating the Trojan War, she relates a biblical story and biblical characters not found in the Homeric epics. In so doing, she subtly positions her epic as superior to that of Homer, a rhetorical strategy precisely different from that of Proba, who claims to recover latent Christian content hidden within Vergil's words.

Second, Eudocia and Ausonius take an active, critical approach to centos and assume that one can identify and remove inferior pieces of the whole. Ausonius explicitly encourages Paulus to assess his cento so thoroughly that, if needed, he should remove Vergilian lines and return them to their original context. Claiming to have done something similar, Eudocia's preface can be read as a detailed account of her critique and redaction of Patricius' cento, which, she claims, contained untruthful or unharmonious elements. By removing these deficiencies and adding harmony to the poem, Eudocia salvages the poem and becomes co-author of the cento, although she repeatedly emphasizes Patricius' authorial hand. Finally, Eudocia describes centos with a blend of visual and oral/aural imagery, which suggests that she and her imagined audience engage centos as physical, readable objects and performed, heard songs. This aural and textual imagery complements Proba and Ausonius' paratextual comments and informs us about the various ways centos were experienced in late antiquity.

Eudocia's verse paraphrase of the Samaritan woman at the well story from the Gospel of John underscores her active hand when rewriting the Bible. In order to update the story for her fifth-century audience, who likely would not have been aware of the socio-cultural conflicts between first-century Jews and Samaritans or the immediate impact resulting from Jesus' ministry to the Samaritans, Eudocia omits these first-century details. She also removes secondary characters from the story, including Jesus' disciples, to focus more directly on the unnamed woman, no longer marked as Samaritan, and on her sexuality, a topic still relevant to late antique Christians. Following late antique sexual norms, Eudocia's woman at the well is given two options: celibacy or marriage. Having chosen neither, she finds herself in a liminal and sexually ambiguous position that thereby elicits Jesus' criticism. This focus on the woman's marital status and sexuality is further complicated by Jesus' "gift of God" metaphor, retained by Eudocia from the Gospel of John but transposed in this episode as a suitable replacement for the living water and food metaphors found in the prose original. This gift imagery becomes increasingly conflated with a marriage gift or dowry, which, from a narrative perspective, symbolically transforms the unnamed woman into Jesus' bride, a common image used for Christian virgins. From the perspective of late antique Christian sexual ethics, this symbolic transformation resolves the woman's sexual ambiguity by providing her with an appropriate sexual status.

The Homeric passages from which Eudocia borrows most heavily when creating the Samaritan woman episode further complicate this reading of the unnamed woman and her sexuality. Specifically, those line clusters originally about Nausicaa and Penelope—two female characters defined by their sexual relationship with Odysseus and other men—underscore the sexual tension found within the prose original and its retelling by Eudocia. A comparison between the unnamed woman and Penelope/Nausicaa potentially undermines any criticism leveled against this woman, since she is intertexually built from lines originally about exceptionally chaste female characters. According to this reading, Jesus' criticism is misplaced. On the other hand, this intertexual play can also be read proleptically as anticipating the woman's redemption after her interaction with Jesus at the well. Since each cento contains nearly unlimited intertextual potential, each reader ultimately must identify and reconcile those complications that inevitably emerge when one retells the Bible with Homeric/Vergilian lines.

Eudocia's second longest extant poem, her three-book epic on the fictional magician Cyprian of Antioch, recounts his conversion to Christianity and his martyrdom during the Diocletianic persecutions. The first book, or *Conversion*, recounts how Cyprian is hired by Aglaidas, an Antiochene aristocrat, to seduce the newly converted Justa, who had already rejected Aglaidas' multiple marriage proposals and had fought off his rape attempts. Cyprian invokes three increasingly powerful demons, culminating in Satan himself, to seduce Justa, but they prove powerless against her prayers and the sign of the cross. As a result of these defeats, Cyprian recognizes God's superior power and decides to convert. As a newly converted Christian, Cyprian redirects his spiritual power toward preaching, healing the sick, and converting Antioch's remaining pagan population. Quickly advancing through the ranks, Cyprian is eventually appointed bishop of Antioch. The second book, or *Confession*, shifts back to Cyprian's conversion moment and takes the form of a speech, in which Cyprian outlines where he learned magic. This journey begins in Athens and

Greece, where Cyprian was raised. As a young man, however, he leaves Greece and travels to Scythia, Egypt, and Babylon, where he rises through the demonic ranks and is eventually appointed Satan's lieutenant. His education complete, Cyprian settles in Antioch, where he provides various services, including erotic magic, for the local community. Cyprian summarizes his assault against Justa, at this point renamed Justina, and his realization of God's authority. This is where our manuscript ends, cutting short Cyprian's inclusion into the Church and the story of his death, alongside Justina, the content of the now lost third book of Eudocia's epic, the *Martyrdom*.

Despite the *Conversion*'s ostensible focus on the Cyprian legend, my reading concentrates on Eudocia's creation of Justa as the story's protagonist and most intertextually rich character. Unlike her literary predecessors, Thecla and Perpetua, Eudocia's Justa experiences little social drama and remains safety ensconced in third-century Antioch. In this regard, Justa's story is one in which "nothing really happens," despite her survival of multiple sexual assaults and demonic attacks. Whereas Thecla and Perpetua undergo gender transformations or bodily modifications, a common late antique literary motif about exceptional women, Justa experiences no gender-bending or gender-blending. In other words, Eudocia creates a Justa who, while explicitly emulating Thecla, is nothing like her. That said, Justa is no two-dimensional character. Rather, her agency is doubly exceptional. Rather than undergoing gender transformations or bodily modifications, Justa imposes these same changes on her male relatives (father) and opponents (Aglaidas and Satan). In so doing, she transforms her father's *oikos* and the liminal space between her house and church into a feminine one, where an explicitly feminine Justa imposes her femininity on those around her. Instead of experiencing social displacement and reintegration like Thecla and Perpetua, Justa displaces others and, in comparison to her intertextual models, emerges as an even more exceptional model, a new feminine ideal.

This reading of Justa complements the treatment of the Samaritan woman at the well episode discussed in the second chapter. Taken together, Justa and the Samaritan woman reveal two ways Eudocia actively retold women's stories. In both cases, she gives her female characters an agency subtly removed from male ones. This is particularly the case with Justa, who manifests autonomous power when she openly defies her family, when she fights off Aglaidas, and when she defeats Satan and his demonic horde. Such exceptional female agency also appears in the woman at the well, who, as a remixed biblical Penelope-Nausicaa hybrid, advances the narrative trajectory by preaching the gospel to her fellow citizens. Her evangelistic speech anticipates, albeit anachronistically, exceptional female characters from the gospel tradition, such as Mary Magdalene, and from early Christian literature, including Thecla, Perpetua, and Justa.

In structure and aim, the *Confession* differs greatly from the *Conversion*. Throughout his Mediterranean tour, Cyprian catalogues his religious and magical education, but his account more directly reflects late antique religious competition and early Christian attempts to discredit rival traditions. As internal narrator, Cyprian repeatedly reminds his audience that each part of his education was empty, powerless, and demonic. This is no reliable picture of late antique paganism or guide for learning magic. Even if Cyprian's account contains some verifiable information about actual rituals of power or historical religious practices, the narrative's underlying competitive rhetoric undermines these details. Rather than mine the text for historically reliable information, my approach examines how Eudocia advances this pro-Christian ideology to her fifth-century audience interested in imagining how the Mediterranean world became "Christianized." Her literary interests with the Cyprian story, to the extent they are recoverable, must be set alongside her politic language at Hammat Gader, as discussed in the first chapter. If Eudocia chose to advance a more nuanced religious identity when it served her purpose, she could just as easily write an epic full of pro-Christian rhetoric and anti-pagan invective.

One way the *Confession* advances its competitive rhetoric is by constructing Cyprian from multiple, well-known itinerant wonder workers, including Pythagoras, Apollonius, and Lucian's Eucrates and Chaldean sorcerer. More than literary models for Cyprian's journey across the Mediterranean, these figures also serve as negative types who remain fully entrenched in their "pagan" ways. By gesturing to these itinerant wonder workers, Cyprian deviates from them through his decision to convert. Here Eudocia's Justa has a different ideological function than her Cyprian. Neither are original characters; in fact, they are both built on well-established literary types. Comparing Justa with her literary predecessors allows her to emerge as an even more exceptional figure, whereas Cyprian's exceptionalism is limited to a specific deviation from his models. Thus, Justa's exceptionalism is made manifest by her entire Christian life, while Cyprian's exceptionalism comes through the single act of conversion. Leading up to their deaths, however, both Cyprian and Justa dedicate their lives to serving Antioch's citizens and meeting their physical and spiritual needs. In this regard, Eudocia's personal investment in euergetistic projects in Antioch dovetails with her literary characters.

It has been nearly forty years since Judy Chicago debuted *The Dinner Party* and the art world was introduced, some for the very first time, to the name Aelia Eudocia. Since then, so much more of Eudocia's poetry has been made available to interested readers through the discovery of new poems and the publication of critical editions and translations. Hardly a household name, Eudocia remains one of antiquity's best surviving yet least studied female poets, and much hard work still remains. Countless avenues of research about her poetry remain open for future generations of scholars. Through this book, I hope to have contributed to our understanding of Eudocia by focusing on her actual words and allowing them to guide my analysis. As a woman who made significant contributions to fifth-century society and helped improved conditions for other women, Eudocia has much to teach twenty-first-century readers, especially those courageous enough to challenge contemporary social, religious, and literary boundaries.

Appendix
Eudocia's *Martyrdom of Cyprian*

Book 1: The Conversion

Proem

1*[1]   When God in heaven brought light to earth
and the true voice of wondrous men was accomplished,
a life-producing radiance filled the whole world
through the words of (other) prophets, the evangelists.
5*   For all robust men embraced one God,
the Heavenly Father, Lord of all, and his Son,
and in the name of the Holy Spirit were washed with water
from the many sins staining their bodies.

Narrative Proper

Once upon a time, there was a venerable girl named Justa.
10*   Her father was Aedesius and her mother, Cledonia,
from the majestic city that Antiochus founded.
Near that city is a laurel-crowned field, pleasant to behold,
and mighty cypress trees wave their boughs,
and silver drops of holy Castalia drip.
15*   There was a certain man, Praulius, the Christ-bearer,
an exceptionally holy man and prudent minister of God,
crowned with good cheer and faith.
He studied the prophetic books and always sang

---

[1]   In order to facilitate a comparison with the Greek editions of Bevengi and Salvaneschi, I maintain their line numbers. Salvaneschi, of course, did not have in his possession the first 99 lines of the *Conversion*. To distinguish line numbers in Bevegni's edition (the first 99 lines of the *Conversion*) from those in Salvaneschi's edition (the final 322 lines), the first 99 lines of the *Conversion* are marked with an asterisk.

the good faith and the holy voice of the prophets.
20*   The noble girl continuously heard him—
for there was a light-bearing window nearby—as she looked from her
        bedroom
into the house of the agreeable minister.
She heard about the great acts of God, the body
that God took on, the message of the great and noble prophets,
25*   the travail of the renowned and glorious Virgin Mary.
She heard about the Magi, how they venerated the glorious Son of
God by the beautiful shining star, which
with its divine light revealed Him lying in a manger;
about the truth and the heavenly citizens'
30*   divinely orchestrated sound of amazing praise to the Lord;
about the awesome power of the divine cross, and how
a mortal race emerged from the dead because Christ suffered;
about how, after His death, He met his disciples;
how He divulged things ordained for each of His followers;
35*   how He returned to His eternal Father's house
and sat on a throne to His right in a position of authority.

The arrow of divine love shot (all) this into the girl's heart,
and she could no longer hide her burning passion within
but desired to see the appearance of the holy man
40*   and to learn the whole truth from his mouth.
And when she did not find a way, she said to her dear mother,
"Listen to your little girl, mother.
We are in distress, because we trust false and wretched demons.
They are made of stone, fresh hewn trees,
45*   burnished gold, radiant silver,
or of the white bones of dead animals
by the hands of strong men. If an
Israelite were here, he would publicly
and effortlessly smash them with a word or prayer."
50*   Cledonia grew angry and, with kind thoughts for demons,
said, "... may your father never
hear your opinions." Justa replied hurtfully,
"Dear mother, you should know this, as well as my God-opposing
        father,
that, since I am struck in my heart with love for God,
55*   I search for Christ His Son, who, according to His Father's testimony,

rules for ever and ever,
the only-begotten Son, almighty Christ, is always present."
And when she said these things, she went back to her bedroom,
as was her habit, to speak intimately with the immortal Christ.

And when dark night covered the paths of the earth,
60*   the mother and father of the wise child, Justa,
(the text is missing some lines here)
his dear and shrewd spouse addressed him first,
relating to him the whole truth about the girl.
In the silent night, they fell asleep at the hour
65*   that compels sweet sleep upon people.
And in their sleep, angels stood gathered round,
and they saw men in their house, more than a hundred,
bearing torches, and Christ, standing in the middle of the angels,
saying, "Come, both of you,
70*   near to me, so I may give you the right to heaven."
The gates of Aedesius' eyes were loosed,
and fleeting, anxiety-banishing sleep left the man.
Terrified, Aedesius' dear heart leapt up.
He took his dear wife, along with the respected girl,
75*   in his hands and went to the holy house of God.
Traveling with the faithful and righteous Praulius,
he stood before the priest of Christ,
the famous Optatus,
and earnestly accomplished the affair: at once with his feet, he
      trampled
80*   his idol, and everyone began to pray in unison
that the one performing the mystery would give them the seal of
      eternal life.
But he refused, until he learned about the
divine message and compassionate girl's desire for Christ.
And Aedesius immediately cut his hair on both sides
85*   from his head and chin—for he was a priest of powerless
idols. They did not let go of the feet of the one performing the
      mystery
until they received the blameless seal,
and Aedesius obtained the position of presbyter,
which he held for twelve whole months plus six,
90*   and then he left human cares behind.

But his holy child went to the houses of God unceasingly.

There was a certain wealthy man, Aglaidas,
extremely well born, who excelled in cunning and
whose heart was possessed by the lawless desire for idols.
95* Upon seeing the very lovely girl habitually rushing to
the houses of almighty God, he was distracted in his thoughts,
and he sent many men and women
to beg her parents that he would take
the holy girl as an equal partner in his bedroom.
1² But she grievously sent away all the young men,
choosing the Lord Christ as her only suitor.
But (Aglaidas) gathered a crowd, since he intended
to defile the holy child by force among the Lord's seats.
5 Those pursuing her shouted loudly,
and everyone rushed out of the rooms with weapons
and made Aglaidas' infantry vanish.
But, because he held pure lust in his heart,
as if struck with blindness, he hid himself to try to grab the girl.
10 But she immediately performed the powerful sign of Christ,
threw the villain on his back, and, with her hands, tore
Aglaidas' body, as well as his cheeks and sideburns.
She tore up his beautiful clothes, and she made him a laughingstock
      to everyone.
After running the same course as glorious Thecla
15 by doing these things, Justa returned to the house of God.

But Aglaidas grew angry and requested of an evil man,
Cyprian, the counselor of impious magic,
by offering to him two talents of gold
and shining silver, that he forcibly compel
20 the virgin, because she was unwilling to consent to sex—
Aglaidas did not know Christ's unflagging power.
The magician pitied the miserable man and, with an invocation,
effortlessly summoned an irksome, evil-working demon.
Arriving immediately, he said, "Why do you call me? Speak!"
25 He answered, "The love for one Galilean girl
horribly tames my heart. Tell me, whether you are

---

2 Here begins the text as edited by Salvaneschi.

powerful enough to bring her to my bed, for I deeply desire her."
The dim-witted adversary agreed to grant this hopeless thing.

And Cyprian directly addressed the villain,
30 "Tell me your accomplishments, so that I may have confidence."
And the demon answered, "I was once the best of the angelic ranks,
but, in obeying my father, I abandoned the highest Lord
of the seven-vaulted sphere. All that I have done,
you shall know— I will relate it. The foundations of the pure heaven
35 through my wickedness I myself shook up, dividing it in two,
and I cast an array of the heavenly host to earth.
I deceived Eve, the mother of mortals, by force;
I separated Adam from delightful paradise;
I myself made the hand of Cain fratricidal;
40 I drenched the earth with blood, and the earth bears thorny
and meager fruit for the race of mortals, all because of me.
I accomplished wonders inimical to God—I made
beds adulterous, I beguiled the human mind
to worship feeble idols, and I inspired men
45 to sacrifice to a horrid bull.
I myself wickedly urged the Hebrews to stretch on a cross
the mighty Word of God, the eternal Son.
I have confounded cities and thrown down their high walls.
With a dance, I derail many marriages with strife.
50 Since I have accomplished all these evils and countless others,
how will I not get this holy and intelligent girl?"

And Cyprian said to the baneful demon, the rejoicer in evil,
"Take this herb, and, in a circle, sprinkle the room
of Aedesius' daughter; I will come later
55 and will place my father's mind into her heart.
As if in a trance, she will obey whatever you want."

At that same time, the pious virgin, with her face to the ground,
in the third hour of the night, sang of the noble God.
But, when the girl deep in her heart began to tremble
60 and perceived the evil worker's treachery
as a fiery burning in her kidneys, she quickly set her thoughts on
her longed-for Lord. With her hand, she quickly crossed
her whole body and yelled,

"Lord of all, glorious God, Father of the immaculate child,
65 Jesus Christ, You who bound the Tartarean,
monstrous serpent in its shadowy lair,
dearest Lord, and You who saved all those chained by him.
With Your hand You delineated the starry sky, and,
in the midst of chaos, You planted the earth on its watery
      foundation.
70 You supplied fiery brands to Titan's progeny,
You yoked the silvery moon to the night,
You fashioned mortal man precisely in Your image
and enjoined him to delight in the garden's pleasure.
By the advice of the most shameful beast, the serpent,
75 man was separated from the wooded plain, but You again
sought and saved him, thanks to Your merciful heart, Lord.
Through Your cross, You made amends for his punishment,
And, in the name of Christ, You cleansed all his sufferings (sins).
For this reason, the inexhaustible earth shines forth.
80 Heaven has been firmly established, the earth has been fixed,
and waters pour forth—the whole course from beginning to end
knows that You are the ruler of all. Come then, save
Your servant according to Your mighty will; let shameful
disgrace not conquer me. O everlasting author, for Your sake
85 I desire to remain a holy virgin.
I love You with all my heart, blessed Jesus,
my praiseworthy master, because You lit
a blazing torch of desire for You and placed it in my heart.
Therefore, never hand Your servant over to
90 the enemy, the abominable, lawless anti-God.
Blessed one, never allow me to transgress Your decrees,
but ward off the conceited sinner, the deceiver."

Having said these things, she quickly
armed her body with the sign of God and immediately set
95 the grotesque demon to flight by saying Christ's name.
She completely routed the scoundrel.

Deeply embarrassed, he returned to the magician.
Cyprian asked the demon, "Where is the girl
I ordered you to bring here as quickly as possible?"

100   And the enemy replied, "Do not ask me about all this openly,
for I saw the terrible sign and became afraid."

But the magician smiled, trusting in his nefarious deeds.
Again, he called another dreaded demon, Beliar.
He said to Cyprian, "I have learned of your command

105   and of this one's dismal failure. Therefore, my father has sent me
as an aide to your distress." Immensely pleased, the magician
answered, "This is the plan, demon: the entire house of the holy
           maiden
bind with a potion. And I will go behind you.
I intend to persuade her quickly." The demon departed, but the most
           holy,

110   devout virgin in the middle of the night was praying
to the Lord and issued forth these words from her mouth,
"In the middle of the night, I rose from my bed
to confess, o Great One, the sins I have committed
before Your justice and unerring judgment.

115   Ruler of creation, endless giver of mercy,
lawgiver and lord of the heavenly host,
before whom the earth trembles and who overthrows
and shames the strength of the nefarious enemy. Father Abraham's
sacrifice You accepted as a splendid hecatomb;

120   You threw down Baal and slew the dragon;
through Your pious servant, Daniel,
You taught the whole Persian race Your divinity.
Through Your only-begotten son, Christ,
You set everything right and established light on earth;

125   after His death, You led dead people back into the light.
I beg you, Lord, do not allow me to come upon evils,
but guard my body, Lord, so that it may be forever unharmed,
and give me the burning torch of virginity,
so that I may know the bridal chamber with my husband,

130   Christ, and I will honor the vows I made—
for He has power and glory with honor. Amen."

While she prayed these things, the demon,
dejected with shame, fled because of her courage.
He returned to the magician, and Cyprian

135   asked, "Tell me demon, where is the girl I ordered you

to bring here?" The demon answered,
"The sign (of the cross), which I saw, conquered me with its power—
it is entirely horrible, overwhelming, unbearable."

Then Cyprian called another demon, more powerful still,
140   who rules all the others, the father of dark-eyed (creatures).
Cyprian said, "Are you such an insignificant weakling, that you will
      give up?"
And Satan bravely answered, "In a moment I will bring
that girl to you—you better be ready."
Cyprian answered, "Tell me the sign
145   by which you will have victory."
Satan said, "First, I will weaken her body with fever.
Then, on the sixth day, once I have antagonized her,
that night I will bring her ready for you."

The fool went and stood before the holy girl,
150   disguised as a young woman and wearing similar clothing.
Sitting on her bed, he said deceptively,
"I have come to you this very morning,
satisfied by my lovely virginity, because
Christ the Lord called me to be consecrated.
155   So, dear girl, tell me this: what reward is there
for lovely virginity, and what payment is offered—
I notice that you look like a corpse—
for a sun-scorched lifestyle and a bone-dry table?"
The esteemed virgin replied, "The immediate
160   prize is negligible, but a greater reward follows."
The plotter of evil said, "Was not Eve a virgin
in the plain of paradise with Adam?
But later, when she had intercourse in the bed
of the first-born, Adam, she was proclaimed mother of children.
165   From then, she produced the entire moral race
and learned all good things." At that very moment, Justa was about
to be persuaded by the demon to go outside,
and the insufferable one gleefully showed her the way.
But the moment she perceived the crafty enemy's deceit,
170   she immediately turned her thoughts to prayer, signed
her body with the cross, issued a call from her mouth,
and cast that guilty, oppressive thing out of her house.

Breathing a bit after the commotion, she said,
"Thank God. A fiery disease was snuffed out."
175 She prayed, "Christ, powerful Lord,
preserve my god-fearing body, Master.
In Your justice, pity me, and give
honor to Your name." The enemy returned once again
to the magician, downcast, terribly distressed.

180 And Cyprian struck him with reproaches,
"Surely you did not fear the sight of a young, doe-eyed girl?
Since you have seen her strength, tell me how great it is."
The enemy said, "Do not ask or request this of me.
I cannot relate how great a sign I saw.
185 Trembling terribly, I turned tail and quickly ran away.
But, if you want to learn more, you have to swear an unbreakable
      oath."
Cyprian answered and asked, "What sort of oath should I swear?"
Satan answered, "By all the powers
I control and possess." Hearing this, Cyprian immediately swore
190 that he would never abandon the arrogant one. Emboldened, Satan
said, "When I saw the sign of the cross of the crucified Christ,
I turned and fled." Cyprian responded,
"Come now, tell me, is He far stronger than you?"
The adversary answered, "Listen to me, and I will tell you the truth:
195 Everything we do here in shameful sin,
delivering mortals to error,
benefits everyone. But in yonder life,
there is a curved instrument of bronze that
lies aflame in their midst. On whomever sins,
200 human or angel, heavenly beings use this instrument to
bring that one to the judgment seat of the crucified Christ."

Cyprian responded, "All right, go away. I am
quickly falling in love with him. Obey me now. I
desire the one who rejoiced in the cross, so that I not suffer these
      things."
205 Satan replied foully, "You just swore an unbreakable oath,
do you want to break it?" Cyprian answered, "Tell me, scoundrel,
what oath did I just now swear to you?" Satan said,
"An oath by my strong powers." The magician responded,

"Enemy, I do not fear you or your deeds.

210 Tonight, I have learned the whole truth from you
because of the virgin's prayers and holy requests
and because of the mighty cross. You are powerless.
Now, on my limbs I place the powerful sign
that you have said is remarkably strong.

215 I also reject your friendship and renounce your counsels."
When he said these things, Cyprian gave honor to Christ
and drove out the shameful demon by saying, "Be gone.
I call upon Christ." The enemy immediately left.

Cyprian gathered his magical books and gave

220 them to strong slaves to carry to the house
of the immaculate God. He followed behind them.
Falling at the feet of the godly priest,
Anthimus, Cyprian supplicated him,
"Servant of the celestial God, I want

225 to enlist my heart in Christ's army and book." Anthimus angrily
answered him, "Away with your wickedness.
Are you not content to do what you want
at a safe distance? Stay away from the Lord's people.
The Almighty's power is invincible."

230 Cyprian responded, "I know in my heart
that Christ's power is effective and mighty.
Tonight, against a holy girl I sent
wicked demons to ensnare her strong-minded
good sense with deceptive bonds.

235 When she perceived them, through prayer and the sign of Christ
she forcefully defeated them. So, bear with me and have pity on me.
Respect your supplicant, most sacred of men, and receive
my books that I, a sinner, used to perform countless evils.
Burn them up and pity my soul."

240 Persuaded, Anthimus took the books and destroyed them all.
Blessing Cyprian, he sent him away with holy words
and strongly encouraged him to enter God's sheepfold.
Cyprian returned home,
destroyed his images of ineffectual idols,

245 and whipped his body throughout the dreary night,
saying, "How can I come before Christ's face,

when I have done so many evils? How can I praise God
with lips used to abuse others
by summoning vile demons?"
250   On the ground, he scattered ashes and begged for God's
mercy in silence, because he feared to raise his voice.

And when the bright, rosy-armed dawn
of the great Sabbath arrived, it was a festive occasion for everyone.
Cyprian came as a neophyte of the mighty God
255   to the holy gathering and humbly prayed,
"Lord, if I am your worthy servant,
grant that I may enter your house and hear a word
from the biblical texts that bodes well for me."
And, as he stepped into temple's threshold, David spoke,
260   the noble son of Jesse: "Behold, Lord, do not cast me aside,
o ruler, nor make it so that I am far from You."[3]
And the great prophet Hosea said these things
under inspiration: "Therefore, make sure he is not a slave."[4] And
      again
David said, "My eyes are set
265   upon the shining dawn that drives away gloomy night,
so that I may always follow your divine words."[5]
In another passage, Isaiah said, "May fear never trouble
your soul, my child, Jacob, whom I love
and selected as the preeminent race of people."[6]
270   God's messenger, Paul, said, "The Lord
Christ purchased us from the turbulent curse
of the first law."[7] And again, the prophet
David, best of lyre players, said, "Who can declare
the power of the immortal one and who can tell to every ear
275   the praises of the all-powerful one?"[8] Then, the Lord's book
of divine words was read, then the priest's
address, then the instructional word for men:
"Exit God's temple, you who are half-initiated."

---

[3]   Psalm 51:11 or (perhaps) Psalm 35:22.
[4]   Hosea 11:1 or (more likely) Isaiah 52:13.
[5]   Psalm 119:148.
[6]   Isaiah 44:1–2.
[7]   Galatians 3:13.
[8]   Psalm 106:2.

Cyprian calmly and silently remained seated,
280 and a certain deacon, Asterius, said to him,
"Exit the Lord's house." But Cyprian answered him,
"I am a servant of the crucified Christ; do you
drive me outside?" The deacon responded, "You are
not yet a fully-initiated servant of the almighty God."
285 Cyprian in turn said, "God is eternally alive
and alone reveals that wicked demons are disgraceful.
He saved the virgin and pitied my heart.
It is not right for me to leave this house
until I have come to faith in Christ."

290 Learning this, God's attendant quickly approached the priest
to tell him the news. The priest summoned Cyprian, as was fitting,
told him many hard words,
and asked him what he had done. He prayed so much that
he shook the cosmos created by God.
295 Finally, he purified him in the divine waters.

On the eighth day, Cyprian became a lector of the revered
books that speak of Christ. And on the twenty-fifth day,
he became a lesser deacon
and guarded the doors of the holy mystery.
300 Fifty days later, he was eminently worthy
of the deaconship. With power, he tamed
the ranks of the godless, impudent, and lawless
and healed terrible afflictions to human bodies.
Indeed, he led into the flock of Christ many
305 who rejected the blind faith of idols.
After a year, he took the post
of priest, and for sixteen years
he waited for the elder's seat.

Then, the blessed bishop Anthimus
310   summoned all the surrounding priests.
When he had told them the will of Christ,
while still alive, he gave the see to Cyprian.
A little while later, Anthimus went to heaven
and handed over the flock, which he had led, to the glorious man.

315 While Cyprian was overseeing the glorious house of God,
 he welcomed the virgin, appointing her deaconess.
 He no longer called her Justa but renamed
 her Justina the blameless and made her mother of all
 tender girls, servants of almighty Christ.
320 Cyprian saved many who had been led astray, the irreligious,
 and persuaded them to desire Christ. He diligently gathered them
 into the flock of the Lord who always has honor. Amen.

Book 2: The Confession

"You who care about the mystery of faith in
 the exalted Christ, see my fresh tears,
 so you may know where my deep pain comes from—
 I speak the truth, and I know that you know it.
5 You who delight in unseemly idols,
 pay attention, because I will point out their deceptions.
 There is no other human like me:
 so impious, so in league with demons,
 such a devotee of worthless idols,
10 as to learn what they are or their strength.

 I am that famous Cyprian, whose
 parents dedicated to Apollo while I was still a child.
 At a young age, I learned the sacred rites of the Beast,
 the stomach-traveling serpent. In my seventh year,
15 I was initiated to Phaethon Mithras,
 and I lived on the acropolis of the noble Athenians.
 I became a citizen, since this was pleasing to my
 parents, who raised me. In my tenth year,
 I lit the torch for the god, and I committed myself to the white
20 suffering of Kore. I also accomplished the serpentine initiations
 of Athena, who lives on the Acropolis. Being initiated as a temple
 servant,
 I went to the glen of Olympus, which ignorant people claim
 is the abode of powerless gods.
 There, I heard the echo and sound of certain words.
25 I beheld herbs and roots—an amazing sight it was—

things which shameless, evil demons hold office over, though
    without effect.
In that place, I perceived the seasons and changing winds.
I learned about many days, which certain rogues,
harsh adversaries, use to fabricate deceptive illusions.

30   I beheld a choir shamelessly singing,
and I saw others in a crowd, performing deeds of Ares.
I also saw ambushes of others and their malicious habits,
and I saw them distraught with fear. I also saw a vast
array of goddesses and gods, because I remained there

35   forty days and another eight after that.
From there, as if from mighty realms,
spirits traveling by air to the earth are sent forth
to make all nations do whatever evils they wish.
I ate a meal from the high branches of blossoming trees

40   once Phaethon had set. Going into my fifteenth year,
I was thoroughly taught about spirits and gods
by seven hierophants
and about empty deeds, the works of lawless demons.
My parents were exceedingly eager that I learn

45   everything on the earth, in the sky, and in the sea,
not only things used for the destruction of men
but also things about lush grass and well-stemmed
plants, and things that oppress man's feeble body,
and things the evil-minded enemy,

50   the ruler of this earth, discovered, the swift-minded serpent
who spitefully disregards the plan of the immortal Ruler.

From there, I came to Argos, the lush pasture of horses.
There was a festival of Dawn, wife of Tithonus, clad in white,
and I became an initiate of the air,

55   of the heaven with its many spheres, [- - -]
of the harmony of the waters and the well-fed earth,
from dewy streams to divine air.
I went as far as Elis, and,
in Sparta, I saw the stout figure of Artemis Tauropolos, in order to
    learn

60   accursed things: volatile nature and destruction,
written stones, cosmic symbols,
and ancient myths. But when I went to the land of Phrygia,

I became very wise and inspired. I
learned from inspecting entrails what was marked on the liver.
65 From the Scythians, I learned about birds and resounding signs,
as well as the wayward paths of animals
and the utterances of those who see the future.
I also learned about the sounds of wooden planks and stones,
as well as the inhumed voices of those long dead.
70 I learned about thuds from doors and palpitations of mortal cares.
I also learned about masses of blood that defile one's limbs
and when worms eat away at the joints.
I learned the exchange of myths, the rhythm of words,
the visible sufferings of the flesh, and the limits of nature.
75 I also learned vows, those true and untrue,
and schemes hostile to men.
No art escaped my notice—nothing chthonic, celestial
or under-worldly, no versatile apparition, no hidden mind,
nothing crafty, cunning, or skillful—
80 I learned everything as far as weak deception, impious deeds,
everything on earth like this.

After these things, when I entered my twentieth year,
I arrived in the land of shadowy men,
Egypt, and went to Memphis.
85 There, I attempted everything inappropriate for a human:
how apotropaic spirits relate to earthly races and how
they are invoked; what stars they desire,
both as a rule and in fact; how they are put to flight;
and how these same spirits keep the murky darkness.
90 And I learned which spirits are their opponents
and how many rulers of dreaded Erebus and enemies of God there
        are.
And I learned how these beings are similar in soul and body
to cattle and fish, as well as what things they care about
and what things they do: swift movement, knowledge,
95 memory, terror, skillful deception, footprints,
secret forgetfulness of many, deeds of the people,
and similar things. I also learned the trembling of the earth,
as well as the origin and roar of rain storms,
the swell of earth and sea—things which, in truth, were imitations,
100 illusions of the Immortal's wisdom.

In that place, I perceived the souls of strong and long-lived
mortals, the shameful monsters, the Giants,
whose souls are dreadfully crushed in the murky darkness.
In a vision, I saw how they bear the earth on their backs,
105 like a man bears a heavy burden of wood on his shoulders.
I saw demons have intercourse with crooked serpents,
and I perceived the biting winds, which bring death for those on
earth.
I saw roaming demons attack the material world
and cast numerous woes upon humans.

110 I saw the earth tortured by a demon
but not resting on unstable water
because of its supports and foundations.
I came to a place where the enemy change their form,
created by the serpent, because of his antagonism toward God's
power,
115 to distort all human life with misery.
From there, many spirits work
impiety against humans, consisting of equal elements, as they travel
the earth.
I also saw there a person possessed by evils,
suddenly come into conflict with a pious man—
120 a crazy person against a wise person, a dishonorable man against an
upright one.
That place had nothing holy nor any activity that should be chosen.

I saw there the gruesome, artificial image of Falsehood.
There was the triple appearance of hideous Lust:
bloody, charred, resembling froth and bile.
125 After that, I saw the likeness of Wrath, winged, wretched,
savage, like a wild animal. Then I saw Deceit,
relentless, secretive, adorned with duplicitous words.
I saw the disgusting image of Hatred, blind
but with four eyes on the back of his head
130 that shun the glorious sight of bright light.
Many feet stick out from his head—
they alone are terrifying. He has no stomach,
for he is ruthless and proceeds without emotion.
Jealousy and dreaded Envy are similar to one another,

135   but baneful Envy has a mouth like a shovel.
      I beheld Morosity, emaciated, nearly a corpse.
      She has many eyes, arrows for pupils,
      with a mind always set on revenge. And
      I saw the appearance of the demon Greed. Starting from the top, he
          has a head
140   that is narrow and long, and he has two mouths,
      one in his midriff and the other on his back.
      He feasts on solid earth and heavy rocks—
      insatiably hungry for flesh and consumed with evil.
      I saw Love for Wealth;
145   she has a greedy and sharp appearance—you would swear you
          saw a scythe.
      Her pupils are always hidden in her eyelids.
      Likewise, I saw Commerce, unsophisticated and quick roving,
      who carries on her shoulders the burden of every hope for wealth.
      I beheld the appearance of Vanity, who has a good spirit
150   and rich flesh. She is not just white bones.
      I saw Idolatry soaring high.
      At the back of her head, she has two thick wings
      which she apparently uses to protect everyone else, but
      which are unable to protect her own limbs.
155   I beheld the deceitful, heavy terror of Hypocrisy,
      who is entirely delicate and has a hollow breast,
      secretly putrefied, blasted by the winds when they bite.
      I also saw the appearance of Delirium, who simultaneously has
      two natures, that of a young man and woman.
160   She is nude, internally shameless, and impotent.
      I saw the wretched demon Recklessness, who has a brazen
      tongue by far larger than his other body parts.
      I also saw Insanity, who has a head like a nut,
      a vacuous soul that accomplishes everything under the sun.
165   Of all these terrible things I noticed one thing—
      their appearance as they shamelessly come down
      through the cosmos—those accursed, evil, monstrously terrible,
      three hundred and sixty-five
      demons of grievous passions who preside over
170   vain glory. I saw the mighty disgrace of Virtue
      and also of Wisdom and empty Justice,
      which they use to divert Greeks from wisdom.

For someone sees an image, and truth completely withdraws.
All of this is shadow and useless dust.
175   For in them, every vice works
to deceive many. But I myself am not supposed
to write endless books. By describing a few of my many deeds,
I have related to you my impiety.

But I will say this in addition: when I was
180   thirty years old, I left the land of shadowy men,
and I arrived at the city of the Chaldeans, an ancient people,
and was eager to learn the course of the air,
which they say rests on flames of fire,
but which learned men think rests on light.
185   There, I learned the periodic nature of stars—
just as if someone plucks an infinite herb from mere buds—
and the celestial ranks formed in battle formations.
They showed me the relationships and homes of each star,
their affection, their food and drink,
190   and their intellectual love dedicated to the light.
They showed me the layers of the silvery heaven,
three hundred and sixty-five of them.
There was among them a "demiurge" of visible nature.
And they provided an explanation: they too obeyed a leader.
195   They revealed to me the plan and the path of those
who conceal a way of life always concerned about hidden things,
and who are only appeased by sacrifices.
Others do not listen at all, nor do they care for libations,
but they only care about the vast expanse of light.
200   Thus, I saw why they continued to
trust in dark counsels—to give light
to dim stars by gradually mixing them.
I was completely astonished when I saw intermediaries,
because they, ethereal and dark, care about happiness.
205   I was amazed when I perceived their customs,
which they mutually establish with each other
by keeping faithful vows in their hearts.
There was piety, love, energy,
and a passionate desire to have intercourse with each other,
210   which their leader, that architect of evils, established.
He made them wise by drawing breath from the air

and an eloquent tongue from the fruitful earth.
With his infernal powers, he taught all the "tricks of the trade."
He blocked the whole line of the cosmos, trusting that
215 they would forget their nature and the loving God.
Cajoling, he put everything up for sale;
that evil-doer rules the earth by dissipating everything.
Believe me, I saw the demon himself
after supplicating him with many libations and sacrifices.
220 Believe me, when I saw him, I spoke with him
and heard his kind words. Among other things,
he called me a youth, beautiful in appearance, just like Jambres,
and an initiate, mighty in deeds, Jambres' equal.
He promised that I would become leader of the cosmos
225 by working with him, because he knew the deeds of my life.
Honoring me, he granted me a grievous troop
of wicked demons and said to me on my way out,
"Cyprian, you are a strong mortal." Rising from his chair,
he sent me forth and amazed the spectators.
230 From that time on, all his priests honored me just like him.
In appearance, he was like richly-worked gold,
with flashing eyes and long hair. On his head,
he wore a garland layered with precious stones,
whose brilliance and splendor illuminated that place.
235 His clothing had a similar embellishment. When he turned, he shook
        the earth.
Around his chair stood many shield-bearers,
holding their gaze to the ground, prepared in army formation.
He illuminated the earth like an Olympian god,
gleaming with stars and making plants grow.
240 By doing everything that God does,
he contends with the sovereign Immortal and his saints.
That is how he apparently deceives the mind of men,
totally feeble, he produces empty shadow,
from which demonic form appears and quickly disappears.
245 Shameful beings are interested in this activity—to be visible
and to take on solid power with flesh. For those who
want these things, libation and the scent of sacrifice provide them.
Dark shades sitting close-by draw smoke
from sacrifices as it rises into the air.
250 This smoke they put on like decorated cloaks,

like beautiful wool or delicate linen ware—
numerous shadowy apparitions from lofty temples—
they wear this air instead of truth.
For this reason, he even needs the sacrifice of an ant
255 and asks for water, rinds, fruits—
everything the nourishing earth produces—
that he might reveal to mortals a mere illusion.
Just as we see in our mind the appearance of the dead
and we seem to converse with those not present,
260 in the same way, the adversary plants his image
in his initiates. He places this image around the faces
and bodies of idols which have no strength.
He pours forth a great storm sure enough, but it is false,
like making fire similar to icy snow,
265 or producing a fish that you can see but not eat,
or radiant gold to be the partner of wretched poverty.
The imitator also fashions material objects:
cities, bedrooms, forested plains,
shaded glens, man-nourishing fields,
270 decorated bedcoverings that mortals make,
things that bring blood-lusty demons all sorts of shadowy things.
Likewise, even sleep-walkers see clearly when they are fast asleep.
These are the works of the sinful demon, this is the work
of godless and irreligious people, those with impure religions.
275 What then do I suffer—wanting to fear
the heavenly God yet dreading the icy demon's
deadly power and his empty boasts,
I am hidden in a shadowy vale? For from a holy girl,
the esteemed virgin Justa, I learned about
280 demons, how totally feeble they are.
For I saw one eccentric in thought, clothed in scales,
boasting unspeakable things, gigantic, a shameful serpent;
yet against her, he did not even have the strength of a fly.
I learned from the most honorable virgin that my lord
285 claims a lot but does nothing true.
A single girl trampled that mighty serpent with her feet.
Oh my! The ruler of deceitful demons
was repelled from entering the girl's bedroom,
and he was trembling terribly. The commander of countless demons
290 did not have the power to barge through the maiden's door.

Pretending to rule everything, he was mastered by a girl;
fantasizing about confounding the earth, he fled from a woman;
having a mischievous heart, he could not defeat a girl.
Thinking he could roar like a devouring lion
295 and scare everyone, like a fly, he was mocked
in the girl's atrium. When I left the land of the Persians
and headed to the great city of Syrian Antioch,
I accomplished many wonders through my terrible, supernatural
    skill.
For some, I provided the cure for love and, for others, the cure for
    jealousy,
300 bitter rivalry, and evil, which affected their flesh.

In that city, there was a certain lover, Aglaidas, who begged me,
as did many others, on his knees for the sake of a girl,
named Justina, that he might have intercourse with her.
That is when a demon first seemed unreliable to me.
305 The many legions he commanded were gathered
around the holy virgin but returned unsuccessful.
The virgin's faith rendered Aglaidas' helper unconscious
and made him powerless.
Aglaidas had many sleepless nights,
310 and I used my magic skills and the enemy's attacks
for seven weeks and another three after that.
Then, the leader of the demonic horde with his servants
waged war against the virgin.
For not only had Eros tamed the young Aglaidas,
315 he also eagerly touched my heart.
It was amazing to see an assemblage of so many demons,
along with the serpent, defeated by the girl's prayers.
But Beliar could not curb our appetite,
although he was struggling greatly and terribly on our behalf.
320 I said to him, "If you have such great power,
let the Eros in our hearts subside,
so that we no longer suffer such pains to no avail."
As I was listening, he ordered the eagle that rules
wantonness to do whatever I said. And he accomplished
325 many things, but he did not manage any more than that.
The lord merely proved that human nature
is stronger than all the abominable demonic hordes.

But when he discovers a human nature at its zenith,
then he thinks highly of himself and swaggers.
330 He no longer looks at the life-giving flower of men
but places credit for it in his own power,
just like a weak and lame fighter,
sitting on a horse familiar with the battle charge,
joyfully assigns most of the credit to himself.
335 For whenever love increases in budding youth,
it raises a spirit more violent than blazing fire.
A great battle took place between me and the demons,
and they fought with one another for some time.
At last, I addressed the serpent with baneful words
340 and said that his honor had suddenly fallen.
Perceiving his inadequacy, he remained silent.
I routed him by shouting mighty things, and he left quickly,
since he knew that his power was inferior and that he was
    ineffectual.
Then, the demon did something amazing to trick Aglaidas:
345 he led in a virgin, but his trick was immediately evident,
since her appearance was nothing like holy Justina.
When I learned these things, I hated the serpent.
And he transformed the leader of guilty men
to have a beauty similar to prudent Justina.
350 And when he approached Aglaidas, Aglaidas happily said,
"The golden beauty of the renowned Justina has arrived."
When he said her name, the demon heard it and fled.
Aglaidas was so scared that his courage failed.

Friends, I myself was present at these wicked
355 events. I saw the girl's desire
for God, the Lord Most High, and I saw the serpent's helplessness.
Along with the serpent, I was shamed, and I never slept,
since I stood by him when he was present. I was turned from a man
    into a woman
and a winged bird. But when I stepped into her atrium,
360 the illusion disappeared, and I returned to being
Cyprian, the believer in worthless magic.
I then made Aglaidas fly.
Down from above, he landed on the girl's roof.
When the holy virgin cast her gaze out of the light-bearing window,

365 she struck down the beautifully-winged bird.
      Aglaidas nearly came to death's door,
      haplessly perched like a bird so high up,
      had the good and wise girl not pitied him
      and addressed him kindly,
370 saying that he should remain silent at home and fear God.
      She then told him to quickly leave the atrium.

      Not a sickness nor a disease, nor any other distressing thing,
      overcame the virgin, for the evil-working demon sent
      countless evils against her. And her parents,
375 when the doctors predicted that her life was coming to an end,
      wasted away with grief. But she said to them, "Dear parents,
      it is not destined for me to die.
      I have an affliction of the heart, not of the body,
      a kind of airborne burning fever
380 smolders within my body." In addition to these,
      we released many other evils against the young virgin's limbs,
      but with the cross of Christ she destroyed
      the arrows of the evil spirit, the deceiver, the enemy.

      Then, I brought about evils for her parents,
385 killing their flocks, herds, and mules;
      the virgin immediately persuaded them,
      "May these things not bother you, but rejoice in the little things,
      because they will multiply for the pure one who speaks blessings."
      The girl's terrible predicament was evident to her neighbors.
390 They ordered the virgin to quickly bring together
      a lawful matrimony, but the young woman
      strengthened her parents' resolve with the sign of the cross.
      At another time, the demon sent a destructive plague upon the
            people
      and issued an oracle to those in the area,
395 saying that he would not stop the irrepressible vengeance until
      Aglaidas led Justa to the bed, as is the custom.
      The handmaid of Christ put an end to the people's cry
      with holy prayers and drove the plague from the city.
      Those near the city who had been tested
400 honored Christ and heaped dishonor on me.
      Saying that I was the bane of the city,

they vehemently hated me, but I
left out of fear for her parents and neighbors alike.

But later, seeing the power and great works of the cross,
405 I had the following thought, which I said to the evil demon,
"Woe, you destructive brood, bearer of every evil,
vessel of impiety; why have you deceived my soul in this way?
You are worthless and powerless, as you yourself know.
If just the thought of the immortal God overpowers you,
410 what will you do when He comes?
If you tremble before the name of Christ, what will you do
when He seeks vengeance for your deeds and destructive actions?
If the mighty power of the divine cross overwhelms you so much,
where will you place your footsteps when He returns?
415 If the *signum crucis* repels you,
how will you be able to save humans from His hand, the force of His
  power?
For surely you do not have an army so great as to defend against
  Him.
Even now, I am well acquainted with your misleading skill,
and I understand your illusion—I know that you are stupid.
420 Your gift is useless and momentary.
Your counsel is soft; your mind is the worst.
There is not a single thing you can do against God;
You only have illusions and things similar to smoke.
You have destroyed my heart and my hope,
425 and you unleashed a swarm concerned with rational thoughts.
Through your terrible evil, you devoured my life;
Through your magical counterfeits, you destroyed my allotted
  nature.
Because you deceived my mind, I have sinned.
I have become senseless and impious and have yielded everything to
  you.
430 I fruitlessly learned wisdom and ancient texts.
By trusting in you, I lost my property and wealth;
along with my parent's riches, you have robbed me of my very
  breath.
If beggars and paupers had eaten as much
as you wasted, lawless one, maybe just a little,
435 I would have God to bless my hopes.

Why did you disrespect me so badly, you evildoer?
I am extremely exhausted, insufferable one—I see the incurable end.
I was a corpse, only appearing to be among the living.
I paid a fortune for a tomb
440 and crossed the threshold of death [- - -]
It is appropriate for me to beg God's holy servants,
who are very pious men,
to receive pity and compassion. If only I
could kiss the footsteps of the venerable child, faithful Justina,
445 so that she thinks positively about my life.
Be gone, Satan, deceiver, lawless one, despot,
you hate the truth and make light of piety."

Growing angry, he moved to kill me with violence.
With all his strength, he attempted to kill me
450 by grabbing my throat. Since no one was around to help me
and I was unable to escape and run from death,
the sign of the most holy girl came to my mind,
that of the bright-shining cross, through which she had obtained
        victory.
I said in a prayer, "Lord God of the glorious girl,
455 come, help me." I immediately stretched out my hand
and placed on my limbs the sign of the cross.
Like an arrow in flight, he fled
and earnestly threatened me by waving his spear.
Having adopted the *signum crucis*,
460 I was invigorated and repeatedly shouted "God."
But the evil-planning beast grew angry and said
in his retreat, "Christ, the one sought in your prayer, will not save
        you
from me, because He hates the impious.
He helps you some now, so that later, with a trick,
465 He can lead you away and condemn you to a wretched fate.
When He leaves you, you know what I will do to you—
you have despised my power. Christ does not welcome
my servants. You have destroyed two things, villain,
our friendship and yourself, for the savior
470 will not help you." When I heard these words,
I was terribly scared, because he
had addressed me with such threats, even if in vain.

Therefore, dear men, who know my lament,
I declare my wretched life to you, so you may look
475 and have pity on me. Tell me if it is possible for me
to placate Christ, if He will listen to my conversion
and lend me aid, so I can flee the shameful path
I previously knew so well." The crowd remained silent for a long
        time.
Finally, someone said to me with a far-reaching shout ...

Bibliography

Accorinti, D., ed. 2016. *Brill's Companion to Nonnus of Panopolis.* Leiden.

Adams, J. N. 1981. "Ausonius, Cento Nuptialis 101-131." *Studi italiani di filologia classica* 53:199-215.

Addey, C. 2014. *Divination and Theurgy in Neoplatonism: Oracles of the Gods.* Farnham.

Aerts, W. J. 1997. "Das literarische Porträt in der byzantinischen Literatur." *Groningen Colloquia on the Novel* 8:151-195.

Afonasin, E. 2016. "Pythagorean Numerology and Diophantus' Arithmetica: A Note on Hippolytus' Elenchos I 2." In Renger and Stavru 2016: 347-359.

Agosti, G. 2001. "L'epica biblica nella tarda antichità greca: autori e lettori nel IV e V secolo." In *La scrittura infinita: Bibbia e poesia in età medievale e umanistica,* ed. F. Stella, 67-104. Florence.

———. 2003. *Nonno di Panopoli. Parafrasi del Vangelo di San Giovanni, Canto quinto.* Florence.

———. 2004. "Alcuni problemi relativi alla cesura principale nell'esametro Greco tardoantico." In *Autour de la césure: Actes du colloque Damon des 3 et 4 novembre 2000,* ed. F. Spaltenstein and O. Bianchi, 61-80. Bern.

———. 2005. "Interpretazione omerica e creazione poetica nella Tarda Antichità." In Κορυφαίῳ ἀνδρί: *Mélanges offerts à André Hurst,* ed. A. Kolde, A. Lukinovich, and A. L. Rey, 19-32. Geneva.

———. 2006. "La voce dei libri: Dimensioni performative dell'epica greca tardoantica." In *Approches de la Troisième Sophistique: Hommages à J. Schamp,* ed. E. Amato, A. Roduit, and M. Steinrück, 33-60. Brussels.

———. 2009. "La Vita di Proclo di Marino nella sua redazione in versi. Biografia e poesia nella scuola Neoplatonica." *Cento Pagine* 3:30-46.

———. 2012. "Greek Poetry." In Johnson 2012a: 361-404.

———. 2014a. "Per uno studio dei rapporti fra epigrafia e letteratura nella tarda antichità." *Il calamo della memoria* 6:13-33.

———. 2014b. "Contextualizing Nonnus' Visual World." In *Nonnus of Panopolis in Context: Poetry and Cultural Milieu in Late Antiquity with a Section on Nonnus and the Modern World,* ed. K. Spanoudakis, 141-174. Berlin.

———. 2016. "Les langues de l'épigramme épigraphique grecque: regard sur l'identité culturelle chrétienne dans l'Antiquité tardive." In *Épigramme dans tous ses états: épigraphiques, littéraires, historiques*, ed. E. Santin and L. Foschia, 276–295. Lyon.

Agosti, G., and F. Gonnelli. 1995. "Materiali per la storia dell'esametro nei poeti cristiani greci." In *Struttura e storia dell'esametro greco*, ed. M. Fantuzzi and R. Pretagostini, 289–434. Rome.

Aitken, E. B., and J. K. Berenson Maclean, eds. 2004. *Philostratus' Heroikos: Religion and Cultural Identity in the Third Century C.E.* Leiden.

Alfieri, A. M. 1987. "Eudocia e il testo di Omero." *Sileno* 13:197–219.

———. 1988. "La tecnica compositiva nel centone di Eudocia Augusta." *Sileno* 14:137–156.

———. 1989. "Note testuali ad Eudocia, Homerocentones." *Sileno* 15:137–139.

Allen, T. W., ed. 1920. *Homeri Opera*. 5 vols. Oxford.

Amat, J. 1996. *Passion de Perpétue et de Félicité suivi des Actes*. Sources Chrétiennes 417. Paris.

Amherdt, D. 2004. *Ausone et Paulin de Nole: correspondance*. Bern.

Amirav, H. 2011. "The Application of Magical Formulas of Invocation in Christian Contexts." In Vos and Otten 2011: 117–127.

Anderson, P. 2002. *"Fame Is the Spur": Memoria, Gloria, and Poetry Among the Elite in Flavian Rome*. PhD diss., University of Cincinnati.

Angelino, C., and E. Salvaneschi, eds. 1982. Σύγκρισις α': *Testi e studi di storia e filosofia del linguaggio religioso*. Genoa.

Anson, J. 1974. "The Female Transvestite in Early Monasticism: The Origin and Development of a Motif." *Viator* 5:1–32.

Appelbaum, A. 2013. *The Dynasty of the Jewish Patriarchs*. Tübingen.

Arbea, A. 2002. "El centón homérico de Eudoxia (s. V d.C.)." *Teología y vida* 43:97–106.

Arcidiacono, C. 2011. *Il centone virgiliano cristiano "Versus Ad Gratiam Domini."* Alessandria.

Ast, R., and J. Lougovaya. 2015. "The Art of Isopsephism in the Greco-Roman World." In Jördens 2015: 82–98.

Aubin, M. 1998. "Reversing Romance? The *Acts of Thecla* and the Ancient Novel." In Hock, Chance, and Perkins 1998: 257–272.

Aull, C. N. 2017. "The Letter Collection of Ausonius." In *Late Antique Letter Collections: A Critical Introduction and Reference Guide*, ed. C. Sogno, B. K. Storin, and E. J. Watts, 131–145. Oakland.

Aune, D. E. 1980. "Magic in Early Christianity." *Aufstieg und Niedergang der Römischen Welt* 2.23.2, 1507–1557. Berlin.

———. 1987. *The New Testament in its Literary Environment*. Philadelphia.

Avi-Yonah, M. 1940. *Abbreviations in Greek Inscriptions*. London.

Badini, A., and A. Rizzi. 2011. *Proba: Il Centone*. Bologna.

Baehrens, A. 1882. *Poetae Latini Minores IV*. Leipzig.

Bailey, R. 2009. *The Confession of Cyprian of Antioch: Introduction, Text, and Translation*. MA thesis, McGill University.

Ballif, M., and M. G. Moran. 2005. *Classical Rhetorics and Rhetoricians: Critical Studies and Sources*. London.

Balmer, J. 1996. *Classical Women Poets*. Newcastle.

Bandini, A. M. 1761. *Graecae ecclesiae vetera monumenta ex bibliotheca Medicae I*. Florence.

Barnes, J. 2016. "The Speaking Body: Metaphor and the Expression of Extraordinary Experience." *Temenos: Nordic Journal of Comparative Religion* 52.2:261–287.

Barnes, T. D. 2006. "An Urban Prefect and His Wife." *Classical Quarterly* 56:249–256.

———. 2010. *Early Christian Hagiography and Roman History*. Tübingen.

Barrier, J. W. 2009. *The Acts of Paul and Thecla: A Critical Introduction and Commentary*. Tübingen.

Barthes, R. 1986. *The Rustle of Language*. New York.

Bassett, S. 2004. *The Urban Image of Late Antique Constantinople*. Cambridge.

Bastiaensen, A. A. R. 2011. "Exorcism: Tackling the Devil by Word of Mouth." In Vos and Otten 2011: 129–142.

Bauman, R. A. 1992. *Women and Politics in Ancient Rome*. London.

Baumann, P. 1999. *Spätantike Stifter im Heiligen Land. Darstellungen und Inschriften auf Bodenmosaiken in Kirchen, Synagogen und Privathäusern*. Wiesbaden.

Bažil, M. 2009. *Centones Christiani: Métamorphoses d'une forme intertextuelle dans la poésie latine chrétienne de l'Antiquité tardive*. Paris.

Beck, H. G. 1966. "Eudokia." *Reallexikon für Antike und Christentum* 6:844–847.

Becker, A. S. 1995. *The Shield of Achilles and the Poetics of Ekphrasis*. Lanham.

Bennema, C. 2017. "Moral Transformation in the Johannine Writings." In *In die Skriflig* 53.3. http://www.scielo.org.za/pdf/ids/v51n3/06.pdf

Bentley, R., ed. 1739. *M. Manilii Astronomicon*. London.

Berenson Maclean, J. K. 2004. "Jesus as Cult Hero in the Fourth Gospel." In Aitken and Berenson Maclean 2004: 195–218.

Bernard, F. 2014. *Writing and Reading Byzantine Secular Poetry, 1025–1081*. Oxford.

Bethe, E. 1900. *Pollucis Onomasticon*. 3 vols. Leipzig.

Betz, H. D. 1992. *The Greek Magical Papyri in Translation, Including the Demotic Spells*. Chicago.

Bevegni, C. 1981. "Note a Eudocia, *De Sancto Cypriano* I 5 e I 32." *Sandalion* 4:183–189.

———. 1982a. "Due note testuali ad Eudocia, *De Sancto Cypriano* I 275 e II 43." *Sandalion* 5:277–282.

———. 1982b. "Eudociae Augustae Martyrium S. Cypriani I 1-99." *Prometheus* 8:249–262.

———. 1990. "Eudociana." *Studi italiani di filologia classica* 8:250–251.

———. 2003. "Per una nuova edizione del *De Sancto Cypriano* dell'imperatrice Eudocia. Primi passi." *FuturAntico* 1:29–46.

———. 2006a. *Eudocia Augusta: Storia di San Cipriano.* Milan.

———. 2006b. "Il *De Sancto Cypriano* dell'imperatrice Eudocia: questioni aperte." *Koinonia* 30:155–168.

Biers, J. C. 1989–1990. "A Gold Finger Ring and the Empress Eudocia." *Muse* 23–24:82–99.

Blessing, C. 2016. "Femineity in the Gospel of John." In *Feminism and Religion: How Faiths View Women and Their Rights,* ed. M. A. Paludi and J. H. Ellens, 129–142. Santa Barbara.

Blume, M. 1989. "À propos de P.Oxy. I,41: des acclamations en l'honneur d'un prytane confrontées aux temoignages épigraphiques du reste de l'empire." In *Egitto e storia antica dall'Ellenismo all'età araba: Bilancio di un confronto,* ed. L. Criscuolo and G. Geraci, 271–290. Bologna.

Boehm, G. 1995. *Beschreibungskunst, Kunstbeschreibung. Ekphrasis von der Antike bis zur Gegenwart.* Munich.

Bonneau, D. 1964. *La crue du Nil, divinité égyptienne.* Paris.

Bourdy, F. 1992. "Du bon usage des bains d'après Oribase." In *Les eaux thermales et les cultes des eaux en Gaule et dans les provinces voisines,* ed. R. Chevallier, 31–38. Tours.

Bovon, F., ed. 1995. *New Testament Traditions and Apocryphal Narratives.* Allison Park.

———. 2003. "Canonical and Apocryphal Acts of Apostles." *Journal of Early Christian Studies* 11.2:165–194.

Bowersock, G. W. 1994. *Fiction as History: Nero to Julian.* Berkeley.

———. 2006. "The Great Teachers of Late Antique Athens." Ἀρχαιογνωσία 14:169–182.

Bowie, E. L. 1994. "The Readership of Greek Novels in the Ancient World." In Tatum 1994: 435–459.

Bowie, E. L., and J. Elsner, eds. 2009. *Philostratus.* Cambridge.

Bradley, K. 2014. "Apuleius' *Apology*: Text and Context." In Lee, Finkelpearl, and Graverini 2014: 23–34.

Bradshaw, P. F. 1992. *The Search for the Origins of Christian Worship: Sources and Methods for the Study of Early Liturgy.* Oxford.

Brakke, D. 2006. *Demons and the Making of a Monk: Spiritual Combat in Early Christianity.* Cambridge, MA.

———, ed. 2009. *Evagrius of Pontus, Talking Back: A Monastic Handbook for Combating Demons.* Collegeville.

Brandt, H. 2000. "Paganism in Late Roman Hagiography?" In *Ethnicity and Culture in Late Antiquity,* ed. S. Mitchell and G. Greatrex, 59–68. London.

Brant, J. 2004. *Dialogue and Drama: Elements of Greek Tragedy in the Fourth Gospel.* Peabody.

Braund, D. 2004a. "Scythians in the Cerameicus: Lucian's *Toxaris.*" In Tuplin 2004: 17–24.

———. 2004b. "Herodotus' Spartan Scythians." In Tuplin 2004: 25–41.

Bremmer, J. N., ed. 1995. *The Apocryphal Acts of John.* Kampen.

———, ed. 1996. *The Apocryphal Acts of Paul and Thecla.* Kampen.

———. 1998a. "The Novel and the Apocryphal Acts: Place, Time and Readership." *Groningen Colloquia on the Novel* 9:157–180.

———, ed. 1998b. *The Apocryphal Acts of Peter: Magic, Miracles and Gnosticism.* Leuven.

———, ed. 2000. *The Apocryphal Acts of Andrew.* Leuven.

———, ed. 2001. *The Apocryphal Acts of Thomas.* Leuven.

———. 2002. "Perpetua and Her Diary: Authenticity, Family and Visions." In *Märtyrer und Märtyrerakten,* ed. W. Ameling, 77–120. Stuttgart.

———. 2004. "The Motivation of Martyrs: Perpetua and the Palestinians." In *Religion im kulturellen Diskurs,* ed. B. Luchesi and K. von Stuchrad, 535–554. Berlin.

———. 2006. "Het martelaarschap van Perpetua en Felicitas." *Hermeneus* 78:128–137.

Bremmer, J., and M. Formisano, eds. 2012. *Perpetua's Passions: Multidisciplinary Approaches to the* Passio Perpetuae et Felicitatis. Oxford.

Bricault, L., M. J. Versluys, and P. G. P. Meyboom. 2007. *Nile into Tiber: Egypt in the Roman World.* Leiden.

Bright, D. F. 1984. "Theory and Practice in the Vergilian Cento." *Illinois Classical Studies* 9:79–90.

Brink, C. O. 1972. "Ennius and the Hellenistic Worship of Homer." *American Journal of Philology* 93:547–567.

Brisson, L. 2013. "Plotinus and the Magical Rites Practiced by the Gnostics." In *Gnosticism, Platonism and the Late Antique World: Essays in Honour of John D. Turner,* ed. K. Corrigan and T. Rasimus, 443–458. Leiden.

Broise, H. 2003. "À propos des thermes de Hammat Gader." *Syria* 80:217–235.

Brown, P. 1981. *The Cult of the Saints: Its Rise and Function in Latin Christianity.* Chicago.

———. 1988. *The Body and Society: Men, Women, and Sexual Renunciation in Early Christianity*. New York.

———. 2002. *Poverty and Leadership in the Later Roman Empire*. Hanover.

———. 2012. *Through the Eye of a Needle: Wealth, the Fall of Rome, and the Making of Christianity in the West, 350–550 AD*. Princeton.

———. 2015. *The Ransom of the Soul: Afterlife and Wealth in Early Western Christianity*. Cambridge, MA.

———. 2016. *Treasure in Heaven: The Holy Poor in Early Christianity*. Charlottesville.

Brubaker, L. 1997. "Memories of Helena: Patterns in Imperial Female Patronage in the Fourth and Fifth Centuries." In *Women, Men and Eunuchs: Gender in Byzantium*, ed. L. James, 52–75. London.

Burkert, W. 1985. *Greek Religion*. Cambridge, MA.

Burman, J. 1991. "The Christian Empress Eudocia." In *Les femmes et le monachisme byzantin*, ed. J. Y. Perreault, 51–59. Athens.

———. 1994. "The Athenian Empress Eudocia." In *Post-Herulian Athens: Aspects of Life and Culture in Athens, A.D. 267–529*, ed. P. Castrén, 63–87. Helsinki.

Burr, E. G. 2000. "Julian 'the Apostate' Against the Galileans." In *Religions of Late Antiquity in Practice*, ed. R. Valantasis, 143–155. Princeton.

Burrus, V. 1987. *Chastity as Autonomy: Women in the Stories of the Apocryphal Acts*. Lewiston.

———. 2004. *The Sex Lives of Saints: The Erotics of Ancient Hagiography*. Philadelphia.

Burton, P. 2007. *Language in the Confessions of Augustine*. Oxford.

Bury, J. B. 1923. *History of the Later Roman Empire: From the Death of Theodosius I to the Death of Justinian (A.D. 395 to A.D. 565)*. 2 vols. London.

Busch, P. 2015. "Magie und das Neue Testament." In Jördens 2015: 69–81.

Busch, S. 1999. *Versus Balnearum: Die antike Dichtung über Bäder und Baden im römischen Reich*. Stuttgart.

Butler, E. M. 1948. *The Myth of the Magus*. Cambridge.

———. 1949. *Ritual Magic*. Cambridge.

———. 1952. *The Fortunes of Faust*. Cambridge.

Bynum, C. W. 1982. *Jesus as Mother: Studies in the Spirituality of the High Middle Ages*. Berkeley.

———. 1991. "Women's Stories, Women's Symbols: A Critique of Victor Turner's Theory of Liminality." In *Fragmentation and Redemption: Essays on Gender and the Human Body in Medieval Religion*, 27–51. New York.

Calef, S. A. 2006. "Thecla 'Tried and True' and the Inversion of Romance." In Levine 2006: 163–185.

Callander, T. 1927. "Inscriptions from Isauria." *American Journal of Philology* 48:235–246.

Cameron, A. 1965. "Wandering Poets: A Literary Movement in Byzantine Egypt." *Historia* 14:470–509.

———. 1970. *Claudian: Poetry and Propaganda at the Court of Honorius.* Oxford.

———. 1982. "The Empress and the Poet: Paganism and Politics at the Court of Theodosius II." *Yale Classical Studies* 27:217–289.

———. 1985. *Literature and Society in the Early Byzantine World.* London.

———. 2000. "The Poet, the Bishop, and the Harlot." *Greek, Roman, and Byzantine Studies* 41:175–188.

———. 2004. "Poetry and Literary Culture in Late Antiquity." In Swain and Edwards 2004: 327–354.

———. 2011. *The Last Pagans of Rome.* Oxford.

———. 2016. "Hypatia: Life, Death, and Works." In *Wandering Poets and Other Essays*, 185–203. Oxford.

Caprara, M. 2005. *Nonno di Panopoli. Parafrasi del Vangelo di San Giovanni, Canto IV.* Pisa.

Carcopino, J. 1968. *De Pythagore aux Apôtres. Études sur la conversion du monde romain.* Paris.

Cardini, M. T. 2010. *Pitagorici antichi: testimonianze e frammenti.* Milan.

Carilli, M. 1975. "Le nugae di Catullo e l'epigramma greco." *Annali della Scuola Normale Superiore di Pisa. Classe di Lettere e Filosofia* 5:925–953.

Cartledge, P. 2002. *The Greeks: A Portrait of Self and Others.* Oxford.

Cartledge, P., and A. Spawforth. 2002. *Hellenistic and Roman Sparta: A Tale of Two Cities.* London.

Castelli, E. 1991. "'I Will Make Mary Male': Pieties of the Body and Gender Transformation of Christian Women in Late Antiquity." In *Body Guards: The Cultural Politics of Gender Ambiguity*, ed. J. Epstein and K. Straub, 29–49. New York.

———. 1999. "Paul on Women and Gender." In Kraemer and D'Angelo 1999: 221–235.

Cavallo, G. 2006. *Lire à Byzance.* Paris.

Chadwick, H. 1948. "The Fall of Eustathius of Antioch." *Journal of Theological Studies* 49:27–35.

Chaniotis, A., and J. Mylonopoulos. 2004. "Epigraphic Bulletin for Greek Religion 2001." *Kernos* 17:187–249.

Christian, T. 2015. *Gebildete Steine: Zur Rezeption literarischer Techniken in den Versinschriften seit dem Hellenismus.* Göttingen.

Ciraolo, L., and J. Seidel, eds. 2002. *Magic and Divination in the Ancient World.* Leiden.

Clark, E. A. 1982. "Claims on the Bones of Saint Stephen: The Partisans of Melania and Eudocia." *Church History* 51:141–156.

———. 1984. *The Life of Melania the Younger: Introduction, Translation, and Commentary*. New York.

———. 1985. "Authority and Humility: A Conflict of Values in Fourth-Century Female Monasticism." *Byzantinische Forschungen* 9:17–33.

———. 1986a. *Ascetic Piety and Women's Faith: Essays on Late Ancient Christianity.* Lewiston.

———. 1986b. "Piety, Propaganda, and Politics in the *Life of Melania the Younger.*" In Clark 1986a: 61–94.

———. 1986c. "The Uses of the Song of Songs: Origen and the Later Latin Fathers." In Clark 1986a: 386–410.

Clark, E. A., and D. F. Hatch. 1981. *The Golden Bough, the Oaken Cross: The Virgilian Cento of Faltonia Betitia Proba.* Chico.

Clark, G. 1993. *Women in Late Antiquity: Pagan and Christian Lifestyles.* Oxford.

Claus, M. 1990. *Mithras. Kult und Mysterien.* Munich.

Clinton, K. 1974. *The Sacred Officials of the Eleusinian Mysteries.* Philadelphia.

Cloke, G. 1995. *"This Female Man of God": Women and Spiritual Power in the Patristic Age, AD 350-450.* New York.

———. 2000. "Women, Worship, and Mission: The Church in the Household," In Esler 2000: 422–451.

Cobb, L. S. 2008. *Dying to Be Men: Gender and Language in Early Christian Martyr Texts.* New York.

Coleman, K. M. 1988. *Statius* Silvae *IV.* Oxford.

Collas, G. F. 1913. *Der Flagellantismus im Altertum.* Leipzig.

Combellack, F. M. 1976. "Homer the Inventor." *Classical Philology* 71:44–55.

Comparetti, D. 1997. *Vergil in the Middle Ages.* London. Orig. pub. 1885.

Connor, C. C. 2004. *Women of Byzantium.* New Haven.

Consolino, F. E. 2017. "Polymetry in Late Latin Poems: Some Observations on its Meaning and Functions." In Elsner and Lobato 2017a: 100–124.

Coon, L. L. 1997. *Sacred Fictions: Holy Women and Hagiography in Late Antiquity.* Philadelphia.

Cooper, K. 1999. *The Virgin and the Bride: Idealized Womanhood in Late Antiquity.* Cambridge, MA.

———. 2013. *Band of Angels: The Forgotten World of Early Christian Women.* New York.

Copeland, K. B. 2014. "Sorceresses and Sorcerers in Early Christian Tours of Hell." In Stratton and Kalleres 2014: 298–315.

Courcelle, P. 1957. "Antécédents autobiographiques des 'Confessions' de saint Augustin." *Revue de philologie et de littérature et d'histoire ancienne* 31:23–51.

———. 1963. *Les Confessions de saint Augustin dans la tradition littéraire. Antécédents et postérité.* Paris.

Crawford, C. 2002. *Tangram Puzzles: 500 Tricky Shapes to Confound and Astound*. New York.

Cribiore, R. 2001. *Gymnastics of the Mind: Greek Education in Hellenistic and Roman Egypt*. Princeton.

———. 2007. *The Schools of Libanius in Late Antique Antioch*. Princeton.

Crisafulli, V. S., and J. W. Nesbitt. 1997. *The Miracles of St. Artemios: A Collection of Miracle Stories by an Anonymous Author of Seventh-Century Byzantium*. Leiden.

Crusius, O. 1899. "Cento." In *Paulys Realencyclopädie der classischen Altertumswissenschaft*. 6:1930–1931. Stuttgart.

Cummins, A., J. H. Diaz, and J. Zahrt. 2016. *Cypriana Old World*. Seattle.

Cumont, F. 1899. *Textes et monuments figurés relatifs aux mystères de Mithra*. 2 vols. Brussels.

———. 1927. "Le nouveau bas-relief de Dieburg." *Journal des Savants* 1927:122–126.

Cuntz, G. 1965. *Itineraria et Alia Geographica*. 2 vols. Turnhout.

Cuntz, O., ed. 1929. *Itineraria Romana Vol. 1: Itineraria Antonini Augusti et Burdigalense*. Leipzig.

Curran, J. 2012. "Virgilizing Christianity in Late Antique Rome." In *Two Romes: Rome and Constantinople in Late Antiquity*, ed. L. Grig and G. Kelly, 325–344. Oxford.

Danesin, C. 2001. "Per un commento al frammento Leidense di Eudocia." *Patavium* 9:49–61.

David, R. 2002. *Religion and Magic in Ancient Egypt*. London.

Davis, S. J. 2001. *The Cult of Saint Thecla: A Tradition of Women's Piety in Late Antiquity*. Oxford.

———. 2002. "Crossed Texts, Crossed Sex: Intertextuality and Gender in Early Christian Legends of Holy Women Disguised as Men." *Journal of Early Christian Studies* 10:1–36.

de Blois, L. 2001. "The Political Significance of Friendship in the *Letters* of Pliny the Younger." In *Aspects of Friendship in the Graeco-Roman World*, ed. M. Peachin, 129–134. Portsmouth.

de Boor, C. 1980. *Theophanes, Chronographia*. Hildesheim.

de Gaiffier, B. 1969. "La lecture des passions des martyrs à Rome avant le IXe siècle." *Analecta Bollandiana* 87:63–78.

de Jong, J. L. 1989. "Renaissance Representations of Cupid and Psyche: Apuleius versus Fulgentius." *Groningen Colloquia on the Novel* 2:75–87.

Delatte, A., and P. Derchain. 1964. *Les intailles magiques gréco-égyptiennes*. Paris.

Delcourt, M. 1961. "Female Saints in Masculine Clothing." In *Hermaphrodite: Myths and Rites of the Bisexual Figure in Classical Antiquity*, 84–102. London.

Delehaye, H. 1921. "Cyprien d'Antioche et Cyprien de Carthage." *Analecta Bollandiana* 39:314–332.

————. 1961. *The Legends of Three Saints: An Introduction to Hagiography.* London.

Demandt, A. 2007. *Die Spätantike. Römische Geschichte von Diocletian bis Justinian 284–565 n. Chr.* Munich.

de Meyier, K. A. 1956. "Membra disiecta d'un manuscrit contenant les soi-disant Centones Homerici." *Scriptorium* 10:93–94.

Damico, A. 2010. *De Ecclesia Cento Vergilianus.* Acireale.

Deming, W. 2004. *Paul on Marriage and Celibacy: The Hellenistic Background of I Corinthians 7.* Grand Rapids.

DesRosiers, N. P., and L. C. Vuong, eds. 2016. *Religious Competition in the Greco-Roman World.* Atlanta.

Deubner, L. 1907. *Kosmas und Damian.* Leipzig.

Dickie, M. 1999. "The Learned Magician and the Collection and Transmission of Magical Lore." In Jordan, Montgomery, and Thomassen 1999: 163–194.

————. 2001. *Magic and Magicians in the Greco-Roman World.* London.

Didot, A. F., ed. 1872. *Epigrammatum Anthologia Palatina.* 3 vols. Paris.

Dieleman, J. 2005. *Priests, Tongues, and Rites: The London-Leiden Magical Manuscripts and Translation in Egyptian Ritual (100–300 CE).* Leiden.

Dihle, A. 1994. *Greek and Latin Literature of the Roman Empire from Augustus to Justinian.* London.

Dindorf, L., ed. 1831. *Ioannis Malalae Chronographia.* Bonn.

Dinkler, E. 1967. *Signum Crucis.* Tübingen.

Di Segni, L. 1997. "The Greek Inscriptions of Hammat Gader." In Hirschfeld 1997: 185–266.

Dix, G. 1945. *The Shape of the Liturgy.* London.

Dodds, E. R., ed. 1963. *Proclus: The Elements of Theology.* Oxford.

Dölger, F. J. 1929–1940. *Antike und Christentum kultur- und religionsgeschichtliche Studien.* 6 vols. Münster.

Domínguez, Ó. P. 2010. *De Alieno Nostrum: el Centón profane en el mundo griego.* Salamanca.

Doublet, G. 1889. "Inscriptions de Paphlagonie." *Bulletin de correspondance hellénique* 13:293–319.

Downey, G. 1941. "The Wall of Theodosius at Antioch." *American Journal of Philology* 62:207–213.

————. 1951. "The Economic Crisis at Antioch under Julian the Apostate." In *Studies in Roman Economic and Social History*, ed. P. R. Coleman-Norton, 312–321. Princeton.

————. 1961. *A History of Antioch in Syria: From Seleucus to the Arab Conquest.* Princeton.

Drake, H. A. 1979. "A Coptic Version of the Discovery of the Holy Sepulchre." *Greek, Roman, and Byzantine Studies* 20:381–392.

Drescher, J. 1946. *Apa Mena: A Selection of Coptic Texts Relating to St. Menas*. Cairo.

Driver, G. R., and L. Hodgson. 1925. *Nestorius: The Bazaar of Heracleides*. Oxford.

Duchesne, L. 1904. *Christian Worship: Its Origin and Evolution. A Study of the Latin Liturgy up to the Time of Charlemagne*. London.

Duncan, A. 2006. *Performance and Identity in the Classical World*. Cambridge.

Dvorjetski, E. 1997. "Medicinal Hot Springs in the Greco-Roman World." In Hirschfeld 1997: 463-476.

——. 2007. *Leisure, Pleasure and Healing: Spa Culture and Medicine in Ancient Eastern Mediterranean*. Leiden.

Dykes, A. 2011. *Reading Sin in the World: The* Hamartigenia *of Prudentius and the Vocation of the Responsible Reader*. Cambridge.

Dzielska, M. 1986. *Apollonius of Tyana in Legend and History*. Rome.

Eck, W. 2014. "The Armed Forces and the Infrastructure of Cities during the Roman Imperial Period – The Example of Judaea/Syria Palaestina." In *Cura Aquarum in Israel II: Water in Antiquity*, ed. C. Ohlig and T. Tsuk, 207-214. Siegburg.

Edwards, M. W. 1991. *The Iliad: A Commentary: Vol. V, books 17-20*. Cambridge.

Edwards, R. 2015. *Discovering John: Content, Interpretation, Reception*. Grand Rapids.

Elsner, J. 2004. "Late Antique Art: The Problem of Concept and Cumulative Aesthetic." In Swain and Edwards 2004: 271-308.

——. 2005. "Piety and Passion: Contest and Consensus in the Audiences for Early Christian Pilgrimage." In *Pilgrimage in Graeco-Roman and Early Christian Antiquity: Seeing the Gods*, ed. J. Elsner and I. Rutherford, 411-434. Oxford.

——. 2017. "Late Narcissus: Classicism and Culture in a Late Roman Cento." In Elsner and Lobato 2017a: 176-204.

Elsner, J., and J. H. Lobato, eds. 2017a. *The Poetics of Late Latin Literature*. Oxford.

——. 2017b. "Notes towards a Poetics of Late Antique Literature." In Elsner and Lobato: 2017a: 1-22.

Elsom, H. 1989. "Apuleius and the Movies." *Groningen Colloquia on the Novel* 2:141-150.

Engelmann, H. 1975. *The Delian Aretalogy of Sarapis*. Leiden.

Engels, D., and P. van Nuffelen, eds. 2014. *Religion and Competition in Antiquity*. Brussels.

Engle, A. 1987. *Light: Lamps and Windows in Antiquity*. Jerusalem.

Esdaile, K. 1909. "Ὁ ἀφ' ἑστίας. Two Statues of a Boy Celebrating the Eleusinian Mysteries." *Journal of Hellenic Studies* 29:1-5.

Esler, P. F., ed. 2000. *The Early Christian World*. 2 vols. London.

Evans-Grubbs, J. 1994. "'Pagan' and 'Christian' Marriage: The State of the Question." *Journal of Early Christian Studies* 2:361-412.

―――. 1995. *Law and Family in Late Antiquity: The Emperor Constantine's Marriage Legislation.* Oxford.

Evelyn-White, H. G. 1919. *Ausonius.* 2 vols. Cambridge, MA.

Fantham, E. 2013. *Roman Literary Culture: From Plautus to Macrobius.* Baltimore.

Faraone, C. A., and D. Obbink, eds. 1991. *Magika Hiera: Ancient Greek Magic and Religion.* New York.

Farnell, L. R. 1909. *The Cults of the Greek States.* 5 vols. Oxford.

Farrell, J., and C. Williams. 2012. "Passio Sanctarum Perpetuae et Felicitatis." In Bremmer and Formisano 2012: 24–32.

Fehribach, A. 1998. *The Women in the Life of the Bridegroom: A Feminist Historical-Literary Analysis of the Female Characters in the Fourth Gospel.* Collegeville.

Feissel, D. 1987. "Bulletin épigraphique. Inscriptions chrétiennes et byzantines." *Revue des Études Grecques* 100:347–387.

―――. 1998. "Gouverneurs et édifices dans les épigrammes de Smyrne au Bas-Empire." *Revue des Études Grecques* 111:125–144.

Ferreiro, A. 2005. *Simon Magus in Patristic, Medieval and Early Modern Traditions.* Leiden.

Festugière, A. J. 1950. *La révélation d'Hermès Trismégiste, vol. 1: L'astrologie et les sciences occultes.* Paris.

―――. 1971. *Collections grecques de miracles.* Paris.

Fideler, D. R. 1993. *Jesus Christ, Sun of God: Ancient Cosmology and Early Christian Symbolism.* Wheaton.

Finn, R. 2006. *Almsgiving in the Later Roman Empire: Christian Promotion and Practice, 313–450.* Oxford.

Flower, M. A. 2008. *The Seer in Ancient Greece.* Berkeley.

Flower, R. 2013. "'The Insanity of Heretics Must be Restrained': Heresiology in the *Theodosian Code.*" In Kelly 2013a: 172–194.

Formisano, M. 2007. "Towards an Aesthetic Paradigm of Late Antiquity." *Antiquité Tardive* 15:277–284.

―――. 2017. "Displacing Tradition: A New Allegorical Reading of Ausonius, Claudian, and Rutilius Namatianus." In Elsner and Lobato 2017a: 207–235.

Formisano, M., T. Fuhrer, and A. Stock, eds. 2014. *Décadence: "Decline and Fall" or "Other Antiquity"?*, ed. M. Formisano, T. Fuhrer, and A. Stock, 171–197. Heidelberg.

Formisano, M., and C. Sogno. 2010. "Petite Poésie Portable: The Latin Cento in its Late Antique Context." In Horster and Reitz 2010a:375–392.

Foskett, M. F. 2002. *A Virgin Conceived: Mary and Classical Representations of Virginity.* Bloomington.

Foucart, P. 1914. *Les Mystères d'Éleusis.* Paris.

Fournet, J. L. 1995. "L''homérisme' à l'époque protobyzantine: l'example de Dioscore d'Aphrodité." *Ktèma* 20:301–315.

Fox, R. L. 2015. *Augustine: Conversions to Confessions.* New York.

Frankfurter, D. 2001. "The Perils of Love: Magic and Countermagic in Coptic Egypt." *Journal of the History of Sexuality* 10:480–500.

———. 2006. *Evil Incarnate: Rumors of Demonic Conspiracy and Ritual Abuse in History.* Princeton.

———. 2010. "Where the Spirits Dwell: Possession, Christianization, and Saints' Shrines in Late Antiquity." *Harvard Theological Review* 103.1:27–46.

———. 2013. "Martyrology and the Paideia of Violence: Brent Shaw on the Realities of Christian Demolition." *Journal of Early Christian Studies* 21:294–298.

Frazer. J. G. 1907. *The Golden Bough.* 10 vols. London.

Frye, D. 2003. "Aristocratic Responses to Late Roman Urban Change: The Examples of Ausonius and Sidonius in Gaul." *Classical World* 96.2:185–196.

Frye, N. 1976. *The Secular Scripture: A Study on the Structure of Romance.* Cambridge, MA.

Futre Pinheiro, M. P., G. Schmeling, and E. P. Cueva, eds. 2014. *The Ancient Novel and the Frontiers of Genre.* Eelde.

Gaddis, M. 2005. *There is No Crime for Those Who Have Christ: Religious Violence in the Christian Roman Empire.* Berkeley.

Gager, J. G. 1992. *Curse Tablets and Binding Spells from the Ancient World.* Oxford.

Gagliardi, D., and E. Scuotto. 1995. *La poesia pagana tardoantica: Antologia degli ultimi autori latini dai novelli a Massimiano.* Naples.

Gamble, H. Y. 1995. *Books and Readers in the Early Church: A History of Early Christian Texts.* New Haven.

Gascou, J. 2006. *Sophrone de Jérusalem: Miracles des Saints Cyr et Jean (BHG I 477-479).* Paris.

Genette, G. 1982. *Palimpsestes. La littérature au second degré.* Paris.

George, J. W. 1992. *Venantius Fortunatus: A Latin Poet in Merovingian Gaul.* Oxford.

Geyer, P. 1965. *Antonini Placentini Itinerarium.* Corpus Christianorum Series Latina 175. Turnhout.

Gitlbauer, M. 1879. "Die Ueberreste griechischer Tachygraphie im Codex Vaticanus Graecus 1809.I." *Denkschriften der kaiserlichen Akademie der Wissenschaften Philosophisch-historische Classe* 28.2:95–109.

Given, J. 2014. *The Fragmentary History of Priscus: Attila, the Huns, and the Roman Empire, AD 430-476.* Merchantville.

Gleason, M. W. 1986. "Festive Satire: Julian's *Misopogon* and the New Year at Antioch." *Journal of Roman Studies* 76:106–119.

Glock, C. Y., and R. Stark. 1966. *Christian Beliefs and Anti-Semitism.* New York.

Goldhill, S. 2008. "Genre." In *Cambridge Companion to the Greek and Roman Novel*, ed. T. Whitmarsh, 185–200. Cambridge.

Golega, J. 1960. *Der homerische Psalter. Studien über die dem Apolinarios von Laodikeia zugeschriebene Psalmenparaphrase*. Ettal.

Gonnelli, F. 1989. "Eudocia, Cassiodoro e Malala." *Vichiana* 18:350–353.

Goold, G. P. 1998. *M. Manilii Astronomica*. Stuttgart.

Gordon, R. 1999. "Imagining Greek and Roman Magic." In *Witchcraft and Magic in Europe: Ancient Greece and Rome*, ed. B. Ankarloo and S. Clark, 161–275. Philadelphia.

Gorman, J. C. 2006. "Sexual Defense by Proxy: Interpreting Women's Fasting in the *Acts of Xanthippe and Polyxena*." In Levine 2006: 206–215.

Gorman, P. 1985. "The 'Apollonios' of the Neoplatonic Biographies of Pythagoras." *Mnemosyne* 38:130–144.

Gotoff, H. C. 1974. "Tibullus. Nunc levis est tractanda Venus." *Harvard Studies in Classical Philology* 78:231–251.

Graf, F. 1991a. "Textes orphiques et rituel bacchique. À propos des lamelles de Pelinna." In *Orphisme et Orphée*, ed. P. Borgeaud and J. Rudhardt, 87–102. Geneva.

———. 1991b. "Prayer in Magical and Religious Ritual." In Faraone and Obbink 1991: 188–213.

———. 1997. *Magic in the Ancient World*. Cambridge, MA.

———. 2014. "Victimology or: How to Deal with Untimely Death." In Stratton and Kalleres 2014: 386–417.

Green, J., and Y. Tsafrir. 1982. "Greek inscriptions from Hammat Gader." *Israel Exploration Journal* 32:77–96.

Green, R. P. H. 1991. *The Works of Ausonius*. Oxford.

———. 1995. "Proba's Cento: Its Date, Purpose, and Reception." *Classical Quarterly* 45:551–563.

———. 1997. "Proba's Introduction to Her Cento." *Classical Quarterly* 47:548–559.

———. 1999. *Decimi Magni Ausonii Opera*. Oxford.

———. 2006. *Latin Epics of the New Testament: Juvencus, Sedulius, Arator*. Oxford.

Greene, E. 2005. *Women Poets in Ancient Greece and Rome*. Norman.

Gregorovius, F. 1881. *Athenaïs. Geschichte einer byzantinischen Kaiserin*. Leipzig.

Guthrie, K. S. 1989. *The Pythagorean Sourcebook and Library: An Anthology of Ancient Writings Which Relate to Pythagoras and Pythagorean Philosophy*. Grand Rapids.

Guthrie, W. K. C. 1939. *On the Heavens*. Cambridge, MA.

———. 1962–1981. *A History of Greek Philosophy*. 6 vols. Cambridge.

Habas, E. R. 1996. "A Poem by the Empress Eudocia: A Note on the Patriarch." *Israel Exploration Journal* 46:108–119.

Haffner, M. 1996. "Die Kaiserin Eudokia als Repräsentantin des Kulturchristentums." *Gymnasium* 103:216–228.

———. 1999. "Tradition und Neuerung in der spätantiken Kultur. Eudokia - Kaiserin zwischen Paganismus und Christentum." *Phasis* 1:64–73.

Hägg, T. 1983. *The Novel in Antiquity.* Berkeley.

———. 1994. "Orality, Literacy, and the 'Readership' of the Early Greek Novel." In *Contexts of Pre-Novel Narrative: The European Tradition,* ed. R. Erikson, 47–81. Berlin.

Haines-Eitzen, K. 2000. *Guardians of Letters: Literacy, Power, and the Transmitters of Early Christian Literature.* Oxford.

———. 2007. "Engendering Palimpsests: Reading the Textual Tradition of the *Acts of Paul and Thecla.*" In Klingshirn and Safran 2007: 177–193.

Hainsworth, B. 1993. *The Iliad: A Commentary.* Vol III, *Books 9–12.* Cambridge.

Halkin, F. 1953. "Inscriptions grecques relatives à l'hagiographie." *Analecta Bollaniana* 71:74–99.

Hansen, G. C. 1995. *Theodore, Kirchengeschichte.* Berlin.

Happ, H. 1986. *Luxorius.* Stuttgart.

Harden, D. B. 1968. "Ancient Glass I: Pre-Roman." *The Archaeological Journal* 125:46–72.

———. 1969. "Ancient Glass II: Roman." *The Archaeological Journal* 126:44–77.

Hardie, P. 2004. "In the Steps of the Sibyl: Tradition and Desire in the Epic Underworld." *Materiali e discussioni per l'analisi dei testi classici* 52:143–156.

Harding, M. 2003. *Early Christian Life and Thought in Social Context: A Reader.* London.

Harich-Schwarzbauer, H., and P. Schierl, eds. 2009. *Lateinische Poesie der Spätantike.* Basel.

Harris, B. F. 1969. "Apollonius of Tyana: Fact and Fiction." *Journal of Religious History* 5:189–199.

Harris, R. J. 1898. *The Homeric Centones and The Acts of Pilate.* London.

Harris, W. V. 1989. *Ancient Literacy.* Cambridge.

Harrison, J. W. 1903. *Prolegomena to the Study of Greek Religion.* Cambridge.

Haskins, E. 2005. "Pythagorean Women." In Ballif and Moran 2005: 315–319.

Hawley, R. 1998. "The Male Body as Spectacle in Attic Drama." In *Thinking Men: Masculinity and its Self-Representation in the Classical Tradition,* ed. L. Foxhall and J. Salmon, 83–99. London.

Haworth, K. R. 1980. *Deified Virtues, Demonic Vices and Descriptive Allegory in Prudentius' Psychomachia.* Amsterdam.

Hecquet-Noti, N. 2009. "Entre exégèse et épopée: Présence auctoriale dans Juvencus, Sédulius, et Avit de Vienne." In Harich-Schwarzbauer and Schierl 2009: 197–215.

Heffernan, T. J. 1995. "Philology and Authorship in the *Passio Sanctarum Perpetuae et Felicitatis*." *Traditio* 50:315–325.

———. 2012. *The Passion of Perpetua and Felicity*. Oxford.

Heinimann, F. 1945. *Nomos und Physis: Herkunft und Bedeutung einer Antithese im griechischen Denken des 5. Jahrhunderts*. Basel.

Henry, R. 1959–1977. *Photius: Bibliothèque*. 8 vols. Paris.

Hershkowitz, P. 2017. *Prudentius, Spain, and Late Antique Christianity: Poetry, Visual Culture, and the Cult of the Martyrs*. Cambridge.

Hertlein, F. C. 1875. *Juliani Imperatoris quae supersunt*. Leipzig.

Hexter, J. H. 1995. *The Judeo-Christian Tradition*. New Haven.

Hinds, S. 1998. *Allusion and Intertext: Dynamics of Appropriation in Roman Poetry*. Cambridge.

———. 2014. "The Self-conscious Cento." In Formisano, Fuhrer, and Stock 2014: 171–197.

Hirschfeld, Y., ed. 1997. *The Roman Baths of Hammat Gader*. Jerusalem.

Hirschfeld, Y., and G. Solar. 1981. "The Roman Thermae at Hammat Gader: Preliminary Report of Three Seasons of Excavations." *Israel Exploration Journal* 31:197–219.

Hock, R. F., J. B. Chance, and J. Perkins. 1998. *Ancient Fiction and Early Christian Narrative*. Atlanta.

Hoffman, J. R. 2004. *Julian's Against the Galileans*. Amherst.

Holman, S. R. 2001. *The Hungry are Dying: Beggars and Bishops in Roman Cappadocia*. Oxford.

———, ed. 2008. *Wealth and Poverty in Early Church and Society*. Grand Rapids.

Holum, K. G. 1982. *Theodosian Empresses: Women and Imperial Dominion in Late Antiquity*. Los Angeles.

———. 1990. "Hadrian and St. Helena: Imperial Travel and the Origins of Christian Holy Land Pilgrimage." In *The Blessings of Pilgrimage*, ed. R. Ousterhout, 66–81. Chicago.

Holum, K. G., and G. Vikan. 1979. "The Trier Ivory, Adventus Ceremonial, and the Relics of St. Stephen." *Dumbarton Oaks Papers* 33:113–133.

Holzberg, N. 1993. "A Lesser Known 'Picaresque' Novel of Greek Origin: The *Aesop Romance* and Its Influence." *Groningen Colloquia on the Novel* 5:1–16.

———. 1995. *The Ancient Novel: An Introduction*. London.

———. 1996. "The Genre: Novels Proper and the Fringe." In Schmeling 1996: 11–28.

Homeyer, H., ed. 1979. *Dichterinnen des Altertums und des frühen Mittelalters*. Paderborn.

Horn, C. 2004. "The Empress Eudocia and the Monk Peter the Iberian: Patronage, Pilgrimage, and the Love of a Foster-mother in Fifth-century Palestine." *Byzantinische Forschungen* 28:197–213.

Hornung, E. 2001. *The Secret Lore of Egypt: Its Impact on the West.* Ithaca.

Horsley, G. H. R. 1987. "Name Change as an Indication of Religious Conversion in Antiquity." *Numen* 34:1–17.

Horster, M., and C. Reitz, eds. 2010a. *Condensing Texts-Condensed Texts.* Stuttgart.

———. 2010b. "'Condensation' of Literature and the Pragmatics of Literary Production." In Horster and Reitz 2010a: 3–14.

Housman, A. E. 1903. *M. Manilii Astronomicon.* 5 vols. Cambridge.

Huber, G. 1990. "Walter Charleton's 'Ephesian Matron': Ein Zeugnis der Petron-Rezeption im England der Restauration." *Groningen Colloquia on the Novel* 3:139–157.

Huizinga, J. 1955. *Homo Ludens.* London.

Hull, R. F. 2010. *The Story of the New Testament Text: Movers, Materials, Motives, Methods, and Models.* Atlanta.

Hultgren, A. J., and S. A. Haggmark. 1996. *The Earliest Christian Heretics: Readings from Their Opponents.* Minneapolis.

Hunink, V. 1997. *Apuleius of Madauros, Pro se de magia.* 2 vols. Amsterdam.

Hunt, E. D. 1982. *Holy Land Pilgrimage in the Later Roman Empire: AD 312-460.* Oxford.

Hunter, D. G. 1992. *Marriage in the Early Church.* Minneapolis.

———. 2000. "The Virgin, the Bride, and the Church: Reading Psalm 45 in Ambrose, Jerome, and Augustine." *Church History* 69:281–303.

———. 2007. *Marriage, Celibacy, and Heresy in Ancient Christianity: The Jovinianist Controversy.* Oxford.

Hylan, S. E. 2015. *A Modest Apostle: Thecla in the History of Women in the Early Church.* Oxford.

Ilievski, P. H. 1993. "The Origin and Semantic Development of the Term *Harmony*." *Illinois Classical Studies* 18:19–29.

Izdebska, A. 2016. "The Pythagorean Metaphysics of Numbers in the Works of the Ikhwān al-Safā' and al-Shahrastāni." In Renger and Stavru 2016: 361–374.

Jackson, H. M. 1988a. "A Contribution Toward an Edition of the *Confession* of Cyprian of Antioch: The *Secreta Cypriani*." *Le Muséon* 101:33–41.

———. 1988b. "Notes on the *Testament of Solomon*." *Journal for the Study of Judaism* 19:19–60.

———. 1996. "Echoes and Demons in the Pseudo-Philonic *Liber Antiquitatum Biblicarum*." *Journal for the Study of Judaism* 27:1–20.

———. 1999. "Erotic Spell of Cyprian of Antioch." In *Ancient Christian Magic: Coptic Texts of Ritual Power*, ed. M. W. Meyer and R. Smith, 153–158. Princeton.

Jacobs, A. S. 2006. "'Her Own Proper Kinship': Marriage, Class, and Women in the Apocryphal Acts of the Apostles." In Levine 2006: 18–46.

James, M. R. 1920. *The Lost Apocrypha of the Old Testament, Their Titles and Fragments.* London.

James, P. 1999. "Prudentius' *Psychomachia*: The Christian Arena and the Politics of Display." In *Constructing Identities in Late Antiquity*, ed. R. Miles, 70–94. London.

Janko, R. 1994. *The Iliad: A Commentary.* Volume 4, Books 13–16. Cambridge.

Janowitz, N. 2001. *Magic in the Roman World: Pagans, Jews and Christians.* London.

———. 2002. *Icons of Power: Ritual Practices in Late Antiquity.* University Park.

Jarratt, S., and R. Ong. 1995. "Aspasia: Rhetoric, Gender, and Colonial Ideology." In *Reclaiming Rhetorica: Women in the Rhetorical Tradition*, ed. A. A. Lunsford, 9–24. Pittsburgh.

Jeffreys, M. 1981. "Byzantine Metrics: Non-Literary Strata." *Jahrbuch der Österreichischen Byzantinistik* 31.1:313–334.

Jensen, B. M. 2012. *The Story of Justina and Cyprian of Antioch as Told in a Medieval Lectionary from Piacenza: Edition with Introduction and Translation.* Stockholm.

Johne, R. 1996. "Women in the Ancient Novel." In Schmeling 1996: 151–207.

Johnson, S. F. 2006a. *The Life and Miracles of Thekla: A Literary Study.* Hellenic Studies 13. Washington, DC.

———, ed. 2006b. *Greek Literature in Late Antiquity: Dynamism, Didacticism, Classicism.* Burlington.

———, ed. 2012a. *The Oxford Handbook of Late Antiquity.* Oxford.

———. 2012b. "Travel, Cartography, and Cosmology." In Johnson 2012a: 562–594. Oxford.

———. 2016a. "Nonnus' Paraphrastic Technique: A Case Study of Self-Recognition in John 9." In Accorinti 2016: 267–288.

———. 2016b. *Literary Territories: Cartographical Thinking in Late Antiquity.* Oxford.

———. 2016c. "'The Stone the Builders Rejected': Liturgical and Exegetical Irrelevancies in the Piacenza Pilgrim." *Dumbarton Oaks Papers* 70:43–57.

Johnson, W. A. 2000. "Toward a Sociology of Reading in Classical Antiquity." *American Journal of Philology* 121:593–627.

———. 2009. "Introduction." In Johnson and Parker 2009: 3–10.

———. 2010. *Readers and Reading Culture in the High Roman Empire: A Study of Elite Communities.* Oxford.

Johnson, W. A., and H. N. Parker, eds. 2009. *Ancient Literacies: The Culture of Reading in Greece and Rome.* Oxford.

Jones, A. H. M. 1964. *The Later Roman Empire, 284–602: A Social Economic and Administrative Survey.* 3 vols. Oxford.

Jones, A. H. M., J. R. Martindale, and J. Morris. 1971. *The Prosopography of the Later Roman Empire.* Volume 1, *A.D. 260–395.* Cambridge.

Jones, C. P. 2006a. "Apollonius of Tyana in Late Antiquity." In Johnson 2006b: 49–64.

———. 2006b. *Philostratus. Apollonius of Tyana: Letters of Apollonius; Ancient Testimonia; Eusebius's Reply to Hierocles.* Loeb Classical Library 485. Cambridge, MA.

Jonnes, L. 2001. "An Inscription of a Homeric Cento." *Epigraphica Anatolica* 33:49–50.

Jordan, D. R., H. Montgomery, and E. Thomassen, eds. 1999. *The World of Ancient Magic.* Bergen.

Jördens, A., ed. 2015. *Ägyptische Magie und ihre Umwelt.* Wiesbaden.

Juergensmeyer, M. 2000. *Terror in the Mind of God: The Global Rise of Religious Violence.* Berkeley.

Jungmann, J. A. 1960. *The Early Liturgy to the Time of Gregory the Great.* London.

Kahlos, M. 2009. *Forbearance and Compulsion: The Rhetoric of Religious Tolerance and Intolerance in Late Antiquity.* London.

Kaldellis, A. 2005. "Julian, the Hierophant of Eleusis, and the Abolition of Constantius' Tyranny." *Classical Quarterly* 55.2:652–655.

———. 2007. "Christodoros on the Statues of the Zeuxippos Baths: A New Reading of the *Ekphrasis.*" *Greek, Roman, and Byzantine Studies* 47:361–383.

Kaper, O. E. 2003. *The Egyptian God Tutu: A Study of the Sphinx-god and Master of Demons with a Corpus of Monuments.* Leuven.

Käppel, L. 1992. *Paian: Studien zur Geschichte einer Gattung.* Berlin.

Karla, G. A., ed. 2009a. *Fiction on the Fringe: Novelistic Writing in the Post-Classical Age.* Leiden.

———. 2009b. "Fictional Biography Vis-à-vis Romance: Affinity and Differentiation." In Karla 2009a: 13–32.

Kazhdan, A. 1995. "Holy and Unholy Miracles Workers." In *Byzantine Magic,* ed. H. Maguire, 73–82. Washington, DC.

———. 2001. "Byzantine Hagiography and Sex in the Fifth to Twelfth Centuries." In Nagy 2001: 245–257.

Keaney, J. J. 1991. *Harpocration: Lexeis of the Ten Orators.* Amsterdam.

Kelly, C., ed. 2013a. *Theodosius II: Rethinking the Roman Empire in Late Antiquity.* Cambridge.

———. 2013b. "Rethinking Theodosius." In Kelly 2013a: 3–64.

Kendall, C. B. 1998. *The Allegory of the Church: Romanesque Portals and Their Verse Inscriptions.* Toronto.

Kennedy, G. A. 1983. *Greek Rhetoric under Christian Emperors.* Princeton.

———. 1989. *The Cambridge History of Literary Criticism.* Volume 1, *Classical Criticism.* Cambridge.

Kennell, S. A. H. 2000. *Magnus Felix Ennodius: A Gentleman of the Church.* Ann Arbor.

Kirk, G. S. 1990. *The Iliad: A Commentary.* Volume II, *Books 5-8.* Cambridge.

Kleinschmidt, A. L. 2013. *Ich-Entwürfe in spätantiker Dichtung: Ausonius, Paulinus von Nola und Paulinus von Pella.* Heidelberg.

Klingshirn, W. E., and L. Safran, eds. 2007. *The Early Christian Book.* Washington, DC.

Knust, J. W. 2006. *Abandoned to Lust: Sexual Slander and Ancient Christianity.* New York.

———. 2011. *Unprotected Texts: The Bible's Surprising Contradictions About Sex and Desire.* New York.

Konstan, D. 1997. *Friendship in the Classical World.* Cambridge.

———. 1998. "The Invention of Fiction." In Hock, Chance, and Perkins 1998: 3–17.

Kortekaas, G. A. A. 1990. "The Latin Adaptations of the 'Historia Apollonii Regis Tyri' in the Middle Ages and the Renaissance." *Groningen Colloquia on the Novel* 3:103–122.

Kraemer, R. S. 1992. *Her Share of the Blessings: Women's Religions among Pagans, Jews, and Christians in the Greco Roman World.* Oxford.

———. 2011. *Unreliable Witnesses: Religion, Gender, and History in the Greco-Roman Mediterranean.* Oxford.

Kraemer, R. S., and M. R. D'Angelo, eds. 1999. *Women and Christian Origins.* New York.

Kretschmar, G. 1977. "Recent Research on Christian Initiation." *Studia Liturgica* 12:87–106.

Kruger, M. J. 2005. *The Gospel of the Savior: An Analysis of P.Oxy 840 and its Place in the Gospel Traditions of Early Christianity.* Leiden.

Kruse, T. 2006. "The Magistrate and the Ocean: Acclamation and Ritualized Communication in Town Gatherings in Roman Egypt." In *Ritual and Communication in the Graeco-Roman World,* ed. E. Stavrianopoulou, 297–315. Liège.

Laird, A. 2006. *Oxford Readings in Ancient Literary Criticism.* Oxford.

Laistner, M. L. W. 1951. *Christianity and Pagan Culture in the Later Roman Empire.* Ithaca.

Lalleman, P. J. 1998. "The Canonical and the Apocryphal Acts of the Apostles." *Groningen Colloquia on the Novel* 9:181–192.

Lalonde, G. 2006. *Horos Dios: An Athenian Shrine and Cult of Zeus.* Leiden.

Lamacchia, R. 1958. "Technica centonaria e critica del testo (a proposito della Medea di Osidio Geta)." *Rendiconti Accademia nazionale dei Lincei, Classe di Scienze morali, storiche e filologiche* 355:258–280.

Lamberton, R. 1986. *Homer the Theologian: Neoplatonist Allegorical Reading and the Growth of the Epic Tradition.* Berkeley.

———. 2001. "The Schools of Platonic Philosophy of the Roman Empire: The Evidence of the Biographies." In *Education in Greek and Roman Antiquity*, ed. Y. L. Too, 433–458. Leiden.

Lambropoulou, V. 1996. "On Harmony: Etymology, Preplatonic Meanings and Elements." *Platon* 47–48:179–193.

———. 1997. "The Concept of Harmony in Greek Thought from Homer to Aristotle 2. Psychology." *Platon* 49:271–296.

———. 1998. "The Concept of Harmony in Greek Thought from Homer to Aristotle 3. Cosmology." *Platon* 50:145–168.

Lampe, G. W. H. 1968. *A Patristic Greek Lexicon.* Oxford.

Lane, E. N., ed. 1996. *Cybele, Attis and Related Cults: Essays in Memory of M. J. Vermaseren.* Leiden.

Lasek, A. M. 2016. "Nonnus and the Play of Genres." In Accorinti 2016: 402–421.

Leaf, W. 1902. *The Iliad.* London.

Ledbetter, G. M. 2003. *Poetics before Plato: Interpretation and Authority in Early Greek Theories of Poetry.* Princeton.

Lee, B. T., E. Finkelpearl, and L. Graverini, eds. 2014. *Apuleius and Africa.* New York.

Leitao, J. 2014. *The Book of St. Cyprian: The Sorcerer's Treasure.* West Yorkshire.

———. 2017. *The Immaterial Book of St. Cyprian.* Seattle.

Leppin, H. 1998. "Aelia Eudokia." *Der Neue Pauly* 4:220–221.

Lerza, P. 1982. "Dio e anti-Dio. Il demone-demiurgo nel S. Cipriano di Eudocia." In Angelino and Salvaneschi 1982: 81–99.

Levine, A., ed. 2006. *A Feminist Companion to the New Testament Apocrypha.* Cleveland.

Lewis, N. D. 2013. *Cosmology and Fate in Gnosticism and Graeco-Roman Antiquity: Under Pitiless Skies.* Leiden.

Liebeschuetz, J. H. W. G. 1972. *Antioch: City and Imperial Administration in the Later Roman Empire.* Oxford.

———. 1994. "The Expansion of Mithraism among the Religious Cults of the Second Century." In *Studies in Mithraism*, ed. J. R. Hinnells, 195–216. Rome.

———. 2006. *Decline and Change in Late Antiquity: Religion, Barbarians and their Historiography.* Burlington.

Lieu, S. N. C. 1989. *The Emperor Julian: Panegyric and Polemic.* Liverpool.

Limberis, V. 1996. *Divine Heiress: The Virgin Mary and the Creation of Christian Constantinople.* London.

Lipsett, B. D. 2011. *Desiring Conversion: Hermas, Thecla, Aseneth.* Oxford.

Littlewood, A. R. 1974. "The Symbolism of the Apple in Byzantine Literature." *Jahrbuch der Österreichischen Byzantinistik* 23:33–59.

Liverani, P. 2011. "Reading Spolia in Late Antique and Contemporary Perception." In *Reuse Value: Spolia and Appropriation in Art and Architecture from Constantine to Sherrie Levine,* ed. R. Brilliant and D. Kinney, 33–52. Farnham.

Livrea, E. 1989. *Nonno di Panopoli. Parafrasi del Vangelo di S. Giovanni, Canto XVIII.* Naples.

———. 1994. "Eudocianum." In *Paideia Cristiana,* ed. M. Naldini, 141–145. Rome.

———. 1996. "La slogatura di Eudocia in un'iscrizione paflagone." *Zeitschrift für Papyrologie und Epigraphik* 113:71–76.

———. 1997a. "I due Taziani in un' iscrizione di Afrodisia." *Zeitschrift für Papyrologie und Epigraphik* 119:43–49.

———. 1997b. "L'imperatrice Eudocia santa?" *Zeitschrift für Papyrologie und Epigraphik* 119:50–54.

———. 1998. "L'imperatrice Eudocia e Roma. Per una datazione del *de S. Cypr.*" *Byzantinische Zeitschrift* 91:70–91.

———. 2000. "La *Gigantomachia* greca di Claudiano: Tradizione manoscritta e critica testuale." *Maia* 52:415–451.

Longo, V. 1969. *Aretalogie nel mondo Greco, Vol. 1: Epigraphi e papiri.* Genova.

Lopez, A. J. 2001. *Textos griegos de maleficio.* Madrid.

Louden, B. 2011. *Homer's Odyssey and the Near East.* Cambridge.

Lowe, D. 2013. "Triple Tipple: Ausonius' *Griphus ternarii numeri.*" In *The Muse at Play: Riddles and Wordplay in Greek and Latin Poetry,* ed. J. Kwapisz, D. Petrain, and M. Szymański, 335–352. Berlin.

Luck, G. 1962. *Hexen und Zauberei in der römischen Dichtung.* Zurich.

———. 2006. *Arcana Mundi: Magic and the Occult in the Greek and Roman Worlds.* 2nd ed. Baltimore.

Ludwich, A. 1882. "Eudokia, die Gattin des Kaisers Theodosios II, als Dichterin." *Rheinisches Museum für Philologie* 37:206–225.

———. 1897. *Eudociae Augustae, Procli Lycii Claudiani Carminum Graecorum Reliquiae.* Leipzig.

MacCormack, S. 1998. *The Shadows of Poetry: Vergil in the Mind of Augustine.* Berkeley.

MacDonald, D. R. 1983. *The Legend and the Apostle: The Battle for Paul in Story and Canon.* Philadelphia.

———. 1994. *Christianizing Homer: The Odyssey, Plato, and the Acts of Andrew.* Oxford.

———. 2000. *The Homeric Epics and the Gospel of Mark.* New Haven.

———. 2001. *Mimesis and Intertextuality in Antiquity and Christianity.* Harrisburg.

MacDonald, M. Y. 1999. "Rereading Paul: Early Interpreters of Paul on Women and Gender." In Kraemer and D'Angelo 1999: 236–253.

Macklin Smith, K. 1976. *Prudentius' Psychomachia: A Re-Examination.* Princeton.

Majani, C. 2006. "*Fons Aponi* in Claudiano, Cassiodoro ed Ennodio: per un'analisi intertestuale." In *Atti della terza giornata ennodiana (Pavia 10-11 Novembre 2004),* ed. F. Gasti, 207–218. Pisa.

Malamud, M. A. 1989. *A Poetics of Transformation: Prudentius and Classical Mythology.* Ithaca.

———. 2011. *The Origin of Sin: An English Translation of the Hamartigenia.* Ithaca.

———. 2012. "Double Double: Two African Medeas" *Ramus* 41:161–189.

Malingrey, A. M. 1972. *Jean Chrysostome: Sur la vaine gloire et l'éducation des enfants.* Paris.

Mangelsdorff, E. A. 1913. "Das lyrische Hochzeitsgedicht bei den Griechen und Römern" *Wissenschaftliche Beilage zum Jahresbericht der Hausa-Schule 1913.* Hamburg.

Mango, C. 2004. "A Fake Inscription of the Empress Eudocia and Pulcheria's Relic of Saint Stephen." *Nea Rhome* 1:23–34.

Mann, W. E., ed. 2006. *Augustine's* Confessions: *Critical Essays.* Lanham.

Maravelia, A. A. 2003. *Η μαγεία στην αρχαία Αίγυπτο. Μεταφυσική πεμπτουσία της χώρας των θεών.* Athens.

Marcos, N. F. 1975. *Los Thaumata de Sofronio: Contribución al estudio de la incubatio cristiana.* Madrid.

Markus, R. A. 1994. "How on Earth Could Places Become Holy? Origins of the Christian Idea of Holy Places." *Journal of Early Christian Studies* 2:257–271.

Marrou, H. I. 1964. *A History of Education in Antiquity.* New York.

Martin, M. 2005. *Magie et magiciens dans le monde gréco-romain.* Paris.

———. 2015. "'Parler la langue des oiseaux': les écritures 'barbares' et mysté-rieuses des tablettes de défixion." In *Écrire la magie dans l'antiquité. Actes du colloque international (Liège, 13-15 octobre 2011),* ed. M. De Haro Sanchez, 251–265. Liège.

Martindale, J. R. 1980. *The Prosopography of the Later Roman Empire.* Volume 2, A.D. 395-527. Cambridge.

Mastrandrea, P. 2001. "L'epigramma dedicatorio del 'Cento Vergilianus' di Proba: Analisi del testo, ipotesi di datazione e identificazione dell'autore." *Bollettino di Studi Latini* 31:565–578.

Mastrangelo, M. 2008. *The Roman Self in Late Antiquity: Prudentius and the Poetics of the Soul.* Baltimore.

———. 2016. "Toward a Poetics of Late Latin Reuse." In McGill and Pucci 2016: 25–45.

Mathews, T. F. 1999. *The Clash of Gods: A Reinterpretation of Early Christian Art*. Princeton.

Matthews, J. 1975. *Western Aristocracies and Imperial Court, AD 364–425*. Oxford.

———. 2006. *The Journey of Theophanes: Travel, Business, and Daily Life in the Roman East*. New Haven.

Mayer, W. 2006a. "Poverty and Society in the World of John Chrysostom." In *Social and Political Life in Late Antiquity*, ed. W. Bowden, A. Gutteridge, and C. Machado, 465–484. Leiden.

———. 2006b. *St. John Chrysostom: The Cult of the Saints*. New York.

———. 2008. "Poverty and Generosity Toward the Poor in the Time of John Chrysostom." In *Wealth and Poverty in Early Church and Society*, ed. S. R. Holman, 140–158. Grand Rapids.

Mayer, W., and P. Allen. 1999. *John Chrysostom*. London.

Mazzarino, S. 1946. *Serena e le due Eudossie*. Roma.

McClanan, A. 2002. *Representations of Early Byzantine Empresses: Image and Empire*. New York.

McGill, S. 2005. *Virgil Recomposed: The Mythological and Secular Centos in Antiquity*. Oxford.

———. 2007. "Virgil, Christianity, and the *Cento Probae*." In Scourfield 2007: 173–93.

———. 2009. "The Rights of Authorship in Symmachus' *Epistulae* I.31." *Classical Philology* 104:229–32.

———. 2014. "Ausonius at Night." *American Journal of Philology* 135:123–48.

———. 2016a. *Juvencus' Four Books of the Gospels: Evangeliorum libri quattuor*. London and New York.

———. 2016b. "Arms and Amen: Virgil in Juvencus' *Evangeliorum libri IV*." In McGill and Pucci 2016: 47–75.

McGill, S., and J. Pucci, eds. 2016. *Classics Renewed: Reception and Innovation in the Latin Poetry of Late Antiquity*. Heidelberg.

McLynn, N. 1992. "Christian Controversy and Violence in the Fourth Century." *Kodai: Journal of Ancient History* 3:15–44.

———. 2006. "Among the Hellenists: Gregory and the Sophists." In *Gregory of Nazianzus: Images and Reflections*, ed. J. Børtnes and T. Hägg, 213–238. Copenhagen.

Mead, G. R. S. 1980. *Apollonius of Tyana: The Philosopher-Reformer of the First Century AD*. Chicago.

Méautis, G. 1931. "Zur ὠκεανέ-Akklamation." *Rheinisches Museum für Philologie* 80:112.

Meimare, I. 1983. "Ύπό επιγραφές της αυγούστης Ευδοκίας (423–460 μ.Χ.)." *Θεολογία* 54:388–398.

Mele, A. 2013. *Pitagora: filosofo e maestro di verità*. Rome.

Merkelbach, R. 1962. *Roman und Mysterium in der Antike*. Munich.

———. 1988. "Eine Akklamation als Hesies-Osiris (Pap.Oxy. 41)." *Zeitschrift für Papyrologie und Epigraphik* 72:65–66.

Migne, J. 1860. "Eudocia Imperatrix Augusta." *Patrologia Graeca* 85:827–864.

Milani, C. 1977. *Itinerarium Antonini Placentini: un viaggio in Terra Santa nel 560–570 d.C.* Milan.

Milavec, A. 2003. *The Didache: Text, Translation, Analysis, and Commentary*. Minnesota.

Miller, P. C. 1993. "The Blazing Body: Ascetic Desire in Jerome's Letter to Eustochium." *Journal of Early Christian Studies* 1:21–45.

———. 2003. "Is There a Harlot in This Text? Asceticism and the Grotesque." *Journal of Medieval and Early Modern Studies* 33:419–436.

———. 2005. *Women in Early Christianity: Translations from Greek Texts*. Washington, DC.

Mioni, E. 1992. *Catalogus codicum graecorum Bibliothecae Nationalis Neapolitanae*. Naples.

Mirecki, P., and M. Meyer, eds. 2002. *Magic and Ritual in the Ancient World*. Leiden.

Misset-van de Weg, M. 2006. "Answers to the Plights of an Ascetic Woman Named Thecla." In Levine 2006: 146–162.

Mitchell, M. M. 2006. "The Emergence of the Written Record." In Mitchell and Young 2006: 177–194.

Mitchell, M. M., and F. M. Young, eds. 2006. *The Cambridge History of Christianity, vol. 1: Origins to Constantine*. Cambridge.

Mitchell, S. 2007. *A History of the Later Roman Empire, AD 284–641: The Transformation of the Ancient World*. Oxford.

Mommsen, A. 1868. *Athenae Christianae*. Leipzig.

———. 1894. *Marcellini V.C. comitis Chronicon ad a. 518: continuatum ad a. 534, cum additamento ad a. 548*. Berlin.

Montserrat, D. 2005. "Carrying on the Work of the Earlier Firm: Doctors, Medicine and Christianity in the Thaumata of Sophronius of Jerusalem." In *Health in Antiquity*, ed. H. King, 230–242. London.

Morales, H. 2009. "Challenging Some Orthodoxies: The Politics of Genre and the Ancient Greek Novel." In Karla 2009a: 1–12.

Morard, F. 1991. "Souffrance et martyre dans les actes apocryphes des apôtres." In *Les Actes apocryphes des apôtres: Christianisme et monde paien*, ed. F. Bovon et al., 95–108. Geneva.

Moraux, P. 1980. "La rédemption racontée en vers homériques." In *Actes du X congrès de l'Association Guillaume Budé, Toulouse 8–12 avril 1978*, 132–133.

Morelli, C. 1910. "L'epithalamio nella tarda poesia latina." *Studi italiani di filologia classica* 18:319–432.

Moreschini, C. 2015. *Apuleius and the Metamorphoses of Platonism*. Turnhout.

Moreschini, C., and E. Norelli. 2005. *Early Christian Greek and Latin Literature: A Literary History*. 2 vols. Peabody.

Moretti, P. F. 2008. "Proba e il Cento nuptialis di Ausonio." In *Debita dona: Studi in onore di Isabella Gualandri*, ed. P. F. Moretti, C. Torre, G. Zanetto, and I. Gualandri, 317–347. Naples.

Morgan, J. R., and R. Stoneman, eds. 1994. *Greek Fiction: The Greek Novel in Context*. London.

Morgan, T. 1998. *Literate Education in the Hellenistic and Roman Worlds*. Cambridge.

Muir, S. C. 2006. "Mending Yet Fracturing: Healing as an Arena of Conflict." In *The Changing Face of Judaism, Christianity, and Other Greco-Roman Religions in Antiquity*, ed. I. H. Henderson and G. S. Oegema, 57–71. Munich.

Mullach, F. G. A., ed. 1860. *Fragmenta Philosophorum Graecorum*. 3 vols. Paris.

Müller, C. W. 1981. "Der griechische Roman." In *Neues Handbuch der Literaturwissenschaft*, ed. E. Vogt, 377–412. Frankfurt.

Müller, J. 2006. *Physis und Ethos: Der Naturbegriff bei Aristoteles und seine Relevanz für die Ethik*. Würzburg.

Müller, M. 2016. *Tod und Auferstehung Jesu Christi bei Iuvencus (IV 570–812): Untersuchungen zu Dichtkunst, Theologie und Zweck der Evangeliorum libri quattuor*. Stuttgart.

Muñoz, L. D. 2001. *Lexico de magía y religión en los papiros mágicos griegos*. Madrid.

Münscher, K. 1912. "Herodes." In *Paulys Realencyclopädie der classischen Altertumswissenschaft* 8:922–954. Stuttgart.

Musurillo, H. 1972. *Acts of the Christian Martyrs*. Oxford.

Mylonas, G. E. 1961. *Eleusis and the Eleusinian Mysteries*. Princeton.

Mynors, R. A. B. 1991. *Collected Works: Adages 2.1.1 to 2.6.100: Desiderius Erasmus, vol. 33*. Toronto.

Naddaf, G. 1992. *L'Origine et l'évolution du concept grec de 'physis.'* New York.

———. 2005. *The Greek Concept of Nature*. Albany.

Nagy, G. 1990. *Pindar's Homer: The Lyric Possession of an Epic Past*. Baltimore.

———, ed. 2001. *Greek Literature*. Volume 9, *Greek Literature in the Byzantine Period*. London.

Nathan, G. S. 2000. *The Family in Late Antiquity: The Rise of Christianity and the Endurance of Tradition*. London.

Netz, R. 2009. *Ludic Proof: Greek Mathematics and the Alexandrian Aesthetic*. Cambridge.

Netz, R., and W. Noel. 2007. *The Archimedes Codex: How a Medieval Prayer Book is Revealing the True Genius of Antiquity's Greatest Scientist*. New York.

Nicholson, O. 2014. "Self-Portrait as a Landscape: Ausonius and His Herediolum." In *Being Christian in Late Antiquity: A Festschrift for Gillian Clark*, ed. C. Harrison, C. Humfress, and I. Sandwell, 235–252. Oxford.

Nieto-Ibáñez, J. M. 1994. "Observaciones sobre la lengua y la métrica de un poema de la emperatriz Eudocia (SEG XXXII 1502)." In *Actas del VIII congreso español de estudios clásicos (Madrid, 23-28 de septiembre de 1991)*, 213–217. Madrid.

Nilsson, M. P. 1947. "Greek Mysteries in the Confession of St. Cyprian." *Harvard Theological Review* 40:167–176.

———. 1950. "Mantique et mystères antiques d'après la Confession de Saint Cyprien." *Revue Archéologique* 35:205–207.

Nock, A. D. 1927. "Hagiographica II. Cyprian of Antioch." *Journal of Theological Studies* 28:411–415.

Noegel, S., J. Walker, and B. Wheeler, eds. 2003. *Prayer, Magic, and the Stars in the Ancient and Late Antique World*. University Park.

Noethlichs, K. L. 2007. "Jews, Heretics or Useful Farm Workers? Samaritans in Late Antique Imperial Legislation." In *Wolf Liebeschuetz Reflected: Essays Presented by Colleagues, Friends, and Pupils*, ed. J. Drinkwater and B. Salway, 57–66. London.

Noreña, C. F. 2014. "Authority and Subjectivity in the *Apology*." In Lee, Finkelpearl, and Graverini 2014: 35–51.

Nugent, S. G. 1985. *Allegory and Poetics: The Structure and Imagery of Prudentius' Psychomachia*. Frankfurt am Main.

———. 1990. "Ausonius' 'Late-Antique' Poetics and 'Post-Modern' Literary Theory." *Ramus* 19.1:26–50.

Ogden, D. 2001. *Greek and Roman Necromancy*. Princeton.

———. 2002. *Magic, Witchcraft, and Ghosts in the Greek and Roman Worlds: A Sourcebook*. Oxford.

———. 2006. "Lucian's Tale of *The Sorcerer's Apprentice* in Context." In Szpakowska 2006: 121–144.

———. 2007. *In Search of the Sorcerer's Apprentice*. Swansea.

Olson, D. R. 2009. "Why Literacy Matters, Then and Now." In Johnson and Parker 2009: 385–403.

Osiek, C., M. MacDonald, and J. H. Tulloch. 2006. *A Woman's Place: House Churches in Earliest Christianity*. Minneapolis.

Ovadiah, A. 1998. "Allegorical Images in Greek Laudatory Inscriptions in Eretz-Israel." *Gerión* 16:383–394.

Pagano, M. 1988–1989. "Il Palazzo dei Giganti nell'agorà di Atene. La residenza della famiglia di Eudocia?" *Annuario della Scuola Archeologica di Atene* 50–51:159–161.

Pagels, E. 1995. *The Origin of Satan*. New York.

Paolucci, P. 2006. *Il Centone Virgiliano* Hippodamia *Dell'* Anthologia Latina. Hildesheim.

Parker, H. N. 1999. "The Observed of All Observers: Spectacle, Applause, and Cultural Poetics in the Roman Theater Audience." In *The Art of Ancient Spectacle*, ed. B. Bergmann and C. Kondoleon, 163–179. New Haven.

Parmentier, M. F. G. 1989. "Non-medical Ways of Healing in Eastern Christianity: The Case of St. Dometios." In *Fructus Centesimus*, ed. A. A. R. Bastiaensen, A. Hilhorst, and C. H. Kneepkens, 279–296. Steenbrugge.

Paschalis, M. 2011. "Apollonius of Tyana as Proteus: *Theios anēr* or Master of Deceit?" In *Holy Men and Charlatans in the Ancient Novel*, ed. S. Panayotakis, G. Schmeling, and M. Paschalis, 133–150. Eelde.

Patlagean, E. 1977. *Pauvreté économique et pauvreté sociale à Byzance, 4e-7e siècles*. Paris.

———. 1997. "The Poor." In *The Byzantines*, ed. G. Cavallo, 15–42. Chicago.

Patzer, H. 1993. *Physis: Grundlegung zu einer Geschichte des Wortes*. Stuttgart.

Pavlovskis, Z. 1965. "Statius and the Late Latin Epithalamia." *Classical Philology* 60:164–177.

———. 1967. "From Statius to Ennodius: A Brief History of Prose Prefaces to Poems." *Rendiconti dell'Istituto Lombardo, Classe di Lettere, Scienze morali e storiche* 101:535–567.

Pearson, B. A. 2007. *Ancient Gnosticism: Traditions and Literature*. Minneapolis.

Pease, A. S. 1920–1923. *M. Tulli Ciceronis De divinatione. Liber primus, liber secundus*. Urbana.

Pelttari, A. 2011. "Symmachus' *Epistulae* 1.31 and Ausonius' Poetics of the Reader." *Classical Philology* 106:161–169.

———. 2014. *The Space That Remains: Reading Latin Poetry in Late Antiquity*. Ithaca.

Penella, R. J. 1979. *The Letters of Apollonius of Tyana: A Critical Text with Translation and Commentary*. Leiden.

Perkins, J. P. 1994. "The *Passion of Perpetua*: A Narrative of Empowerment." *Latomus* 53:837–847.

———. 1995. *The Suffering Self: Pain and Narrative Representation in the Early Christian Era*. London.

———. 2007. "The Rhetoric of the Maternal Body in the *Passion of Perpetua*." In *Mapping Gender in Ancient Religious Discourses*, ed. T. Penner and C. V. Stichele, 313–332. Leiden.

Pernot, L. 1993. *La rhétorique de l'éloge dans le monde gréco-romain*. 2 vols. Paris.

Perry, B. E. 1967. *The Ancient Romances: A Literary-Historical Account of Their Origins*. Berkeley.

Pervo, R. 1987. *Profit with Delight: The Literary Genre of the Acts of the Apostles*. Philadelphia.

———. 1996. "The Ancient Novel Becomes Christian." In Schmeling 1996: 685–711.

Peterson, E. 1929. "Die Bedeutung der ὠκεανέ-Akklamation." *Rheinisches Museum für Philologie* 78:221–223.

Petschenig, M., et. al. 1888. *Poetae Christiani Minores*. Vol. 1. Leipzig.

Pierleoni, G. 1962. *Catalogus codicum graecorum Bibliothecae Nationalis Neopolitanae*. Naples.

Pietersma, A. 1994. *The Apocryphon of Jannes and Jambres the Magicians: P. Chester Beatty XVI*. Leiden.

Pignani, A. 1985. "Il modello omerico e la fonte biblica nel centone di Eudocia imperatrice." *Koinonia* 9:33–41.

———. 1987. "'Eudokia' del Padre, 'apostolê' ed 'hupakoê' del Figlio nel Homerocento di Eudocia imperatrice." In *Talariskos: studia graeca Antonio Garzya sexagenario a discipulis oblata*, ed. A. Garzya, 209–223. Naples.

Plant, I. M. 2004. *Women Writers of Ancient Greece and Rome*. Norman.

Pohlenz, M. 1978. *Die Stoa: Geschichte einer geistigen Bewegung*. 2 vols. Göttingen.

Pollmann, K. 2004. "Sex and Salvation in the Vergilian Cento of the Fourth Century." In Rees 2004a: 79–96.

———. 2017. *The Baptized Muse: Early Christian Poetry as Cultural Authority*. Oxford.

Popescu, V. 2014. "Lucian's *True Stories*: Paradoxography and False Discourse." In Futre Pinheiro, Schmeling, and Cueva 2014: 39–58.

Prete, S. 1978. *Decimi Magni Ausonii Burdigalensis Opuscula*. Leipzig.

Pucci, J. 1998. *The Full-Knowing Reader: Allusion and the Power of the Reader in the Western Literary Tradition*. New Haven.

———. 2016. "Ausonius on the Lyre: *De Bissula* and the Traditions of Latin Lyric." In McGill and Pucci 2016: 111–131.

Pucci, P. 1986. *Odysseus Polutropos: Intertextual Readings in the "Odyssey" of Homer*. Ithaca.

Quack, J. F. 2015. "Dämonen und andere höhere Wesen in der Magie als Feinde und Helfer." In Jördens 2015: 101–118.

Quinn, J. M. 2002. *A Companion to the Confessions of St. Augustine*. New York.

Quispel, G. 1956. "An Unknown Fragment of the Acts of Andrew (Pap. Copt. Utrecht N. 1)." *Vigiliae Christianae* 10:129–148.

———. 1974. "Faust: Symbol of Western Man." In *Gnostic Studies*, Vol 2., 288–307. Istanbul.

Raabe, R., ed. 1895. *Vita Petri Iberi*. Leipzig.

Bibliography

Racionero, Q. 1998. "Logos, Myth and Probable Discourse in Plato's Timaeus." *Elenchos* 19:29–60.

Radermacher, L. 1927. *Griechische Quellen zur Faustsage: der Zauberer Cyprianus; die Erzählung des Helladius; Theophilus.* Sitzungsberichte der Österreichischen Akademie der Wissenschaften, Philosophisch-historische Klasse, Vol. 206, Issue 4. Wien.

Rapp, C. 2007. "Holy Texts, Holy Men, and Holy Scribes: Aspects of Scriptural Holiness in Late Antiquity." In Klingshirn and Safran 2007: 194–222.

Reardon, B. P. 1991. *The Form of Greek Romance.* Princeton.

Rees, R. D., ed. 2004a. *Romane memento: Vergil in the Fourth Century.* London.

———. 2004b. "Praising in Prose: Vergil in the Panegyrics." In Rees 2004a: 33–46.

———. 2017. "The Poetics of Latin Prose Praise and the Fourth-Century Curve." In Elsner and Lobato 2017a: 313–344.

Renberg, G. H. 2016. *Where Dreams May Come: Incubation Sanctuaries in the Greco-Roman World.* 2 vols. Leiden.

Renger, A., and A. Stavru, eds. 2016. *Pythagorean Knowledge from the Ancient to the Modern World: Askesis, Religion, Science.* Göttingen.

Rey, A. L. 1998. *Centons homériques (Homerocentra). Patricius, Eudocie, Optimus, Côme de Jérusalem. Introduction, texte critique, traduction, notes et indexes.* Paris.

Reydams-Schils, G. 2015. "Hellenistic and Roman Philosophy." In *A Companion to Ancient Education,* ed. W. M. Bloomer, 123–133. New York.

Rhee, H. 2005. *Early Christian Literature: Christ and Culture in the Second and Third Centuries.* London.

Rice, T. T. 1957. *The Scythians.* London.

Richardson, N. J. 2006. "Literary Criticism in the Exegetical Scholia to the *Iliad*: A Sketch." In Laird 2006: 176–210.

Riedweg, C. 2005. *Pythagoras: His Life, Teaching, and Influence.* Ithaca.

Roberts, M. 1985. *Biblical Epic and Rhetorical Paraphrase in Late Antiquity.* Liverpool.

———. 1989a. "The Use of Myth in Latin Epithalamia from Statius to Venantius Fortunatus." *Transactions of the American Philological Association* 119:321–348.

———. 1989b. *The Jeweled Style: Poetry and Poetics in Late Antiquity.* Ithaca.

———. 1993. *Poetry and the Cult of the Martyrs: The Liber Peristephenon of Prudentius.* Ann Arbor.

———. 2004. "Vergil and the Gospels: The *Evangeliorum Libri IV* of Juvencus." In Rees 2004a: 47–61.

———. 2009. *The Humblest Sparrow: The Poetry of Venantius Fortunatus.* Ann Arbor.

———. 2017a. "Lactantius's Phoenix and Late Latin Poetics." In Elsner and Lobato 2017a: 373–390.

———. 2017b. *Venantius Fortunatus, Poems.* Cambridge, MA.

Robiano, P. 2016. "The *Apologia* as a *mise-en-abyme* in Philostratus' *Life of Apollonius of Tyana*." In *Writing Biography in Greece and Rome: Narrative Technique and Fictionalization*, ed. K. de Temmerman and K. Demoen, 97–116. Cambridge.

Robinson, M. 2011. *A Commentary on Ovid's Fasti, Book 2*. Oxford.

Rodman, R. C. 1997. "Who's on Third? Reading *Acts of Andrew* as a Rhetoric of Resistance." *Semeia* 79:27–44.

Roller, L. E. 1999. *In Search of God the Mother: The Cult of Anatolian Cybele*. Berkeley.

Román López, M. T. 1995. "La magia hindú y su proyección hacia occidente en el mundo antiguo." *Espacio, tiempo y forma* 8:85–126.

Rondholz, A. 2012. *The Versatile Needle: Hosidius Geta's Cento "Medea" and its Tradition*. Berlin.

Ronot, H. 1973. *Bourbonne-les-Baines. Guide thermal et touristique*. Langres.

Rose, E. 2005. "Hagiography as a Liturgical Act: Liturgical and Hagiographic Commemoration in the Early Middle Ages." In *A Cloud of Witnesses: The Cult of the Saints in Past and Present*, ed. M. Barnard, P. Post, and E. Rose, 161–183. Leuven.

———. 2008. "Medieval Memories of the Apostolic Past: Reception and Use of the Apocryphal Acts in the Liturgical Commemoration of the Apostles." *Apocrypha* 19:123–145.

Rosenblum, J. D., L. C. Vuong, and N. P. DesRosiers, eds. 2014. *Religious Competition in the Third Century CE: Jews, Christians, and the Greco-Roman World*. Göttingen.

Roskam, G. 2014. "John Chrysostom on Pagan Euergetism: A Reading of the First Part of *De inani gloria et de educandis liberis*." *Sacris Erudiri* 54:147–169.

Rossi, M. A. 1984. "The Passion of Perpetua, Everywoman of Late Antiquity." In *Pagan and Christian Anxiety*, ed. R. C. Smith and J. Lounibos, 53–86. New York.

Rousselle, A. 1983. *Porneia: De la maîtrise du corps à la privation sensorielle, IIe–IVe siècles de l'ère chrétienne*. Paris.

Rücker, M. 2014. "*Pharmakeía und crimen magiae": Frauen und Magie in der griechisch-römischen Antike*. Göttingen

Rücker, N. 2009. "*Ausonio possis considere portu* (Verg. Aen. 3,378). Ausonius, Paulinus, Ovid und Vergil: Spätantike Briefdichtung neu gelesen." In Harich-Schwarzbauer and Schierl 2009: 83–108.

———. 2012. *Ausonius an Paulinus von Nola: Textgeschichte und literarische Form der Briefgedichte 21 und 22 des Decimus Magnus Ausonius*. Wiesbaden.

Ruether, R. R. 1998. *Women and Redemption: A Theological History*. Minneapolis.

Ruiz-Montero, C. 1996. "The Rise of the Greek Novel." In Schmeling 1996: 29–86.

Russell, J. B. 1981. *Satan: The Early Christian Tradition*. Ithaca.

Sabattini, T. A. 1973. "S. Cipriano nella tradizione agiografica." *Rivista di studi classici* 21:181–204.

Bibliography

Salanitro, G. 1995. "Eudocia e Omero. Appunti sulla tradizione manoscritta degli Homerocentones." In *Studia classica Iohanni Tarditi oblata*, ed. L. Belloni, G. Milanese, and A. Porro, 1257–1262. Milan.

———. 1997. "Osidio Geta e la poesia centonaria." *Aufstieg und Niedergang der Römischen Welt* 2.34.3:2314–2360.

Salisbury, J. E. 1997. *Perpetua's Passion: The Death and Memory of a Young Roman Woman*. New York.

Saller, R. 1989. "Patronage and Friendship in Early Imperial Rome: Drawing the Distinction." In *Patronage in Ancient Society*, ed. A. Wallace-Hadrill, 49–62. London.

Salvaneschi, E. 1981. "'Ex allou allo.' Antico e tardo antico nelle opere di Eudocia Augusta." In *Desmos koinônias: Scritti di filologia e filosofia, per Gianfranco Bartolini nel secondo anniversario della scomparsa 1979-1981*, ed. G. Fabiano and E. Salvaneschi, 123–188. Geneva.

———. 1982a. "Un Faust redento." In Angelino and Salvaneschi 1982: 1–10.

———. 1982b. "De Sancto Cypriano." In Angelino and Salvaneschi 1982: 11–80.

Salvatore, A. 1953. "Rapporti tra nugae e carmina docta nel canzoniere catulliano." *Latomus* 12:418–431.

Sambursky, S. 1958. "Philoponus' Interpretation of Aristotle's Theory of Light." *Osiris* 13:114–126.

Sandnes, K. O. 2009. *The Challenge of Homer: School, Pagan Poets and Early Christianity*. London.

———. 2011. *The Gospel 'According to Homer and Virgil': Cento and Canon*. Leiden.

Sauer, E. 2005. *Coins, Cult and Cultural Identity: Augustan Coins, Hot Springs and the Early Roman Baths at Bourbonne-les-Bains*. Leicester.

Sauer, J. 1924. "Das Aufkommen des bärtigen Christustypus in der frühchristlichen Kunst." In *Strena Buliciana*, ed. F. Bulić, 303–329. Zagreb.

Scarborough, J. 1990. "The Pharmacology of Sacred Plants, Herbs, and Roots." In Faraone and Obbink 1990: 138–174.

Scharf, R. 1990. "Die 'Apfel-Affäre' oder gab es einen Kaiser Arcadius II.?" *Byzantinische Zeitschrift* 83:435–450.

Scheiber, A. 1984. "Parallels to a Topos in Eudocia's Poem." *Israel Exploration Journal* 34:180–181.

Schelkle, K. H. 1954. "Cento." In *Reallexicon für Antike und Christentum*, ed. T. Klauser, 972–973. Stuttgart.

Schembra, R. 1993. "La 'quarta' redazione degli Homerocentones." *Sileno* 19:277–293.

———. 1994. "L'Omero 'cristiano.' Varianti di cristianizzazione e 'doiades' nella 'quarta' redazione degli Homerocentones." *Sileno* 20:317–332.

———.1995. "Analisi comparativa delle redazioni lunghe degli Homerocentones." *Sileno* 21:113–137.

———. 1996. "Genesi compositiva della III Redazione degli Homerocentones." *Sileno* 22:291–332.

———. 1997. "La duplice versione del centone 'peri tês anastaseôs' nella III Redazione degli Homerocentones." *Eikasmos* 8:171–179.

———. 1998. "Note critiche a M,D. Usher, Homeric Stitchings." *Sileno* 24:241–260.

———. 2000a. "Analisi comparativa delle redazioni brevi degli Homerocentones." *Orpheus* 21:92–122.

———. 2000b. "La tradizione manoscritta della I Redazione degli Homerocentones." *Byzantinische Zeitschrift* 93:162–175.

———. 2001a. "La genesi delle edizioni a stampa della I Redazione degli Homerocentones." *Byzantinische Zeitschrift* 94:641–669.

———. 2001b. "Note critiche e metodologiche ad A.-L. Rey, Centons homériques, Paris 1998." In *Poikilma: Studi in onore di Michele R. Cataudella in onore del 60. compleanno*, ed. M. R. Cataudella and S. Bianchetti, 1177–1193. La Spezia.

———. 2002. "Il riuso cristiano del modello omerico negli Homerocentones." In *Omero tremila anni dopo. Atti del congresso di Genova 6-8 luglio 2000*, ed. F. Montanari, 505–510. Roma.

———. 2003. "I centoni omerici online e su CD-rom. Alla scoperta dei rapporti di intertestualità con Omero e i Vangeli." *Gaia* 7:425–438.

———. 2006. *La prima redazione dei centoni omerici: Traduzione e commento.* Alessandria.

———. 2007a. *La seconda redazione dei centoni omerici: Traduzione e commento.* Alessandria.

———. 2007b. *Homerocentones.* Turnhout.

Schenkl, C. 1888. *Poetae Christiani Minores.* Vienna.

Schmeling, G., ed. 1996. *The Novel in the Ancient World.* Leiden.

———. 1998. "The Spectrum of Narrative: Authority of the Author." In Hock, Chance, and Perkins 1998: 19–30.

Schneemelcher, W. 1991. *New Testament Apocrypha, Vol. 2: Writings Relating to Apostles, Apocalypses, and Related Subjects.* Louisville.

Schneiders, S. M. 2003. *Written That You May Believe: Encountering Jesus in the Fourth Gospel.* New York.

Schottenius Cullhed, S. 2010. "Typology and the Cento of Proba." *Quaderni Urbinati di Cultura Classica* 95:43–51.

———. 2014. "Proba and Jerome." In Formisano, Fuhrer, and Stock 2014: 199–222.

———. 2015. *Proba the Prophet: The Christian Virgilian Cento of Faltonia Betitia Proba.* Leiden.

———. 2016. "Patterning Past and Future: Virgil in Proba's Biblical Cento." In McGill and Pucci 2016: 97–110.

Schroeder, C. T. 2006. "The Erotic Asceticism of the *Passion of Andrew*: The Apocryphal *Acts of Andrew*, the Greek Novel, and Platonic Philosophy." In Levine 2006: 47–59.

Schulte, F. S. 1914. *Joannis Chrysostomi: De Inani Gloria et de Educandis Liberis*. Münster.

Schürer, E. 1973–1987. *The History of the Jewish People in the Age of Jesus Christ (175 BC–AD 135)*. 3 vols. Edinburgh.

Schwendner, G. 2002. "Under Homer's Spell: Bilingualism, Oracular Magic, and the Michigan Excavation at Dime." In Ciraolo and Seidel 2002: 107–118.

Scourfield, J. H. D., ed. 2007. *Texts and Culture in Latin Antiquity. Inheritance, Authority, and Change*. Swansea.

Shanzer, D. 1986. "The Anonymous Carmen Contra Paganos and the Date and Identity of the Centonist Proba." *Revue des Études Augustiniennes* 32:232–248.

———. 1994. "The Date and Identity of the Centonist Proba." *Recherches Augustiniennes* 27:75–96.

———. 2009. "Literature, History, Periodization, and the Pleasures of the Latin Literary History of Late Antiquity." *History Compass* 7.3:917–954.

Shaw, B. 1993. "The Passion of Perpetua." *Past and Present* 139:3–45.

———. 2011. *Sacred Violence: African Christians and Sectarian Hatred in the Age of Augustus*. Cambridge.

Shaw, T. M. 1998. *The Burden of the Flesh: Fasting and Sexuality in Early Christianity*. Minneapolis.

———. 2000. "Sex and Sexual Renunciation." In Esler 2000: 401–421.

Sheridan, J. A. 1998. "Not at a Loss for Words: The Economic Power of Literate Women in Late Antique Egypt." *Transactions of the American Philological Association* 128:189–203.

Shewring, W. H. 1931. *The Passion of SS. Perpetua and Felicity: A New Edition and Translation of the Latin Text Together with the Sermons of S. Augustine upon These Saints*. London.

Shorrock, R. 2011. *The Myth of Paganism: Nonnus, Dionysus and the World of Late Antiquity*. London.

Sigerist, H. E. 1961. *A History of Medicine*. New Haven.

Sigismund-Nielson, H. 2012. "Vibia Perpetua—An Indecent Woman." In Bremmer and Formisano 2012: 103–117.

Simelidis, C. 2016. "Nonnus and Christian Literature." In Accorinti 2016: 289–307.

Simon, M. 1986. *Verus Israel: A Study in the Relations Between Christians and Jews in the Roman Empire (AD 135–425)*. London.

Sineri, V. 2011. *Il Centone di Proba.* Acireale.

Sivan, H. 1992. "The Dedicatory Presentation of Late Antiquity: The Example of Ausonius." *Illinois Classical Studies* 17:83–101.

———. 1993. *Ausonius of Bordeaux: Genesis of a Gallic Aristocracy.* London.

Snyder, J. M. 1989. *The Woman and the Lyre: Women Writers in Classical Greece and Rome.* Carbondale.

Söder, R. 1932. *Die Apokryphen Apostelgeschichten und die romanhafte Literatur der Antike.* Stuttgart.

Sowers, B. 2012. "Thecla Desexualized: The Saint Justina Legend and the Reception of the Christian Apocrypha in Late Antiquity." In *"Non-canonical" Religious Texts in Early Judaism and Early Christianity,* ed. J. H. Charlesworth and L. M. McDonald, 222–234. New York.

———. 2015. "Pudor et Dedecus: Rhetoric of Honor and Shame in Perpetua's Passion." *Journal of Early Christian Studies* 23.3:363–388.

———. 2016. "Amiticiae and Late Antique Nugae: Reading Ausonius' Reading Community." *American Journal of Philology* 137:511–540.

———. 2017. "Historiolae: Narrative Charms in Magical Texts and Literature in Late Antiquity." *History of Religions* 56.4:426–448.

Spaeth, B. S. 2014. "From Goddess to Hag: The Greek and the Roman Witch in Classical Literature." In Stratton and Kalleres 2014: 41–70.

Springer, C. P. E. 1988. *The Gospel as Epic in Late Antiquity: The Paschale Carmen of Sedulius.* Leiden.

Stabryła, S. 2005. "Fides in Prudentius' Psychomachia." In *Studies of Roman Literature,* ed. J. Styka, 19–28. Kraków.

Stambursky, S. 1976. "The Source and Reality of the Term 'Gematria.'" *Tarbits* 45:268–271.

Stanislaus, S. A. 1938. "The Scriptures in Hexameter." *Classical Weekly* 32:99–100.

Stark, R. 1996. *The Rise of Christianity: A Sociologist Reconsiders History.* Princeton.

Stephens, S. A. 1994. "Who Read Ancient Novels?" In Tatum 1994: 405–418.

Stevenson, J. 2005. *Women Latin Poets: Language, Gender, and Authority from Antiquity to the Eighteenth Century.* Oxford.

Stratton, K. B., and D. S. Kalleres, eds. 2014. *Daughters of Hecate: Women and Magic in the Ancient World.* Oxford.

Streete, G. P. C. 2006. "Buying the Stairway to Heaven: Perpetua and Thecla as Early Christian Heroines." In Levine 2006: 186–205.

Struck, P. T. 2002. "The Poet as Conjurer: Magic and Literary Theory in Late Antiquity." In Ciraolo and Seidel 2002: 119–131.

Styers, R. 2004. *Making Magic: Religion, Magic, and Science in the Modern World.* Oxford.

Swain, S., and M. Edwards, eds. 2004. *Approaching Late Antiquity: The Transformation from Early to Late Empire.* Oxford.

Szpakowska, K., ed. 2006. *Through a Glass Darkly: Magic, Dreams and Prophecy in Ancient Egypt.* Oxford.

Tatum, J., ed. 1994. *The Search for the Ancient Novel.* Baltimore.

Taylor, J. H. 2001. *Death and the Afterlife in Ancient Egypt.* Chicago.

Tebben, J. R. 1994. *Concordantia Homerica, Pars I: Odyssea.* 2 vols. Hildesheim.

———. 1998. *Concordiantia Homerica, Pars II: Ilias.* 3 vols. Hildesheim.

Thébert, Y. 2003. *Thermes romains d'Afrique du Nord et leur contexte méditerranéen. Études d'histoire et d'archéologie.* Rome.

Thomas, C. M. 1998. "Stories Without Texts and Without Authors: The Problem of Fluidity in Ancient Novelistic Texts and Early Christian Literature." In Hock, Chance, and Perkins 1998: 273–291.

———. 2003. *The Acts of Peter, Gospel Literature, and the Ancient Novel: Rewriting the Past.* Oxford.

Thomassen, E. 1999. "Is Magic a Subclass of Ritual?" In Jordan, Montgomery, and Thomassen 1999: 55–66.

Thompson, T. 1914. *The Offices of Baptism and Confirmation.* Cambridge.

Thurn, J. 2000. *Ioannis Malalae Chronographia.* Berlin.

Toepffer, I. 1889. *Attische Genealogie.* Berlin.

Torrance, A. 2013. *Repentance in Late Antiquity: Eastern Asceticism and the Framing of the Christian Life, c. 400–650 CE.* Oxford.

Totti, M. 1985. *Ausgewählte Texte der Isis- und Sarapis-Religion.* Hildesheim.

Treggiari, S. 1991. *Roman Marriage: "Iusti Coniuges" from the Time of Cicero to the Time of Ulpian.* Oxford.

Trevett, C. 1999. "Spiritual Authority and the 'Heretical' Woman: Firmilian's Word to the Church in Carthage." In *Portraits of Spiritual Authority: Religious Power in Early Christianity, Byzantium and the Christian Orient,* ed. J. W. Drijvers and J. W. Watt, 45–62. Leiden.

———. 2006. *Christian Women and the Time of the Apostolic Fathers (AD c. 80–160): Corinth, Rome and Asia Minor.* Cardiff.

Trimpi, W. 1971. "The Ancient Hypothesis of Fiction: An Essay on the Origins of Literary Theory." *Traditio* 27:1–78.

Troisgros, H. 1975. *Borvo et Damona. Divinités gallo-romaines des eaux thermales.* Bourbonne-les-Bains.

———. 1994. *Bourbonne-les-Bains et sa region.* Langres.

Trzcionka, S. 2007. *Magic and the Supernatural in Fourth-Century Syria.* London.

Tsatsos, J. 1977. *Empress Athenais-Eudocia: A Fifth Century Byzantine Humanist.* Brookline.

Tupet, A. M. 1986. "Rites magiques dans l'antiquité romaine." *Aufstieg und Niedergang der römischen Welt* 2.16.3:2592–2675.

Tuplin, C. J., ed. 2004. *Pontus and the Outside World: Studies in Black Sea History, Historiography and Archaeology*. Leiden.

Turner, V. 1974. *Dramas, Fields and Metaphors: Symbolic Action in Human Society*. Ithaca.

———. 1979. *Process, Performance and Pilgrimage: A Study in Comparative Symbology*. New Delhi.

———. 1981. "Social Dramas and Stories About Them." In *On Narrative*, ed. W. J. T. Mitchell, 137–164. Chicago.

Turner, V., and E. Turner. 1978. *Image and Pilgrimage in Christian Culture: Anthropological Perspectives*. New York.

Tuzlak, A. 2002. "The Magician and the Heretic: The Case of Simon Magus." In Mirecki and Meyer 2002: 416–426.

Usher, M. D. 1997. "Prolegomenon to the Homeric Centos." *American Journal of Philology* 118:305–321.

———. 1998. *Homeric Stitchings. The Homeric Centos of the Empress Eudocia*. Lanham.

———. 1999. *Homerocentones Eudociae Augustae*. Stuttgart.

van Beek, C. I. M. I. 1936. *Passio Sanctarum Perpetuae et Felicitatis*. Nijmegen.

———. 1938. *Passio Sanctarum Perpetuae et Felicitatis, Latine et Graece*. Florilegium patristicum 43. Bonn.

Van Dam, R. 1993. *Saints and Their Miracles in Late Antique Gaul*. Princeton.

van der Paardt, R. T. 1989. "Three Dutch Asses." *Groningen Colloquia on the Novel* 2:133–140.

Van Deun, P. 1993. "The Poetical Writings of the Empress Eudocia: An Evaluation." In *Early Christian Poetry: A Collection of Essays*, ed. J. den Boeft and A. Hilhorst, 273–282. Leiden.

van Minnen, P. 2006. "Saving Hagiography? Egyptian Hagiography in its Space and Time." *Church History and Religious Culture* 86:57–91.

Van Rengen, W. 1984. "Deux défixions contre les bleus à Apamée (VIe siècle apr. J.-C.)." In *Apamée de Syrie*, ed. J. Balty, 213–234. Brussels.

Vergnières, S. 1995. *Éthique et politique chez Aristote: φύσις, ἦθος, νόμος*. Paris.

Veyne, P. 1990. *Bread and Circuses: Historical Sociology and Political Pluralism*. London.

Vidman, L. 1970. *Isis und Sarapis bei den Griechen und Römern*. Berlin.

Vierow, H. 1999. "Feminine and Masculine Voices in the *Passion of Saints Perpetua and Felicitas*." *Latomus* 58:600–619.

von Albrecht, M. 1997. *A History of Roman Literature from Livius Andronicus to Boethius*. 2 vols. Leiden.

von Dobschütz, E. 1912. *Das Decretum Gelasianum de libris recipiendis et non recipiendis.* Leipzig.

Vorster, J. N. 2006. "Construction of Culture Through the Construction of Person: The Construction of Thecla in the *Acts of Thecla.*" In Levine 2006: 98–117.

Vos, N. 2011. "Demons Without and Within: The Representation of Demons, the Saint, and the Soul in Early Christian Lives, Letters, and Sayings." In Vos and Otten 2011: 159–182.

Vos, N., and W. Otten, eds. 2011. *Demons and the Devil in Ancient and Medieval Christianity.* Leiden.

Watts, E. 2006. *City and School in Late Antique Athens and Alexandria.* Berkeley.

———. 2013. "Theodosius II and His Legacy in Anti-Chalcedonian Communal Memory." In Kelly 2013a: 269–284.

———. 2015. *The Final Pagan Generation.* Oakland.

———. 2017. *Hypatia: The Life and Legend of an Ancient Philosopher.* Oxford.

Wehrli, F. 1965. "Einheit und Vorgeschichte der griechisch-römischen Romanliteratur." *Museum Helveticum* 22:133–154.

Welzen, H. 2016. "The Transformation of the Temple in the Fourth Gospel." *HTS Teologiese Studies* 72.4.

Werblowsky, R. J. Z. 1973. *Lucifer and Prometheus: A Study of Milton's Satan.* New York.

Wessling, B. 1988. "The Audience of the Ancient Novels." *Groningen Colloquia on the Novel* 1:67–79.

West, M. L. 2003. *Homeric Hymns, Homeric Apocrypha, Lives of Homer.* Cambridge, MA.

Westerbrink, A. G. 1970. "Catullus' Epithalamia." *Hermeneus* 41:166–175.

Whitby, M. 2002. *Sparta.* London.

Whitby, M. 2003. "The Vocabulary of Praise in Verse-Celebration of 6th-century Building Achievements: *AP* 2.398–406, *AP* 9.656, *AP* 1.10 and Paul the Silentiary's *Description of St Sophia.*" In *Des géants à Dionysos: Mélanges de mythologie et de poésie grecques offerts à Francis Vian,* ed. D. Accorinti and P. Chuvin, 593–606. Alessandria.

———. 2006. "The St. Polyeuktos Epigram (*AP* 1.10): A Literary Perspective." In *Greek Literature in Antiquity,* ed. S. F. Johnson, 159–187. Burlington.

———. 2007. "The Bible Hellenized: Nonnus' Paraphrase of St. John's Gospel and 'Eudocia's' Homeric centos." In Scourfield 2007: 195–231.

———. 2009. "Review of Schembra (2007a)." *Byzantinische Zeitschrift* 102:811–815.

———. 2013. "Writing in Greek: Classicism and Compilation, Interaction and Transformation." In Kelly 2013a: 195–218.

———. 2016. "Nonnus and Biblical Epic." In Accorinti 2016: 213–239.

Whitby, M., and M. Whitby, eds. 1989. *Chronicon Paschale 284–628 AD.* Liverpool.

White, D. 1982. "Property Rights of Women: The Changes in the Justinian Legislation Regarding the Dowry and the Parapherna." *Jahrbuch der Österreichischen Byzantinistik* 2:539–548.

White, P. 1978. "Amicitia and the Profession of Poetry in Early Imperial Rome." *Journal of Roman Studies* 48:74–92.

———. 1993. *Promised Verse: Poets in the Society of Augustan Rome*. Cambridge.

Whitmarsh, T. 2005. "The Greek Novel: Titles and Genre." *American Journal of Philology* 126:587–611.

Wiemer, H. 1995. *Libanios und Julian*. Munich.

———. 2004. "Akklamationen im spätrömischen Reich: Zur Typologie und Funktion eines Kommunikationsrituals." *Archiv für Kulturgeschichte* 86:27–73.

Wiesen, D. S. 1971. "Virgil, Minucius Felix and the Bible." *Hermes* 99:70–91.

Wilburn, A. T. 2012. *Materia Magica: The Archaeology of Magic in Roman Egypt, Cyprus, and Spain*. Ann Arbor.

Wilken, R. L. 1967. "The Homeric Cento in Irenaeus, 'Adversus Haereses' I, 9,4." *Vigiliae Christianae* 21:25–33.

———. 1984. *The Christians as the Romans Saw Them*. New Haven.

Wilkinson, J. 2002. *Jerusalem Pilgrims Before the Crusades*. Oxford.

Williams, C. 2012. "Perpetua's Gender. A Latinist Reads the *Passio Perpetuae et Felicitatis*." In Bremmer and Formisano 2012: 54–77.

Williams, M. A. 2000. "Negative Theologies and Demiurgical Myths in Late Antiquity." In *Gnosticism and Later Platonism: Themes, Figures, and Texts*, ed. J. D. Turner and R. Majercik, 277–302. Atlanta.

Wilson, E. F. 1948. "Pastoral and Epithalamium in Latin Literature." *Speculum* 23:35–57.

Wilson, N. G. 1994. *Photius: The* Bibliotheca. London.

Wilson-Kastner, P., ed. 1981. *A Lost Tradition: Women Writers of the Early Church*. Washington, DC.

Wipszycka, E. 1996. *Études sur le christianisme dans l'Égypte de l'antiquité tardive*. Rome.

Wire, A. C. 2004. "Hearing Women's Voices Through Paul's Letters." In *Dem Tod nicht glauben: Sozialgeschichte der Bibel*, ed. F. Crusemann, 544–557. Gütersloh.

Yasin, A. M. 2009. *Saints and Church Spaces in the Late Antique Mediterranean: Architecture, Cult, and Community*. Cambridge.

Yegül, F. 1992. *Baths and Bathing in Classical Antiquity*. Cambridge, MA.

Zahn, T. 1882. *Cyprian von Antiochien und die deutsche Faustsage*. Erlangen.

Zanker, P. 1995. *The Mask of Socrates: The Image of the Intellectual in Antiquity*. Berkeley.

Index Locorum

Subject Index